THE MILITARY HISTORY OF THE THIRD WORLD SINCE 1945

A Reference Guide

CLAUDE C. STURGILL

Greenwood Press
Westport, Connecticut • London

Library of Congress Cataloging-in-Publication Data

Sturgill, Claude C.
    The military history of the Third World since 1945 : a reference
guide / Claude C. Sturgill.
      p.   cm.
    Includes bibliographical references and index.
    ISBN 0–313–28152–1 (alk. paper)
    1. Developing countries—History, Military. 2. Military history,
Modern—20th century.   I. Title.
D883.S79 1994
355′.009172′4—dc20   93–35391

British Library Cataloguing in Publication Data is available.

Library of Congress Catalog Card Number: 93–35391
ISBN: 0–313–28152–1

First published in 1994

Greenwood Press, 88 Post Road West, Westport, CT 06881
An imprint of Greenwood Publishing Group, Inc.

Printed in the United States of America

♾️

The paper used in this book complies with the
Permanent Paper Standard issued by the National
Information Standards Organization (Z39.48—1984).

10 9 8 7 6 5 4 3 2 1

Contents

Figures and Tables

FIGURES

TABLES

Acknowledgments

I would especially like to thank Mr. Robert Lane, head librarian of the Fairchild Library in the Air University at Maxwell Air Force Base, Alabama. He and his staff were of invaluable help during my 1991–1992 stay as a visiting professor at the Air War College.

The Research Library of the University of Florida has, as always, given me every possible aid and latitude in the use of its massive collections.

My wife Sue has helped in the preparation of the typescript and given me the invaluable help of her knowledge of computer science.

General Military Patterns within the Third World since 1945

World War II was the great starting event for the Third World on its long road to independence and beyond. This conflict keyed each of these countries to its present status. Until 1940, the colonial powers' military machines had proven impregnable to any resistance. The non-Christian and the Latin American worlds knew their masters. The cultural and political shock of the North European troops surrendering to the Japanese in Asia was incalculable. The ease with which the French, British, and Belgians in World War II nearly lost a war to the Germans gave ideas to black Africans everywhere. U.S. preoccupation with Pacific and European enemies promoted better relations with the Latin Americans. In 1945, North European countries did not have the manpower or powder to back up their claims to renewed sovereignty over pre-1940 empires.

Several aspects complete the picture of the beginning of the crumbling of the old European overseas empires. The United States of America—by far the greatest military, industrial, and economic power to emerge from World War II—pursued two polices with devastating effect on the old colonial empires. The United States did not want the old empires restored after 1945. President Woodrow Wilson's concept of self-determination for all peoples reigned, and the administrations of presidents Harry Truman, Dwight Eisenhower, John Kennedy, Lyndon Johnson, Richard Nixon, and Gerald Ford opposed all forms of old-style European colonialism (imperialism) throughout the world.

The British retreated from Burma, India, Sri Lanka, and finally the Middle East. The French lost disastrous colonial wars in Indo-China and Algeria. The United States found itself in a new position of worldwide authority in the role of police officer or peacekeeper. By 1960, Americans found their garrisons were all over the world. Americans stood guard in Europe, in Asia, and in Latin America. Their military advisor groups were all over the world, including Africa and the vast reaches of the Pacific.

Americans tried to believe that the reason for all this interference in the internal affairs of the new sovereign nations in the Third World was to fight the growing specter of worldwide communism. President Reagan called the Soviet Union "The Evil Empire." A second reason was that the steadying hand of the French, British, Dutch, and American colonial masters was gone. Nearly all the newly independent nations of the Third World rather quickly adopted military-style dictatorships or governments in which only the military could guarantee the survival of any form of a civil government. The United States hoped these new nations would form American-style democratic governments.

Simply put, Americans could let the people in every Third World country decide for themselves, even if they picked a communist form of government, or could offer economic and educational aid to support any of these new democratic governments.

At the first glimmering of a rebel group supported by a Communist group anywhere in the world, the United States would first send military aid and then a few military advisors in military aid groups. Next special forces would be sent to train and bolster U.S.-supported forces, whether they were rebel or government sponsored.

At the extreme, as in Grenada and Panama, the United States used overwhelming military force in direct belligerent activities where democratic interests were threatened. The military history of the United States is replete with examples of where "the world was made safe for democracy." The U.S. history in the Third World since 1945 has not always been positive. Even with the collapse of the Warsaw Pact and the "evil empire" of the Soviet Union, Americans are involved militarily in faraway places like Somalia, Taiwan, Mainland China, and India, among others.

Some historical overview is necessary to explain how the United States began interfering in the affairs of sovereign nations throughout the world, bent upon teaching them to live their lives "the American way."

One place to start is the signing of the United Nations's Charter in San Francisco on June 26, 1945. This was a time when the victorious great allied powers, Russia, the United States, Great Britain, France, and non-Red China tried war criminals in Germany and Japan.

The United States cut back its military establishment from fourteen million to more than one million, and Americans settled back to peace and prosperity in a free world. The Russians occupied much of Eastern Europe and decided to keep it. Non-Red Chinese forces under Chang Kai-Chek lost a civil war to Red Chinese forces led by Mao Zedong. By 1949, the "hated political doctrine of communism" seemed victorious everywhere, the doctrine of democracy appeared on the run throughout the world.

The United States relied on the Marshall Plan to rebuild Western Europe, sustained Chang Kai-Chek (Nationalist China) on the island of Taiwan, drew a line in the sand around the world, and warned the evil Russian Communists that they would not be permitted to advance one more square inch without a fight.

During the years immediately after World War II, the Russians developed an atomic bomb, and the two superpowers (United States and Russia) approached nuclear parity. The arms race went on, despite some ups and downs in how much either side spent of a given year's national budget for military purposes, not ending until 1993. This was called the Cold War. Americans agreed that it was better than a shooting war, and out of this came the belief that democracy had to succeed across the world with no loss or as little loss of American lives as possible.

During this period, India, Burma, Pakistan, and Sri Lanka gained their independence from the British. Black African states gradually obtained freedom, with little colonial resistance except in Rhodesia, Kenya, and the Congo.

The French freed their African colonies but set up the French Speaking Economic Community, thus for all practical purposes continuing French colonialism in Africa except in Algeria. The Algerian Independence Movement and French internal politics eventually led the French to leave. Indo-China became independent, at least in the north, as a result of poor French military leadership. The Dutch surrendered to the independence movement in the Dutch East Indies, which became the Republic of Indonesia.

Imperialism held on in two places. In the Republic of South Africa, whites continued to fight a rear-guard action against granting black citizens full political rights. Colonial business as usual continued also in the Caribbean and in Central and South America, where the United States has excused its multiple interventions since 1945.

The decade of 1950–1959 was supposedly a decade of U.S. prominence in the world. Yet the Korean conflict, 1950–1953, saw the United States fail when its forces accepted what was in actuality a stalemate. Everything remained the way it was before the "police action" began. Despite 136,000 American casualties, Congress never declared war but called the conflict a U.S. peace-keeping action. During this same period, Arab leftist governments came to power in Egypt and Iraq. U.S. and European oil interests were taken over by the Arab states. Real trouble started over the question of the continued existence of Israel.

From 1960 to 1969, the United States went through its next "police action" in Vietnam. The Soviet Union established political ties and military bases in Cuba, Egypt, Algeria, and Guinea. Pro-Western military revolts occurred in Zaire, Ghana, and Indonesia.

The 1970s were bad years for the United States, which first left Vietnam and then abandoned its puppet government to the North Vietnamese. Pakistan broke into two as Bangladesh became independent. The last remaining

European colonies in Africa, the Spanish Sahara, Djibouti, and Zimbabwe (Rhodesia) became free. Internal conflicts erupted in Angola and Ethiopia, with Russian backing. France interfered in Chad, Zaire, and Mauritania.

During the period from 1980 to 1989, the United States openly and often violently interfered in the Middle East, Israel, Central America, Africa, and South Africa; fought international terrorism; and outproduced the Soviets in the arms race to the point where their economy fell apart. These years marked the assassination of heads of state, including Egypt's President Anwar el-Sadat, India's Prime Minister Indira Gandhi, Lebanon's Premier Rashid Karami, and Pakistan's President Mohammed Zia ul-Haq.

Certain major events in U.S. military history have colored relations with the nations of the Third World throughout the period 1945–1993: the Korean War, the Vietnam War, the Arab-Israel conflicts, and Desert Storm. The other aspect of our military relationships with the nations of the Third World since 1945 is something known by a number of different names. These we call "international peacekeeping and disarmament activities," a term used as a catch-all phrase both to hide covert military operations and to describe legitimate operations, as in sending the "Blue Helmets" on the Israel–Syrian border to keep the two sides from shooting at each other. These events and phenomena are further described in Chapters 2 and 3.

The rest of this reference guide is organized by countries under the various regions within the Third World. The influence of the U.S. militarily in each country is the main theme covered in each entry. However, the military influence of other countries is included where significant, as with France in Chad, Belgium in Zaire, the Soviet Union in Cuba, and England in Oman.

The Effects of the Korean, Vietnamese, Arab–Israeli, and Desert Storm Operations

The United States effectively went through four tests of its military mettle and its diplomatic courage between 1946 and 1993. What might have been a more orderly progress of independence movements with the final establishment of sovereign governments throughout the Third World was overshadowed by the Cold War behavior of the United States and the Union of Soviet Socialist Republics. In no place was this conflict more intense than in the emerging Third World countries. Korea and Vietnam are Asian appendages of the ancient Chinese Empire. The Arabs and the Israelis are Semites sprung from the same Indo-European stock that swept into the Middle East before the Greeks became known. The most recent expression of Western diplomatic efforts and adroit military skill was the crushing of the Iraqi Army by a U.N. force really commanded, equipped, led, and controlled by the United States. Such conflicts so affecting the Third World occurred in Africa, where the contest of wills was between communism and democracy, unity and tribal independence, white and black, European-trained elites and the native groups.

Perhaps the worldwide reverberations of the four major military events in the Korean, Vietnamese, Arab-Israeli, and Desert Storm conflicts are even more significant because they showed the near total involvement of the United States and how it operated as a militant democratic superpower determined to set up a New World Order based on its own set of rules and precepts.

The Korean War of 1950–1953 was the first major military confrontation between the United States and the Soviet Union. Military operations began on June 15, 1950, when the North Korean Army attacked South Korea and

President Harry S. Truman hurried American units to the support of South Korean forces. The General Assembly of the United Nations voted to condemn the North Koreans as aggressors. In 1950, the North Koreans nearly chased the South Koreans and the Americans into the sea, but the Americans landed well behind the North Korean Lines and swept the country clean of most opposition all the way to the Chinese border on the Yalu River. At that point, the Red Chinese government of Mao Zedong, fearing a possible effort by Chang Kai-Chek (with American support) to overrun mainland China, entered the Korean War. Back south almost to the sea again went the U.N. forces, composed of Australians, Canadians, French, Turks, Americans, South Koreans, and Nationalist Chinese, among others. In 1951, a U.N. counterattack drove the Chinese and the remnants of the North Korean Army to a line just north of Seoul. This eventually became the current international boundary between North and South Korea. The peace at negotiations at Panmunjon seemed to drag on forever. Finally an armistice was signed on July 27, 1953.

The entire Korean conflict saw as many as 400,000 U.S. troops deployed on the peninsula at one time and cost some 147,000 plus combat casualties representing, much more than a normal police action in a remote corner of the Third World. Though the world's two great opposing super systems, Communist Russia and democratic United States, clashed, atomic weapons were not used. The Korean police action as a conflict of states, butchering of innocents, brainwashing of prisoners, and the use of irregular troops led to the belief internationally that either superpower would use all means possible to impose its system upon the entire world. The superpowers then decided that each preferred to play the role of distant big brother than to risk manpower and expose new technology and to risk the chance of the use of nuclear weapons. The superpowers and their first line allies continued, nonetheless, to interfere in the independence and development of the new states in the Third World.

Vietnam came as a surprise to both superpowers since neither realized the determination of a few hundred devout followers of the French-educated Vietnamese leader Ho Chi Min. Neither power nor its first line allies, such as France on one side and Mainland China on the other, understood the Vietnamese people's determination to rid themselves of "foreign control." It took Ho and his followers forty-five years of bitter struggle against France, Japan, the United States and its puppet regime in Saigon to win.

The independence movements in the Third World since 1945 have been based largely on getting the Westerners, as former colonialist rulers and Europeans out of their countries. "Yankee go home" has a connotation far wider than North America. The stunning political, diplomatic, and military defeat of the United States and its puppet South Vietnamese government did not go unnoticed in the Third World. In addition, U.S. citizens were not willing to lose their own lives to maintain any form of imperialism outside the United States.

Yet the superpowers did offer the new governments of the Third World needed technical advisers, building materials, capital, and teachers so that they could leap from backward colonial situations into the consumer-conscious world of the late twentieth century. This assistance could come only from the superpowers and their close allies, and all the trappings of the military were equally blended into the care packages. Military advisors, military volunteers, and armaments on credit flowed into the Third World, along with material aid to build peaceful economies. The worldwide struggle between communism and democracy continued in the Third World. How this played out in each of the developing nations of the Third World unfolds below in a country-by-country fashion.

The closest the United States and the Soviet Union have come to actual blows after the Korean military action has occurred in the almost regular little wars between the Israelis and the Arab states. Arab–Israeli warfare goes back to the destruction of Jerusalem in the first century A.D. Only a few Jews lived in the Holy Land until after World War II, when the Western allies let thousands of Jews into Palestine. Since 1945, this area has seen wars from 1945 to 1948, from 1948 to 1949, in 1956, in 1967, in 1969, from 1968 to 1970, from 1970 to 1973, in 1973, and in 1982 — not to mention various border clashes between Israel and Jordan, Syria, Lebanon, and Egypt. The plight of displaced Arab Palestinians has complicated the situation further.

This series of little wars has been important in the military history of the Third World because of the involvement of the superpowers. The Russians have equipped the Syrians, the Lebanese factions and, from time to time, the Egyptians. The United States equips the Israelis and, from time to time, the Jordanians and the Egyptians. Although the dead and wounded totals in these little wars have never been in the hundreds of thousands, a major Israeli–Arab conflict might involve all the countries of the Near East. Then the greatest percentage of the world's proven oil reserves could go up in smoke. The price of a gallon of gasoline is also important to the superpowers, Europe, Japan, and the First World as a whole.

The collapse of the Soviet Union beginning in 1988 leaves only the United States as a superpower to smite the enemies of democracy. This was demonstrated in relation to Iraq, Desert Shield, and Desert Storm.

This military intervention by the U.N. forces was led, supplied, and ordered by the United States. With or without the foreknowledge of the U.S. Department of State, Iraq attacked and overran Kuwait in a matter of hours on August 2, 1990. This sparked an international crisis; the United States feared for its Saudi Arabian oil reserves. The United Nations, coached by the United States, imposed a ban on all trade with Iraq. The United States froze Iraqi assets, and other nations were called upon to do the same. Several months of diplomatic warfare followed, while the Iraqi Army dug in and went on a rampage in Kuwait. The allies, especially the United States, began shipping a large army to Saudi Arabia. Saddam Hussein refused to leave Kuwait, and George Bush said he should do so or war would ensue. On January 16, 1991, air attacks pounded the Iraqi Army in Kuwait and selected military targets in Iraq. The U.N. coalition began a ground attack on February 27, 1991, to retake Kuwait. Given little Iraq resistance, in a few days the war was over. The United States had won, and Americans were elated.

Meanwhile, the Third World saw how the remaining superpower could be dangerous when its own economic interests were threatened.

□ □ **3**

International Peace-Keeping and Disarmament Activities

The Soviet Union and the United States alone have tried since 1945 to settle serious disagreements among themselves, as well as within the Third World, by peaceful means. In listing the most important efforts the United States has made to keep or make peace without brandishing military muscle, it is important to note first the Helsinki Security Conference of July 30 to August 2, 1975, binding the superpowers to recognize certain basic human rights.

There have been many arbitration efforts throughout the Third World— in Angola, Nigeria, Morocco-Sahara, the Contadora Peace Initiatives in Central America, with varying degrees of success. The Arabs and Israelis keep talking.

The Geneva Conference on Disarmament, mainly on nuclear missiles, has met off and on since 1975 and has been successful since the Soviet empire began to fall to pieces in 1988. Iceland, Britain, and Portugal have seemingly settled their "Cod War" over fishing rights in so-called Icelandic waters. The British–Argentine War over the Falkland Islands in 1982 showed especially those in Latin America and in the Third World that the United States would side with its European allies over matters of primary concern. The major result of this war was the replacement of the military dictatorship in Argentina with a more democratic regime.

For decades the United States has propped up reactionary regimes with few outward signs of democracy. The United States sanctifies a war against the Indian majority in Guatemala, gives military aid went to Islamic fundamentalist freedom fighters in Afghanistan but not to the Southwest Africa People's Organization of the African National Congress, maintains pressures for free elections in Nicaragua, and mines harbors and arms Contra insurgents against a government with which the United States has been clandestinely at war. The hatred for the United States and its local allies builds support in many Third World countries for local revolutionary movements and parties.

The fear of Maoist-type repression helps create allies for the United States in the Third World. Whenever radical change relating to property or privilege threatens the established ruling class there, the United States stands with them against any real redistribution of wealth or social reform.

Third World leaders, trained in Western universities in the First World, often have little understanding of political or social movements in their own countries or direct ties to local leaders. These elites tend to be pessimistic about practical reforms. They tend to believe that their countries will remain underdeveloped since world trade terms are often unequal and exploitative, causing them to develop independently. Thus they need more military hardware from industrially advanced countries and are then more dependent on them. This is turn deprives the Third World populations of needed agricultural and industrial development.

The issue of aid to the underdeveloped nations of the Third World is complex; much takes place that does more harm than good; it is still linked to the Cold War or to the support of entrenched conservative interests. Third World nations quickly devote bigger shares of their pitifully sparse national incomes to military hardware.

Perhaps a new international program like the United States's Marshall Plan deployed in Europe after World War II should be developed to fight hunger and political repression around the world and to bring about essential economic and social reform.

The Middle East

Billions of gallons of proven oil reserves sit under the sands of the Middle East. The nations of this region—Israel, Egypt, Yemen, Lebanon, Syria, Jordan, Saudi Arabia, Oman, Iran, Bahrain, Kuwait, Cyprus, Turkey, Qatar, and the United Arab Emirates—have all suffered, at least since the seventh century A.D., from deep religious divisions, both Christian and Moslem. The world has not been confronted to date with one great oil super-power. The industrial nations such as Germany, France, Italy, England, the United States, Canada, and Japan exploited the oil reserves of the Middle East powder keg. Even OPEC, the fabled cartel of oil-producing nations, has been little more than an occasional indirect threat to the northern nations.

Some Middle Eastern countries, such as Israel, Jordan, and Egypt, have few oil reserves. Thus they are "energy have-not nations."

But burn the important oil reserves in the other Middle Eastern countries— as in Saudi Arabia, Iraq, or Kuwait—and the industrial world as it presently exists would soon grind to a halt. The overthrow of the Shah of Iran in 1979, the American hostage crisis in Iran from 1979 to 1981, the Iran–Iraq War from 1980 to 1988, and the Desert Storm operation in 1990–1991 received major media attention in the United States and across the world. The "easy life" in the United States could last only a generation until we exhausted our own reserves. Oil wars would erupt across the world. The Middle East is indeed a powder keg because of its one great natural resource, proven oil reserves.

The current political economic system in the Middle East is a direct out-growth of World War II. In 1945, Britain controlled Egypt, Palestine, and Jordan in various ways. France held sway in Syria and had deep seated influence in Lebanon. The Soviet Union and the United States both controlled parts of Iran. Saudi Arabia and its appendage kingdoms of Oman, Bahrain, Kuwait, Qatar, and the United Arab Emirates were largely dependent on the British for arms, as was the area called Yemen or Aden. Turkey was an independent country, having remained neutral during World War II.

The industrial explosion in the First World immediately after World War II caused the need for crude oil to double, double, and double again. Western oil producers—Texaco, Aramco, British Petroleum, Gulf, and Fina—exploited the region's oil, usually splitting profits 50–50 with the ruling families.

As the oil business boomed, the rulers of these countries began to take over the enterprises by expropriation. In 1951, Mussadegh in Iran nationalized the entire oil industry, from the hole in the ground to pumping the crude into the bellies of foreign oil tankers. Other oil-producing nations eagerly followed suit. By the early 1970s, the industrialized West was on the outside looking in. Only the United States and the Soviet Union had proven oil reserves that would last them for a generation or two. The United States felt it wiser to use dollars to buy foreign oil and leave its own proven reserves in the ground. The Soviet Union often sold oil, sometimes at cut rate prices, to build up its scarce foreign exchange.

The very fact that the governments of the Middle East have a one-cash-crop economy has caused most of the military problems of this part of the world since 1945. It is easy for the industrialized nations to barter guns in exchange for oil. The beginning of the Cold War saw the United States and its allies and the Soviet Union and its allies compete for the oil-rich reserves of this entire area. This simply assured that Middle Eastern countries would build military machines far out of proportion to their true defense needs. In some ways, the Middle East possesses offensive forces geared more to making war than to assuring peace.

The Israeli–Palestinian problem adds a quantum leap in the belief of the nations of this region that they must prepare for war at any moment against a troublemaker, from time to time, Israel, Iraq, Iran, or the Palestinians.

The internal divisions in Lebanon create further instability in the area. The population is divided between warring factions of Christians and Moslems, further splintered into rival groups. The Middle East powder keg is always smoldering.

The Middle East is always ripe for intervention from someone within or out of the region. For example, the French, the Israelis, and the British intervened in Suez in 1956. Iran and Iraq fought from 1980 to 1988. The Jews and the Arabs have sporadic shoot-outs. Desert Storm proved that the United States and its industrialized allies would also not hesitate to intervene if oil reserves seemed threatened (see Figure 4.1).

PALESTINE AND ISRAEL

Israel is a tiny part of the Middle East, about the same size as the state of New Jersey, with a population of about 4.7 million, 82 percent Jewish and 14 percent Moslem. Israel maintains a Western-style democracy. Military

Figure 4.1
Arms Transfer Agreements, 1983–1990 (In Billions of U.S. Dollars)

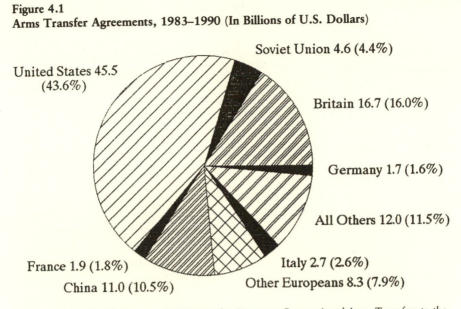

Soviet Union 4.6 (4.4%)

United States 45.5
(43.6%)

Britain 16.7 (16.0%)

Germany 1.7 (1.6%)

All Others 12.0 (11.5%)

France 1.9 (1.8%)

China 11.0 (10.5%)

Italy 2.7 (2.6%)

Other Europeans 8.3 (7.9%)

Source: Richard F. Grimmett, *CRS Report for Congress: Conventional Arms Transfers to the Third World, 1983–1990,* Congressional Research Service, The Library of Congress, August 2, 1991, pp. 48–49.

forces number some 140,000 constantly under arms, with a trained standby militia which is described as all other Israelis.

The history of the Jewish state in Israel since 1945 has been one of bitter survival. Faced with determined Arab opposition from three sides, the Jews have fought for their very existence time and again. Israel still exists for two reasons: (1) the utter determination of most Jews everywhere that there will never again be another Holocaust, and (2) the continuing economic and military support from the United States in the form of money, technicians, and outright gifts of military hardware. These two policies are likely to continue well into the future.

Israel has proved its mettle in many wars with its Arab neighbors. The Israeli military forces have gone on the theory that they must pound their enemies into the ground.

On May 14, 1948, the state of Israel was proclaimed. On the very next day, neighboring Arab states sent in their armies. The result was a series of armistice agreements negotiated by the United Nations under which Israeli territory increased by 50 percent. In October 1956, Israel invaded the Gaza Strip and the Sinai Peninsula. This was part of their arrangements with the British and the French in the Suez intervention. Israeli forces evacuated these areas only after the United Nations sent in peace-keeping forces.

In May 1967, terrorist acts by Arab extremists forced President Gamal Nasser of Egypt to move some 80,000 troops into the Sinai. He sent the

U.N. peacekeepers away and closed the Strait of Tiran, blocking Israel's only port on the Gulf of Aqaba. A defense treaty was signed between Jordan and Egypt on May 30.

Seeing the handwriting on the wall, Israeli defense forces attacked Egypt, Jordan, and Syria on June 5, 1967. The Arab forces survived through the intervention of the United States. Israel retained control of the Sinai Peninsula, the Gaza Strip, the Golan Heights in Syria, and the West Bank of the Jordan.

In early 1969, fighting broke out between Israel and Egypt along the Suez Canal. The United States helped end these hostilities. The Yom Kippur War started on October 6, 1973, when Egyptian and Syrian forces attacked Israel. Caught by surprise, the Israelis called up their reserves and pushed their adversaries back to the 1967 cease-fire lines.

Both the United States and the Soviet Union then took part in a series of peace negotiations, reminding their client states where their support came from. In March 1974, the Israeli Army withdrew from the banks of the Suez Canal. Syria and Israel signed a flimsy cease-fire on May 31, 1974. U.S. efforts to reconcile Israel with the Arab states bore fruit with an interim agreement between Israel and Egypt in 1975. In November 1977, Egyptian President Anwar Sadat visited Jerusalem. President Jimmy Carter led President Sadat and Israeli Prime Minister Menachem Begin to sit down together and talk at Camp David in 1978, and there has been a kind of peace between Israel and Egypt ever since.

Along the Israeli-Lebanese border, however, Palestine Liberation Front guerrillas, supported by Syrian troops, often cause serious trouble. The Palestinian Liberation Front has also caused serious outbreaks of civil disobedience within Israeli territory in recent years. Peace talks between the Palestine Liberation Organization and the Israeli government continue in Washington, D.C.; and this leads to some calm in the Middle East. The permanent settlement of Israel's right to exist, the extent of its territory, and the future of the displaced Palestine Arab peoples remain in question.

The military involvement of the United States in supporting Israel has been a U.S. foreign policy commitment since the end of World War II. As shown in Figure 4.2, the United States has committed enormous funds for military financing.

Added to this military hardware is approximately another $1.2 billion per year, so the total U.S. commitment averages close to $3 billion per year. Other countries have sold weapons to Israel, especially France, but none has given as much as the United States. Yet the Israeli government has managed to maintain more than just a semblance of resistance to U.S. foreign policy in the Middle East, especially after the recent oil war with Iraq over Kuwait.

The United Nations maintains a disengagement military force of some 1,130 in the Golan Heights between Israel and Syria. Other U.N. peacekeeping forces observe Israel's borders with Lebanon, Syria, and Egypt.

Over the years, Israel has provided for her own military defense, as shown in Figure 4.3 (p. 16).

Figure 4.2
U.S. Commitment of Funds to Military Financing, 1985–1993

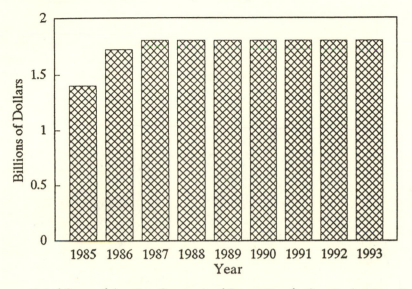

Source: United States of America, *Congressional Presentation for Security Assistance Programs,* Washington, D.C.: GPO. Various years and paging.

EGYPT

Egypt has a population of about 55 million, most of whom live at or below the marginal survival level. Over 20 percent of the total population live in the capital, Cairo. Egypt is a vast desert, except for the Nile Valley and delta where an estimated 95 percent or more of the population live. Egypt is a Moslem country with a form of democratic government. Egypt is often at gunpoint hostility with Israel, Libya, and Iraq. Only 40 to 50 percent of Egyptians can read or write.

Egypt is one of the oldest nations in the world, with recorded history stretching back to 6,000 years before Christ. A local ruler by the name of Menes united Egypt by military force about 3100 B.C. The military assumed its present importance in Egyptian society at this time. Conquered by the Persians in 525 B.C., the Greeks in 332 B.C., the Romans by 30 B.C., the Arabs in A.D. 642, and falling under Western European influence with the arrival of the British Army in 1882, Egypt was not to know true independence until after 1945.

Only in 1952 did the Egyptian Army overthrow the last of the British puppet rulers, King Farouk I. With this revolution began modern Egyptian history with the rule of Lieutenant Colonel Gamal Nasser. A pan-Arab socialist state developed. Close ties grew with the Soviet Union and Eastern

Figure 4.3
Israel's Military Defense Expenditures (In Billions of U.S. Dollars as a Percentage of GNP)

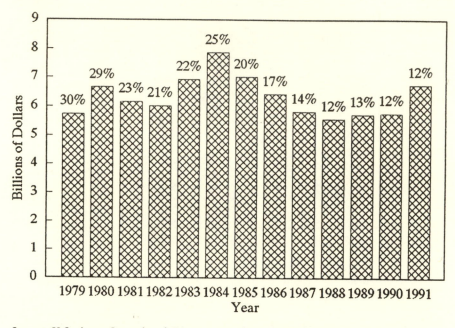

Source: U.S. Arms Control and Disarmament Agency, *World Military Expenditures and Arms Transfers,* Washington, D.C.: GPO, November 1991, p. 67. The figures for 1990 and 1991 are based on Huldt et al. *The Military Balance 1992–1993,* London: International Institute for Strategic Studies, 1992, p. 111.

Europe, especially Czechoslovakia, and armaments and military advisors rolled in.

When the Western-controlled World Bank withdrew its aid in 1956, Nasser nationalized the Suez Canal. This led to a combined Israeli, British, and French invasion that same year. Only heavy U.S. diplomatic pressure forced the withdrawal of these allied forces after the Egyptian defeat. The Egyptian military forces, Soviet led and equipped, fought very badly. Nasser's continued pan-Arab policies led to the Israeli attack in 1967 that almost totally destroyed the Egyptian armed forces. Only U.S. diplomatic intervention kept the Israelis from driving into Cairo.

Upon Nasser's death in 1970, Anwar el-Sadat became president with the military's help. He concluded a new treaty of friendship with the Soviet Union, but he sent the Soviet military advisors packing. In 1973, he made war on Israel. Although he lost, the Egyptian Army did well on the battlefield. With U.S. aid, Sadat began negotiating with Israel in 1974; and by 1977 he had signed two peace treaties over the Sinai and the Suez Canal. He visited Jerusalem in 1977, and went to Camp David for a meeting with Jimmy Carter and Menachem Begin of Israel. This opened the present era of reasonable relations with Israel. President Sadat also permitted greater political freedom through the formation of real opposition political parties and the growth of capitalistic investments. He was assassinated on October 6, 1981, by religious dissidents who hated what they called his "pro-Jew" policy.

His successor, Hosni Mubarak, has continued Sadat's policies of non-alignment, gradual democratization of the country, and peace with Israel. Egypt also joined the allied powers led by the United States in the war with Iraq over the issue of Kuwait. Cooperation remains firm between Egypt and the West.

There is no doubt that the security of the present Egyptian government rests with the loyalty of the Egyptian armed forces. These military units are equipped with a "potpourri" of weapons from both Western and Soviet bloc manufacturers. In recent years American and Egyptian military units have held joint training exercises in the desert. About 1,000 U.S. soldiers are peacekeepers on Egypt's Sinai peninsula. U.S. aid to Egypt is on a par with that given to Israel, as is shown in Figure 4.4. It is interesting to note that Egypt owed the United States $11.7 billion on June 30, 1988. The importance placed on the armed forces by the Egyptian government is shown by

Figure 4.4
U.S. Aid to Egypt (In Billions of U.S. Dollars)

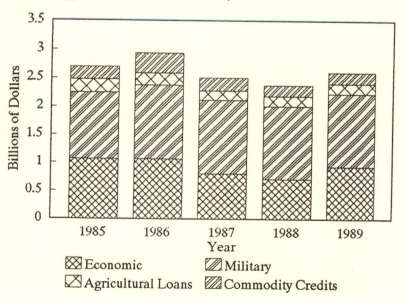

Source: U.S. Department of Commerce, *Foreign Economic Trends and Their Implications for the United States, Egypt,* Washington, D.C.: May 1989.

the following. In 1991, the Egyptian armed forces contained 420,000 actives, of which about 150,000 were draftees. Their ready reserve totaled another 604,000. That gave the Egyptian government the capacity to call upon more than 1,000,000 soldiers in time of war—nearly 2 percent of the total population. There is a U.N. peace-keeping force on Egypt's border with Israel.

The Egyptians pay an imposing sum, both in actual cost and as a percentage of GNP for their military establishment, as is shown in Figure 4.5.

YEMEN

The Independent Islamic Republic of Yemen was established by a merger of the Yemen Arab Republic and the People's Democratic Republic of Yemen on May 22, 1990. With an almost wholly desert surface, Yemen must support an estimated population of 12.4 million mainly on some proven oil reserves. More than one million Yemenites live and work abroad in other Arab countries, although many returned home during the Desert War with Iraq.

Figure 4.5
Egypt's Military Defense Expenditures (In Billions of U.S. Dollars as a Percentage of GNP)

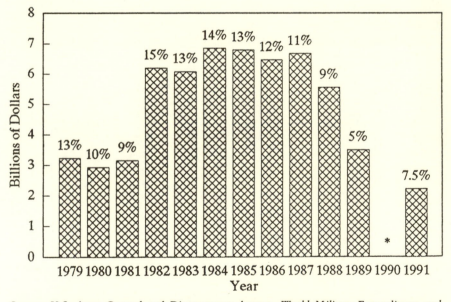

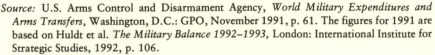

Source: U.S. Arms Control and Disarmament Agency, *World Military Expenditures and Arms Transfers,* Washington, D.C.: GPO, November 1991, p. 61. The figures for 1991 are based on Huldt et al. *The Military Balance 1992–1993,* London: International Institute for Strategic Studies, 1992, p. 106.
*Figures for 1990 are unavailable.

After World War II, what had been generally called Aden split into the Yemen Arab Republic (North Yemen) and the People's Democratic Republic of Yemen (South Yemen). North Yemen, about the size of Nebraska, remained under the traditional sheik and tribal form of government. In 1984, large oil reserves were proven in North Yemen. South Yemen, about the size of Wisconsin, adopted a more socialist outlook.

The proven oil reserves and the diminished British influence led to the outbreak of war between the two Yemens in 1979, and the Arab League intervened on several occasions to end border fighting. Conditions have been better under unification, but the new Yemen remains a military state. Many Yemenites are now expatriates, anxious to return home to overthrow the new republic.

In 1990, at the time of unification, Yemen went through protracted reorganization of its armed forces. Some 65,000 are regulars, but this figure may include as many as 45,000 draftees. The army reserves are perhaps as large as 40,000. There is a better armed and trained Central Security Agency (Security Police) of some 20,000 men.

The United States does not support Yemen's military security arrangements except with a trickle of supplies through Saudi Arabia and a small military mission. Before unification, the United States sold North Yemen some $348,068,000 worth of military hardware.[1] The Soviet Union was active in South Yemen.

Figures are not available as yet for the economic or military programs of the new Independent Islamic Republic of Yemen.

LEBANON

Lebanon, a country about the size of New Jersey with a population of somewhere between two and three million, is a military morass. A longstanding political compromise between various Moslem and Christian factions fragmented in 1975–1976 when the Lebanese armed forces dissolved into warring religious groups. Although the United States supported the efforts of the Lebanese central government to rebuild its army, the entire program collapsed in 1984. The United States remains committed to supporting what is called the central government and has sent in well over $200 million in humanitarian aid since 1975. However, the terrorist bombings of the U.S. Embassy and the U.S. Marine Corps barracks near Beirut's international airport in 1983 worsened U.S.–Lebanon relations.

Various internal military factors, as well as the presence of the normally Soviet-backed Syrian Army since 1977 and large numbers of Palestine Liberation Organization soldiers, have kept Lebanon in a constant warlike condition with neighboring Israel. A U.N. peace-keeping force of 5,300 men has served along the Lebanon–Israel border for years with varying results.

There is little hope for a return to peacetime conditions within Lebanon until Syrian and Israeli forces leave.

The summary of *The Congressional Security Assistance Program for 1993* shows a total of $20,997,000 going to Lebanon, of which none are earmarked for military financing.[2] Figures of support for the armed forces of the central Lebanese government after 1983 are either unavailable or unreliable.

The military situation in Lebanon since 1984 is best described as a civil war among multiple religious elements of the population with varying support levels from three interventionist powers—Israeli, Syria, and the United States. It remains to be seen if the U.N. peace-keeping forces (Blue Helmets) can maintain some semblance of public order.

SYRIA

Syria is about the size of North Dakota. Some two million of a total population of ten million live in the capital Damascus. Syrians in large measure are either Sunni Moslems or Christians, but the Kurdish minority remains a difficult problem for the government of President Hafez al-Assad. Since 1945 Syria has been preoccupied with three military problems: (1) maintaining some sort of government amid various warring army factions since the French withdrawal of 1946, (2) ending the existence of Israel, and (3) meddling in the internal affairs of Lebanon. Syria formed part of the United Arab Republic (with Egypt) from 1958 until 1970 when it ended, after the utter rout of its armed forces by the Israelis in June 1967.

The Syrian Army, largely trained and equipped by the Soviet Union, has seen as many as 5,000 Soviet soldiers stationed in the country at one time. The Syrian military forces still maintain a far-left political orientation. During the Iran–Iraq War of 1980–1988, Syria aligned itself with Iraq. Many Syrians work in Iraq and other Moslem countries. Without their sending large sums of money home, Syria's depressed economy might collapse. There is a U.N. peace-keeping force on the borders between Lebanon and Israel.

Because of the twenty-year Syrian–Soviet assistance pact signed in 1980, the U.S. Congress forbade, by a 1983 law, any aid to Syria. Syria is not listed in *The Congressional Presentation for Security Assistance Programs for Fiscal Year 1993.*

Syrian military expenditures have been heavy over the years, as is shown in Figure 4.6. There are scattered reports that Syrian society is becoming totally militarized. For example, Elizabeth Picard wrote, "The persistent war and heavy military rule do not have only negative effects on Syrian finance. Experts sometimes praise the leading role of the Syrian Army in national economy when it enters farming and building. They notice that public societies with military status have been exceptionally successful."[3]

Figure 4.6

Syria's Military Defense Expenditures (In Billions of U.S. Dollars as a Percentage of GNP)

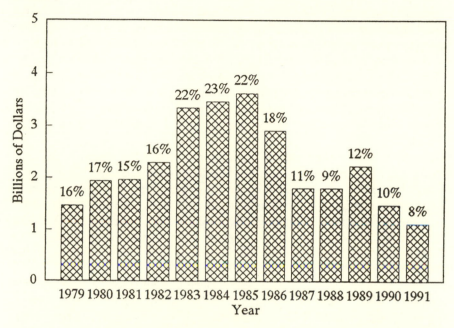

Source: U.S. Arms Control and Disarmament Agency, *World Military Expenditures and Arms Transfers,* Washington, D.C.: GPO, November 1991, p. 83. The figures for 1990 and 1991 are based on Heisbourg et al. *The Military Balance 1991–1992,* London: International Institute for Strategic Studies, 1991, p. 120, and Huldt et al. *The Military Balance 1992– 1993,* London: International Institute for Strategic Studies, 1992, p. 122.

IRAQ

Iraq is about the size of California. Nearly 25 percent of the sixteen million population live in the capital, Baghdad. Longstanding ethnic problems between the ruling Moslem groups and the Kurds keep the northern frontier provinces on the Turkish and Iranian borders in turmoil. Iraq gained independence in 1932, joined the United Nations in 1945, and helped found the Arab League. A military takeover in 1958 killed King Faysal II and many of the political leadership. The leader of this takeover was General Abdul Quasim, assassinated in February 1963. A series of further internal military actions led to Saddam Hussein becoming President and Chairman of the Revolutionary Command Council in July 1979.

Saddam Hussein controls all aspects of the country, working through the Ba'ath political party. His government is neither democratic nor Communist;

it is Iraqi and intensely nationalist. Iraqi's economy is based solely on its ability to sell oil via its nationalized petroleum industry.

The 1980–1988 Iran–Iraq War weakened the economy by increasing Iraqi's foreign debt unbearably. It has been charged that the United States aided Iraq in its war with Iran and largely looked the other way when Iraq prepared to grab Kuwait in order to use its oil to reduce the foreign debt.

As a result of the war with Iran, Saddam Hussein established his "People's Army." This army was estimated, before the Desert Storm operations in 1991, to contain nearly 400,000 regulars with a ready reserve of another 600,000. Armed mainly with second-rate Soviet equipment, the Iraqi Army was literally pounded into the ground by the U.N. forces led by the United States.

Since the end of the Desert War, Saddam Hussein has remained the only real power in Baghdad. He is often at odds with the United Nations over provisions of the armistice that ended the Desert War. There is a 500-man U.N. force stationed in the demilitarized zone between Iraq and Kuwait.

If there was heavy U.S. military aid to Iraq during the brief period between the resumption of full diplomatic relations in 1984 and the invasion of Kuwait in 1990, it is not revealed in the annual reports of the *Congressional Presentation for Security Assistance Programs.*

Iraq's military expenditures have not been known since 1979, when they totaled $5.414 billion, or 8 percent of the gross national product. It is interesting to note the growth figures of the Iraqi Army that are public knowledge, as shown in Figure 4.7. All source materials seem to think that this figure has remained near the one-million level. Obviously, by 1989 Saddam Hussein had called all his reserves to active service that lasted at least to the end of the Desert War in 1991.

JORDAN

Jordan is about the size of Indiana. Nearly 65,000 of a total population of only three million live in the capital city of Aman. Jordan is governed by a constitutional monarchy which recognizes only one political party, the Arab National Union. The British retired from Jordan on May 14, 1948. Three days later, the State of Israel came into being. Several Arab states, including Jordan, tried to help the Arab Palestinian nationalists opposed to the new Jewish state. This resulted in a type of warfare that really continued until April 3, 1949. Jordan remained in control of the West Bank of the Jordan River.

Jordan joined the Arab world in a treaty with Egypt in May 1967; and unfortunately, Jordan participated in the Six Day War against Israel in 1967. This war cost Jordan all control over the West Bank of the Jordan River. Nearly one million Palestinian refugees flooded into Jordan.

Tension between these refugees and the Jordanian government erupted into violence in September 1970. Included were such acts of terrorism as

Figure 4.7
Iraq's Military Strength in Millions of Men

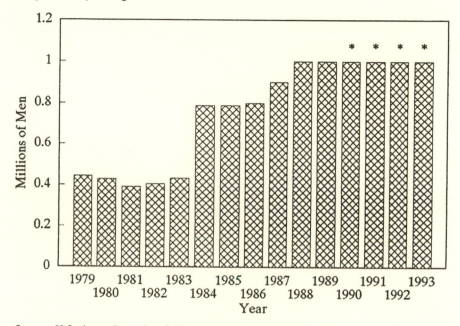

Source: U.S. Arms Control and Disarmament Agency, *World Military Expenditures and Arms Transfers,* Washington, D.C.: GPO, November 1991, p. 67.
*Figures for 1990–1993 are my own estimates.

taking civil aviation airliners hostage. Syrian forces even posed as Palestinian troops. It was not until July 1971 that government forces broke the back of the Palestinian resistance.

King Hussein I, who rules in Jordan, has a difficult role. Only 10 percent of his country's land can grow crops. Jordan, like Israel, has no oil; but she does have excellent phosphate deposits. A primary source of national income is money from Jordanians working in other countries. The Jordanian kingdom in recent years has walked a tightrope between Israel, Syria, Iraq, and Saudi Arabia. In such circumstances, it is not surprising that Jordan has come to depend upon the U.S. military almost as much as Israel.

From 1952 to 1988, Jordan received $1.5 billion in economic aid. U.S. security assistance began in 1950. It has been in the form of foreign sales credits for arms, education of military personnel, and other services. From 1950 to 1988, these forms of military aid amounted to $1.3 billion.

In more recent years, U.S. military assistance programs have been generous, as shown in Figure 4.8 (p. 24).

On her own side, the kingdom of Jordan has expended considerable money to arm and train her military forces, as shown in Figure 4.9 (p. 25).

Figure 4.8
U.S. Military Assistance Programs to Jordan (In Millions of U.S. Dollars)

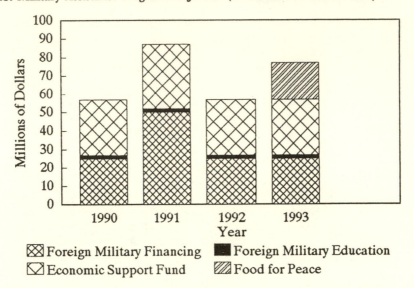

Source: United States of America, *Congressional Presentation for Security Assistance Programs, Fiscal Years 1990–1993,* Washington, D.C.: GPO.

Like all Arab states, some of Jordan's military forces are draftees. Most of Jordan's military equipment is of British make. Jordan also has a barely trained militia of some 250,000 men and women.

King Hussein I managed to stay out of the 1990–1991 war over Kuwait, but he came under heavy criticism for permitting Iraq to use Jordan's highway for truck convoys. The common opinion in the United States was that he had little choice.

SAUDI ARABIA

Saudi Arabia is about the size of the Old South. Some 4.5 million Saudis live in seven cities, out of a population of only 11 million. More than 4 million of the inhabitants of Saudi Arabia are foreign workers. The kingdom of Saudi Arabia has one of the largest proven oil reserves in the world. The United States has long since accepted the responsibility for the defense of the Saudi government. Saudi Arabia, strictly governed in accordance to Islamic Law, sees no need for a constitutional form of government.

The modern Saudi state was founded by Ibd Saud in 1902 by military conquest. The Saud family continued to expand its holdings until the British and French, under mandate from the League of Nations, drew boundaries

Figure 4.9
**Jordan's Military Expenditures as a Percentage of Gross National Product and
Numbers of Military Troops**

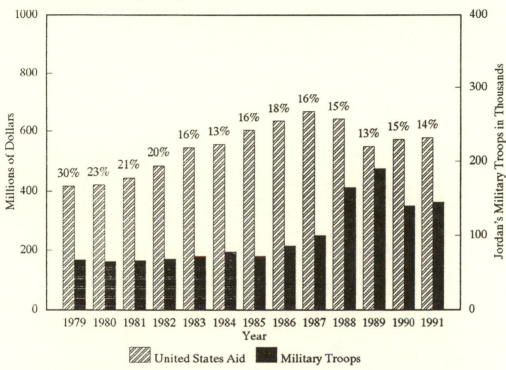

Source: U.S. Arms Control and Disarmament Agency, *World Military Expenditures and
Arms Transfers,* Washington, D.C.: GPO, November 1991, p. 69. The figures for 1990 and
1991 are based on Heisbourg et al. *The Military Balance 1991–1992,* London: International
Institute for Strategic Studies, 1991, p. 110, and Huldt et al. *The Military Balance 1992–
1993,* London: International Institute for Strategic Studies, 1992, p. 112.

in the sand with Jordan, Iraq, and Kuwait in the 1920s. The boundaries
with the United Arab Emirates and Yemen were established in the 1960s.

Although the oil reserves were proven in the 1930s, it was not until after
1945 that the spectacular rise in wealth began. Saudi Arabia would prefer
not to participate in the Arab League's wars with Israel. It is often a reluc-
tant and foot-dragging participant. Saudis prefer to remain at home and
count their oil-revenue-produced U.S. dollars. Nevertheless, Saudi Arabia
has become the heart and soul of the Organization of Petroleum Exporting
Countries (OPEC) and often acts to moderate extremist demands for price
increases from such countries as Iran and Iraq.

The history of Saudi Arabia since 1945 has been an uneasy one. King Faisal was assassinated by a member of the royal family in March 1975; and there is constant, sinister behind-the-scenes maneuvering within the family. Government is by consensus among the council of ministers appointed by the king. The king himself is the highest court in the land.

The Saudi military contains some 76,500. They have American and British armaments. The Saudi National Guard has 35,000 trained actives reinforced by 20,000 tribesmen, some still on camels. There is a frontier force of some 11,000. A small special security force of less than 1,000 men acts on direct orders from the king.

Saudi Arabia is one of the few Middle Eastern countries in which the military does not play a dominant role in politics. The most recent threats to internal security were these: In 1969, the Committee for the Liberation of Saudi Arabia staged an unsuccessful revolt. All the members were arrested but released after light jail terms. In 1979, a group of several hundred insurgents seized the Grand Mosque in Mecca. On the sixth day, Saudi troops stormed the mosque killing 102 while losing 127 soldiers. Some 16 civilian hostages also lost their lives. In January 1980, after a secret trial, 63 of the convicted insurgents were beheaded at public executions held in several cities throughout the country.

Saudi Arabia was the major staging ground for the U.N. forces in the Gulf War with Iraq over Kuwait. Although the Saudis did well, they learned that their military forces were too small; and they plan to triple their present military forces. Perhaps the Saudis are tired of being counted as a second-rate military power. More likely, they worry that the United States will continue to withdraw its military presence from around the world. Since 1945, the Saudi government has been spending the greatest part of its oil income on building a modern infrastructure for the country. There is little likelihood that the United States will abandon the Saudis militarily as long as the oil flows.

American military aid to the Saudis has been strictly on a "cash basis." Between 1950 and 1990, U.S. military sales agreements with Saudi Arabia amounted to $38,109,204,000.[4] For example, after the Iraqi invasion of Kuwait in 1991, the United States quickly sold Saudi Arabia F-15 jet fighter-bombers, M-60 tanks, and Stinger missiles to mention only a few weapons systems. U.S. arms sales to Saudi Arabia are complicated by Israeli opposition.[5]

Saudi Arabian military expenditures, heavily criticized by both the United States and Arab League partners, are shown in Figure 4-10.

For a peaceful government whose true wish is to improve living conditions for its own people, these figures are very large. They are about two to three times larger than expenditures by the U.S. government. Saudi Arabia has pressing human problems. Even with strict, rigorously enforced royal edicts, only 80 percent of Saudi children attend elementary school. Literacy is limited to about 60 percent for men and 40 percent for women.

Figure 4.10
Saudi Arabia's Military Defense Expenditures (In Billions of U.S. Dollars as a
Percentage of GNP)

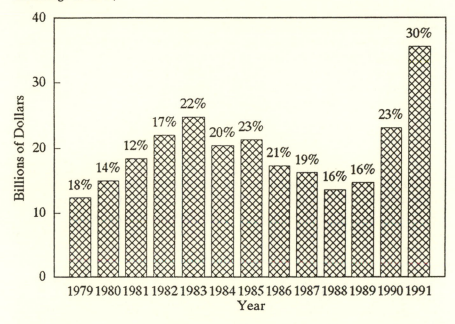

Source: U.S. Arms Control and Disarmament Agency, *World Military Expenditures and Arms Transfers*, Washington, D.C.: GPO, November 1991, p. 79. The figures for 1990 and 1991 are based on Huldt et al. *The Military Balance 1992–1993*, London: International Institute for Strategic Studies, 1992, p. 120.

OMAN

Located near the end of the horn of the Arabian Gulf, Oman is about the size of New Mexico and has a population of only 1.3 million. Oman is an important Middle East state since all oil tankers from Iran and Iraq must pass through the nearby Strait of Hormuz. Most army equipment is of British manufacture, and Omani and British armies often hold joint training exercises. The United States also has permission to build bases and store stocks of ammunition and other military hardware on Omani territory. The country is relatively wealthy from its oil production, but its proven reserves should last only another 25 years.

Among noteworthy political events since 1945 was the inclusion of Oman in the British sphere of influence by treaty in 1951. The British helped put down the traditionally rebellious internal Muscat tribes in the 1950s. On July 23, 1970, Sultan Said ibn Taimur was overthrown by his son. Oman opened its air bases to U.N. forces during the Gulf War.

The well-equipped Omani armed forces contain about 31,000 men and some 3,700 foreigners. The Royal Guard is at the 4,000 level; there is a Home Guard of some 3,500, plus several other small contingents.

The United States has furnished military assistance and economic support to Oman in recent years, as can be seen from Table 4.1.

Oman invests a substantial portion of her gross national product in her own defense, as shown in Figure 4.11.

During this same time, the Omani Armed Forces grew from 13,000 to 29,000 men. Oman suffers from a severe budget strain to keep its military at such highly trained and equipped effectiveness.

IRAN

Iran is a bit bigger than Alaska. It has a population of about 50 million, of whom 93 percent are Shi'a Muslims. Less than one-half of the population is literate. The present government is an Islamic Republic established in 1979. Iran entered the modern world with the discovery of oil in 1908. In 1925, Reza Shah Pahlavi began his sixteen-year rule as a result of military conquest. In 1942, the military forced his abdication in favor of his son, Mohammad Reza Pahlavi. During World War II, Iran was a supply route to the Soviet Union. In 1945, Soviet troops refused to quit two northern provinces until pressured by the British, the Americans, and the United Nations.

The year 1951 saw Premier Mohammad Mossadeq nationalize the British-dominated oil industry. Massadeq tried a military takeover in 1953 but was himself arrested by the Shah. Iran began a series of reforms to westernize in 1961. These reforms were sharply criticized by conservative Shi'a Muslim leaders. One of these leaders, the Ayatollah Khomeini, led a successful revolution in 1979. By 1982, most of the vestiges of the Shah's government were gone, as were many of its leaders and followers.

Table 4.1
U.S. Aid to Oman (In U.S. Dollars)

	1991	1992	1993
Military Financing		5,000,000	1,000,000
International Military Education	100,000	100,000	110,000
Economic Support Fund	15,000,000	15,000,000	15,000,000
Totals	15,100,000	20,100,000	16,110,000

Source: United States of America, *Congressional Presentation for Security Assistance Programs, Fiscal Years 1991–1993,* Washington, D.C.: GPO, 1991–1993.

Figure 4.11
Oman's Military Defense Expenditures (In Billions of U.S. Dollars as a Percentage of GNP)

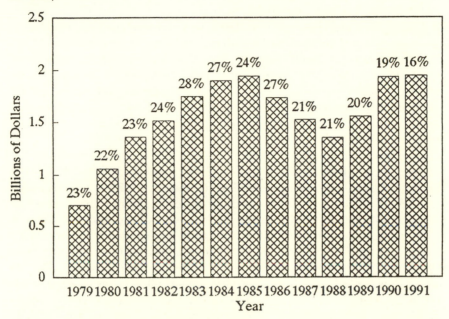

Source: U.S. Arms Control and Disarmament Agency, *World Military Expenditures and Arms Transfers,* Washington, D.C.: GPO, November 1991, p. 76. The figures for 1990 and 1991 are based on Huldt et al. *The Military Balance 1992–1993,* London: International Institute for Strategic Studies, 1992, p. 118.

As a result of the storming of the U.S. embassy in Teheran by Revolutionary Guards in 1979 and the holding of 62 U.S. citizens as hostages, diplomatic relations were broken off with Iran in April 1980. Iranian assets in the United States were frozen. The hostages were released in 1981, and Iran's money in U.S. banks was restored some time later.

The Iran–Iraq War began in 1980 over control of the Shatt Al-Arab waterway, which is part of the boundary between the two nations. Both nations use parts of this waterway to move oil to foreign markets. The war continued until 1988, resulting in hundreds of thousands of casualties on both sides. Each side accused the other of using biological and chemical warfare.

This war left Iran with an enormous debt and a weakened government. Many of the Western industrialized nations, including both Britain and the United States, had turned elsewhere for foreign oil purchases they might make.

In November 1986, prominent U.S. political leaders offered to furnish Iran with modern armaments. In return Iran would use her good offices to obtain the release of U.S. hostages held by Shi'a Moslem groups in Lebanon. This sparked a political crisis in the United States. It may also have resulted in the release of the hostages. A U.S. Navy warship accidentally shot down an Iranian civil airliner in 1986.

During the Desert War of 1990–1991, Iran remained neutral, although it gave sanctuary to most of Iraq's outdated air force.

Relationships between Iran and the United States continue guarded. Before the 1979 revolution, the United States provided billions of dollars in arms sales and military assistance to the Shah's government. American military advisors were plainly visible throughout the country, as were American teachers and technicians. Iran formed a part of the electronic spy network on the Soviet Union.

Over the years, Iran has undoubtedly spent a great deal of money on her military forces. Between 1979 and 1982 this amounted to possibly 6 to 8 percent of gross national product. The figures after 1982 are not available in uniform reliable form from source to source but seem to be in the 20 to 50 percent range, especially during the last years of the Iran–Iraq War.

Estimates vary widely about the strength of Iran's military forces. A composite and conservative estimate is that Iran maintains a total military force of about 500,000 men, plus some 200,000 Revolutionary Guards. There is also a Popular Militia, which appears to include all men over the age of 14. There are some armed opposition groups to the present government, especially that of the Kurdish minority. All opposition groups are small, ill armed, and almost without training. There is no provable U.S. involvement in any of these antigovernment groups.

BAHRAIN

The tiny oil-producing state of Bahrain is about four times the size of Washington, D.C. It really is an archipelago consisting of 33 islands. People live on only 5 of them. Geographically Bahrain sits across the Persian Gulf from Iran. The 500,000 people of this tiny country are governed by an Emir in the traditional Arab way. They are mostly Arabs, divided between the Shi'a (60 percent) and Sunni (30 percent) sects. Over one-half the work force are expatriates.

Bahrain obtained her independence from Britain in 1971. The local government purchased a controlling interest in the country's oil production in 1975.

Bahrain has a total 7,500 men in her armed forces. They are supplied with recent military hardware. There is an internal police force of some 9,000 men in this well-governed Arab state.

The United States does not give military aid to Bahrain. The *Congressional Presentation for Security Assistance Programs, Fiscal Year 1993* says:

"The F93 request for Foreign Military Financing would support the purchase of spare parts and associated support for Bahrain's existing inventory of C-130 aircraft."[6] The United States had sold Bahrain $971.5 million worth of military hardware as of September 1991.

In her own defense, Bahrain spends at the levels shown in Figure 4.12.

KUWAIT

This tiny, oil-rich Arab nation was the flash point in the Desert War of 1990–1991. The Iraqi Army of Saddam Hussein overran this tiny country in a matter of hours. Iraq's refusal to restore Kuwait's independence led to the Desert Shield–Desert Storm U.N. Operations of 1990–1991. Kuwait was liberated while the Iraqi Army was soundly defeated.

Figure 4.12
Bahrain's Military Defense Expenditures (In Millions of U.S. Dollars as a Percentage of GNP)

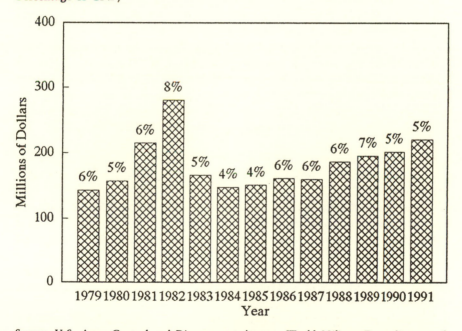

Source: U.S. Arms Control and Disarmament Agency, *World Military Expenditures and Arms Transfers*, Washington, D.C.: GPO, November 1991, p. 53. The figures for 1990 and 1991 are based on Heisbourg et al. *The Military Balance 1991–1992*, London: International Institute for Strategic Studies, 1991, p. 103, and Huldt et al. *The Military Balance 1992–1993*, London: International Institute for Strategic Studies, 1992, p. 105.

Kuwait is ruled by the Al-Sabah dynasty under the guise of a constitutional monarchy. Elections in 1992 may eventually lead to some political change. There is a growing women's civil rights movement. There are fewer than 700,000 Kuwaitis in a population of nearly two million. The others are foreign workers from Iraq, India, Egypt, the United States, and Britain, among others. More than 70 percent of the Kuwaitis are literate. Although a member of the Arab League, Kuwait maintains an ambiguous attitude toward Israel. Even after the war, Kuwait remains one of the richest nations in the world. There are 500 U.N. troops stationed in the demilitarized zone between Kuwait and Iraq.

United States current military support "consists solely of Foreign Military Sales Cash or commercial sales. Kuwait's planned purchases are designed to replace and upgrade equipment lost during the Iraqi occupation."[7] The United States negotiated sales agreements with Kuwait for $3.75 billion in military equipment in the period 1950–1991.[8]

Kuwait's present military forces total 8,000 to 10,000 men in all branches, including the royal guard and the security police. Some 300 to 400 U.N. troops from at least 30 countries are still in Kuwait to observe the rules of the armistice ending the 1991 Desert War. Kuwait's military equipment is still not up to world standards except for her air force, which has been reequipped with French Mirage jets.

Unlike most members of the Arab League, Kuwait spends her money on infrastructure and on producing the good life for her population. Kuwait's military expenditures over the years have been modest. Between 1979 and 1989, they were never less than 3 percent and never more than 6 percent of GNP. Kuwait prefers to depend on foreign allies, especially Saudi Arabia and the United States, for security. To date this has been a successful defense policy.

QATAR

Qatar is an oil-rich Arab nation about the size of both Connecticut and Rhode Island. The population is about 250,000. The government is a traditional Moslem emirate. Qatar is located on a peninsula in the Persian Gulf just across from Iran. The British left Qatar in 1971.

This Arab sheikdom has a modest military establishment of perhaps 7,500. French Mirage jet fighter aircraft are the best part of the country's military hardware. Qatar purchases most of her military equipment from the French and the British. However, the *Congressional Presentation for Security Assistance Programs 1993,* notes: "In FY93 and beyond, Qatar and the US will be working to improve our security relationship in the aftermath of Operation Desert Shield/Storm. The Qataris have expressed a need to upgrade their air defense system, and have specifically indicated a desire to acquire Patriot missiles and . . . a system to protect the Amir's plane."[9]

Qatar's contributions to her own defense averaged 8 percent of GNP in 1979–1980. The sheikdom has not released any defense figures since 1980.

UNITED ARAB EMIRATES

The United Arab Emirates occupy space along the Persian Gulf stretching from Oman to Qatar. The entire country is about the size of Maine. The British left this region in 1971. Bahrain and Qatar left the federation in September 1971. The oil companies were nationalized in 1975. At present the United Arab Emirates are a loosely joined federation of seven Moslem sheikdoms with a population of about 1,300,000. These emirates sit on a pool of oil and are major suppliers of the Japanese, among others.

These oil-rich emirates maintain a standing military establishment of some 44,000, of which as many as 15,000 may be foreigners. Most of their better military equipment is of French and British manufacture. The United Arab Emirates do not actively participate in American military assistance programs.

From 1979 to 1989, the United Arab Emirates averaged spending 7 percent of their GNP on military expenditures of all kinds. Obviously the emirates prefer to spend their oil revenues on more peaceful pursuits.

NOTES

1. FMS Control and Reports Division, Comptroller, DSAA, *Foreign Military Sales, Foreign Military Construction Sales and Military Assistance Facts, as of September 30, 1991,* Washington, Data Management Division, Comptroller DSSA, 1992.

2. United States of America, *Congressional Presentation for Security Assistance Programs, Fiscal Year 1993,* Washington, GPO, Jointly prepared by the Department of State and the Defense Security Agency, 1992.

3. Elizabeth Picard, "Assad's Syria," *Journal of Defense and Diplomacy,* August 1986, p. 45.

4. *Foreign Military Sales, September 30, 1991.*

5. *Congressional Presentation, Fiscal Year 1993.*

6. Ibid., p. 104.

7. Ibid., p. 220.

8. *Foreign Military Sales, September 30, 1991.*

9. *Congressional Presentation, Fiscal Year 1993,* p. 287.

□ □ **5**

The Indian Ocean Area

This immense area of the world is home to civilizations that predate those of Egypt and Europe. Nearly 1.2 billion people inhabit India, Pakistan, Afghanistan, Sri Lanka, Bangladesh, Bhutan, Maldive Islands, and Nepal. Every independent nation in this area has internal and external feuds that often erupt into border conflicts and sometimes even into declared wars. The conflicts in this part of the world predate colonial times and the 1500s.

Portuguese, Spanish, and British imperialist holdings kept some control over large areas from about 1750 until 1945. For nearly two centuries, the white colonial powers built up a class of native civil servants and curried favor with the most reasonable of the native rulers. The Europeans believed that they were performing a civilizing mission.

As independence rushed into this area after 1945, many vestiges of Western rule remained; all these nations have constitutions and some form of elected representation. Yet there are impossible overpopulation problems, and old tribal and religious problems continue to this day: the India–Pakistan feud, Sri Lanka's tribal wars, and (despite the departure of the Soviet Army and the collapse of the Soviet puppet government in Kabal) the civil war in Afghanistan, which keeps the country in near complete chaos. Even the tiny Maldive Islands have internal problems.

The dominant problem in this area is the longstanding confrontation between India and Pakistan, which led to war over the province of Kashmir and the breaking away of Bangladesh from Pakistan.

There is mass poverty in this badly overpopulated portion of the world. For example, Bangladesh's 118 million people average a per capita income of $180. Feeding the present starving millions is beyond this area's governments.

Figure 5.1 (p. 36) illustrates the real problem of this part of the world.

Even the centuries-old problems of racial, religious, and tribal hatreds pale before such overwhelming poverty. The governments of India, Pakistan,

Figure 5.1
Indian Ocean Area, Total Population and per Capita Income (In U.S. Dollars)

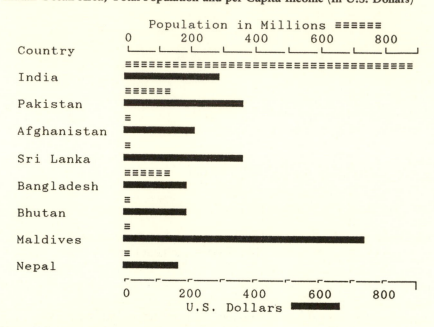

Note: U.S. 1990 per capita income was $21,800.

Afghanistan, Sri Lanka, Bangladesh, Bhutan, the Maldive Islands, and Nepal cannot afford to buy even one round of ammunition. Yet what they did buy and receive from the United States, France, Britain, Israel, and the former Soviet Union since 1945 is described in the balance of this chapter.

INDIA

India is the largest country in this part of the world with a land area larger than Alaska, Texas, and Montana and an estimated population of 884 million. India has a democratic form of government and became independent from Britain in 1947. The major trading partners have been the United States, the Soviet Union, Britain, Iran, and Iraq.

India joined the United Nations and the British Commonwealth of Nations in 1947. The ethnic feuding between a Hindu majority and a Muslim minority led to the creation of Pakistan at the time of independence from Britain. India and Pakistan have rarely been friendly, and at times they have been close to total war. The focal point of this dispute has been control of the province of Kashmir. In 1947, the Hindu ruler of the Moslem majority in

Kashmir decided to join India. Brief open wars occurred over Kashmir in 1947–1948 and in 1965.

In 1971, India and Pakistan also fought over East Pakistan until this province became the independent state of Bangladesh, when friction cooled. However, the Soviet invasion of Afghanistan (1979–1988) caused great concern in India. Pakistan rapidly built up her armed forces with U.S. military aid.

Indian politics is dominated by the mainly Hindu Congress Party, led first by Gandhi and now by his heirs. The continued border troubles with Pakistan, added to a few border clashes with China over Tibet and Nepal, give the military a key roll in Indian society. A Sikh revolt in 1984 killed Prime Minister Indira Gandhi. A short civil war resulted in which the Indian Army killed thousands of Sikhs.

In 1990–1991, there were repeated clashes between Indian Army units and independence movement groups in Kashmir. The Sikhs remain an unsettling ingredient in Indian society, where hatreds based on religion are an important element. A U.N. military observer group remains along the Indian–Pakistani cease-fire line in Kashmir.

A Third World government with this record of external and internal violence must maintain a strong military presence. Thus India has accepted both economic and military aid from all available sources. The Soviet Union was a reliable supplier of military aid to India before the end of the Cold War. From 1951 to 1984, the United States provided India with about $12 billion in humanitarian aid. In 1990, India began to show interest in possible military aid from the United States. The *Congressional Presentation for Security Assistance Program, Fiscal Year 1993* says: "The proposed . . . program will contribute to our overall goal of increasing military-to-military ties. Its emphasis on resource management courses, technical training and professional military education for mid- and senior-level officers builds on the Indian Armed Forces' tradition of respect for democracy and civilian control of the military" (p. 195).

The Indian armed forces number more than one million. Their military equipment is of various capabilities, depending on when purchased and from whom. The Indian Army has a fierce reputation of loyalty to the national government. It has excellent fighting qualities. It does not hesitate to open fire on unruly elements within the country.

Since 1979, India has spent 3 percent of her gross national product supporting an army that grew from 444,000 to 1.3 million in 1991. India's GNP increase of $97 billion to $287 billion from 1979 to 1991 was offset by a corresponding growth in population. The poverty of the Indian population in comparison to that of the industrialized First World increased accordingly.

Until the border problems with both Pakistan and China are resolved,

India continues to spend large sums of money she cannot afford on her military.

PAKISTAN

Pakistan has a population of some 113 million. It is about the size of California. It borders India, China, the former Soviet Union, Afghanistan, and Iran. This is the reason the military has remained the dominant factor in Pakistani society. Pakistan was created out of the Moslem majority parts of British India in 1947. There were two parts of Pakistan separated by Republic of India territory. In 1970, East Pakistan became Bangladesh as a result of a local revolt supported by the Indian Army. Pakistan is an Islamic republic with universal adult suffrage. A series of sometimes bloodless and sometimes bloody military takeovers occurred in 1948, 1951, 1958, and 1962. Actual democratic forms were reestablished in 1970.

The loss of Bangladesh in 1971 led to the election of Zulfigar Ali Bhutto as president. He was active with the other Islamic nations as well as throughout the Third World. He brought state socialism to Pakistan. He did not call for another election until 1977.

A restless army removed Bhutto from office. Martial law began. Actual democratic government emerged again in 1985. Further complications occurred. President Mohammed Zia ul-Haq died when his official plane exploded in 1988. Benazir Bhutto, a woman, was elected president in a 1988 free election. She was soundly beaten in a similar free election in 1990. In 1991, the Pakistani parliament began passing legislation to replace current secular law with the Islamic Koran.

The Russian presence in Afghanistan from 1979 to 1988 caused immense economic dislocation in Pakistan. Several million Afghan refugees arrived in Pakistan. The country was the staging ground for Afghan resistance fighters. The United States furnished these Afghan military units with weapons training, and various other forms of military support. Pakistan chose these same years to build up her own military forces. This decision caused fear around her frontiers, especially in India. There is a U.N. observer group along the Indian–Pakistani cease-fire line in Kashmir.

U.S. aid to Pakistan from 1950 to 1991 amounted to about $5 billion.[1] All military debts owed the United States were forgiven in 1989. Military aid was suspended in October 1990. It will not be resumed until Pakistan returns to a democratic form of government. Yet, the United States intends to send $55,681,000 in economic aid to Pakistan in 1993 under the Food for Peace, Peace Corps, and International Narcotics Control funds.[2]

Currently Pakistan maintains 565,000 men in her active armed forces. She claims a reasonably ready reserve of another 500,000. All males have a military obligation of a possible eight years active service. Most of their equipment is of U.S. manufacture. There are several French weapons beginning to appear, especially Mirage fighter bombers. Pakistan is participating in U.N. peace-keeping activities in Kuwait. She has nearly 1,000 military advisors working in Saudi Arabia.

Her main enemy continues to be India. Her most critically pressing problem is dealing with the Afghan refugees. With the Russian departure from Afghanistan and the recent fall of the Communist government in Kabul, the Afghani freedom fighters have begun fighting among themselves. There are reasonable fears that this will spread across the frontier into the Afghan refugee camps in Pakistan.

Pakistani defense spending is shown in Figure 5.2.

AFGHANISTAN

The population of Afghanistan must be about 16 million, counting refugees still in Pakistan and Iran. Modern Afghanistan began with Ahmad Shah Durrani in 1747. This dynasty lasted until the Communist takeover in 1978. Germany, Russia, and Britain all tried to influence Afghanistan, with disastrous results for themselves. Although Britain did effectively control

Figure 5.2
Pakistan's Military Defense Expenditures (In Billions of U.S. Dollars as a Percentage of GNP)

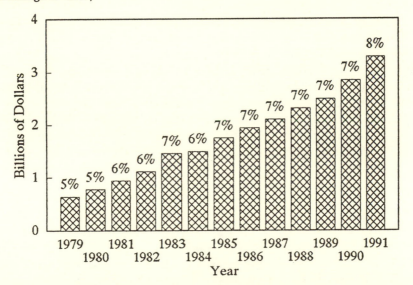

Source: U.S. Arms Control and Disarmament Agency, *World Military Expenditures and Arms Transfers,* Washington, D.C.: GPO, November 1991, p. 76. The figures for 1990 and 1991 are based on Heisbourg et al. *The Military Balance 1991–1992,* London: International Institute for Strategic Studies, 1991, p. 175, and Huldt et al. *The Military Balance 1992–1993,* London: International Institute for Strategic Studies, 1992, p. 135.

Afghani foreign affairs, she never managed to exercise military control. Neither did the Russians. The Germans tried to play up anti-British feelings during World War I. Afghanistan remained neutral.

Despite some attempts to modernize Afghanistan from 1920 to 1978, the essential political fact of this underdeveloped, underpopulated land remained intact. Numerous tribes continue to rule Afghanistan. Independent tribal leaders give their allegiance to the Shah in Kabul with curt nods of their heads when it pleases them to do so.

The Marxist takeover in April 1978 brought on immediate civil war. In December 1978, Russian troops entered the country. By 1980 there were 85,000 Russian troops in Afghanistan. They controlled the cities and the main connecting highways. The Afghani freedom fighters operated mainly from refugee camps in Pakistan and Iran. They fought the Russians and the Afghani Communists with everything from rocks to rockets. The United States furnished the freedom fighters with military equipment and training. When the Russians backed out in 1989 they took 120,000 of their troops home.

After the Russians left, the Afghani Communist government fell to the freedom fighters. Now the various groups of freedom fighters are warring with each other for control of the country. Politics in Afghanistan today clearly resembles politics in Afghanistan in 1747.

There cannot have been any economic growth in Afghanistan, at least not since 1979. The United States did give possibly as much as $500 million to the humanitarian aid of Afghani refugees.[3]

The now nonexistent Afghani Communist Army was 40,000 strong. It had Soviet equipment. Its air force had Soviet MIG 23 fighter bombers. The Afghani freedom fighters divide into at least thirteen major groups. Many of these groups still operate from refugee camps in Iran and Pakistan. The numbers of these freedom fighters has between estimated to be from 40,000 to 375,000 men. The Afghani military situation is one big mess.

Afghani Communist government spending on military defense is shown in Figure 5.3. Figures are unavailable after 1984. Estimates of damages and casualty figures in the present war are unreliable and hence unavailable.

SRI LANKA

Sri Lanka has a population of about 17 million. It is an island off the southwestern coast of India almost the same size as West Virginia. It is a country of extraordinary lush green mountains, wide valleys, and rushing rivers. Sri Lanka was formerly called Ceylon. It was here that the British colonial masters developed the best of their most famous products, tea.

All this peacefulness ended with independence in 1948. Sri Lanka has her India–Pakistan border feud. Unfortunately, her trouble is internal. The Sinhalese form some 75 percent of the population. There is a minority ethnic group called the Tamils, about 25 percent of the population. These two

Figure 5.3
Afghanistan's Military Defense Expenditures (In Millions of U.S. Dollars as a
Percentage of GNP)

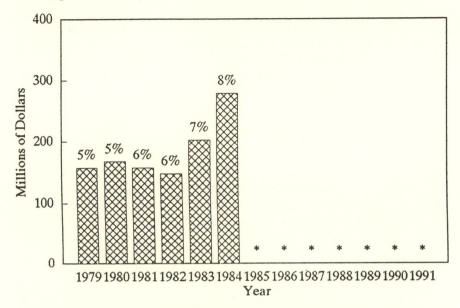

Source: U.S. Arms Control and Disarmament Agency, *World Military Expenditures and
Arms Transfers,* Washington, D.C.: GPO, November 1991, p. 52.
*Figures after 1984 are unavailable.

groups simply hate each other. They have done so for many centuries. Certainly the Sinhalese military forces are trying to force assimilation on the minority Tamils.

Sri Lanka has been strongly democratic. The Sri Lanka Freedom party and the United National party often alternate ruling. As racial violence grew, this political compromise collapsed by 1989.

As early as 1956, there were occasional outbreaks of violence as the Tamil group became more radicalized. They were easily influenced by the local Communists. By 1983, Sinhalese soldiers died in their terrorist actions. Hundreds of Tamils died in the capital city of Colombo. Thousands of Tamils were left homeless in these same purges. The dominant role of the military in Sri Lankan society dates from these episodes.

By 1987, the internal terrorist and counterterrorist actions reached such epidemic heights that the Sri Lankan government asked for military intervention by India. India sent in troops and mediators. Several concessions to the Tamils raised hopes for peace.

The compromise collapsed when the Tamil militants refused to disarm. By late 1988, the Tamil minority raised serious insurrections throughout the country. The Sri Lankan government's troops struck back with great ferocity.

Yet to be restored is the calm of British colonial rule. About 25,000 have died in this civil war since 1983. The armed forces of the Sri Lankan government are small and inadequate for its needs. A total of 90,000 men are counted. Only 25,000 are in the standing establishment. British armaments prevail. There are also 30,000 national police controlled by the defense department. During these years of civil war, many communes have accepted the training of their men as home guards.

Their opposition now amounts to probably less than 2,000 very well trained and reasonably well armed guerrillas. They call themselves the Lieration Tigers of Tamil Eelam. "The Tigers" received military aid from the Soviet Union until 1989.

The United States provided only $2 million for military sales, construction, and assistance during the period 1950–1991.[4] The U.S. government is cool to further aid because "In the course of anti-insurgency operations, Sri Lankan security forces have sometimes used excessive force and violated human rights." There is a proposed training program for Sri Lankan military personnel intended to improve their human rights performance.[5]

Sri Lankan provision for her military forces is shown in Figure 5.4.

The Sri Lankan government's key to winning the civil war is the use of its large security force. They are pounding "the Tamil Tigers" into the ground. Such a series of localized military actions often takes many years. It is a cheap way to win a civil war. The British did the same thing in Malaya after 1945.

BANGLADESH

Bangladesh, with a population of 118 million and a per capita annual income of $180, is one of the poorest nations in the world. The literacy rate is only 30 percent. Only 60 percent of the children receive any form of primary education at all. Poor is the only justifiable description of Bangladesh. This country needs peace.

The British divided their possessions in India into the Republic of India and the Islamic Republic of Pakistan in 1947. Pakistan existed in eastern and western halves. About 1,000 miles of Indian territory separated the two parts of Pakistan. The majority Bengal population in East Pakistan resisted assimilation attempts by the national government, located in West Pakistan. The introduction of Urdu as the only official language greatly distressed the Bengals.

By 1954, West Pakistan was ruling Bengal by a form of martial law. Conditions deteriorated year by year until open civil war began in 1971 with the declaration of the Peoples' Republic of Bangladesh. Open fighting between the rebels and the West Pakistan garrisons saw millions of Bengals flee into India. Finally war began between India and Pakistan in November 1971.

Figure 5.4
Sri Lanka's Military Expenditures as a Percentage of Gross National Product and Numbers of Military Troops

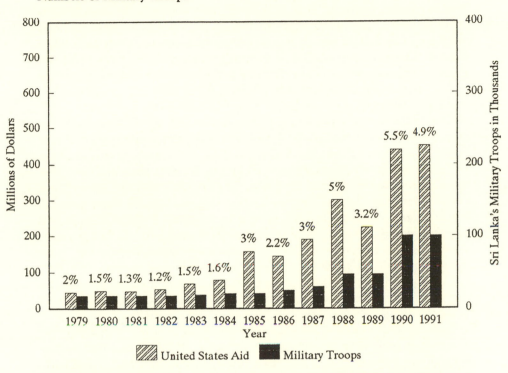

Source: U.S. Arms Control and Disarmament Agency, *World Military Expenditures and Arms Transfers,* Washington, D.C.: GPO, November 1991, p. 81. The figures for 1990–1991 are based on Huldt et al. *The Military Balance 1992–1993,* London: International Institute for Strategic Studies, 1992, p. 137.

The Indian Army, with the help of tens of thousands of Bengal rebels, overwhelmed the West Pakistani garrisons. West Pakistan could not send reinforcements across 1,000 miles of Indian territory. By the end of 1971 Bangladesh was a newly independent nation.

The Bangladeshi government is of a democratic variety run by a series of very strong leaders. Sheikh Mujibur Rahma actually ran the country until 1977. In that year some form of martial law became the normal way of life. Ziaur Rahman took control. He died at the hands of the dissident military in 1981. Lieutenant General H. M. Erchad seized power in 1982. A system of "on again–off again" martial law maintains law and order. Erchad declared Bangladesh an Islamic Republic in 1988.

In 1988, 1989, and 1991 natural disasters such as monsoon-induced flooding and whole series of cyclones made the Bangladeshi people even poorer.

In 1991, some 8,000 U.S. military personnel helped the Bangladeshi government in a humanitarian fashion after the series of cyclones killed at least 150,000 people and left millions homeless. The Soviet Union initially helped arm the army. Mainland China also gives military and economic aid. Between 1950 and 1991, the United States made some $3.4 million worth of military sales agreements with Bangladesh.[6] In 1992, the United States provided a total of $2.1 billion in various security aid programs. The 1993 plans recognize: "The military plays a critical role as the backbone of relief operations in this disaster-prone country, and supports the country's efforts at building a democratic system."[7]

The civil war that started in the Hill Tracts as early as 1971 intensifies the tragedy of Bangladesh. The Hill Tracks are the most sparsely populated region of this ravaged country. Thirty-two local tribes make up a population of 600,000. Most of these tribes have old-style tribal governments. They are also almost 100 percent Buddhist. The Hill Tracks population began resisting attempts by the Bangladeshi Army to incorporate them into the Muslim state. The tribes began raiding army outposts. By 1990 the attempts to put down this revolt on the part of the Moslem majority reached genocide proportions. Apparently there is no possible compromise solution. How many hill tribesmen remain under arms is unknown.

Consequently the military remain the most important element in Bangladeshi society. Without a strong armed force loyal to the central government, it would collapse overnight.

This explains why Bangladeshi armed forces are over the 100,000 mark. About 90 percent of these troops are in the army. Bangladesh also maintains a strong border guard force of more than 30,000 men. Another 20,000 more are in the national security police controlled by the department of defense.

Bangladesh's own defense efforts are shown in Figure 5.5. Bangladesh is dependent on worldwide charity to feed her population. She fights her Hill tribesmen as the British did their Malayan Communist guerrillas after 1945.

BHUTAN

Bhutan is a small country, about the size of Vermont and New Hampshire. Geographically it is squeezed between China and India. The estimated population is 1.5 million. The capital, Thimpu, has a population of less than 25,000. Most of the population farm for a living.

Bhutan is a monarchy without a constitution. Under a 1949 treaty, Bhutan agreed to be guided by India; but not until 1971 did Bhutan even open a diplomatic office in New Delhi. In 1978 this delegation became a full embassy. Bhutan is now a member of the United Nations and a full member of several other international and regional associations. The United States does not have any diplomatic relations with Bhutan. The road and air networks link Bhutan only with India.

Figure 5.5
Bangladesh's Military Expenditures as a Percentage of Gross National Product and
Numbers of Military Troops

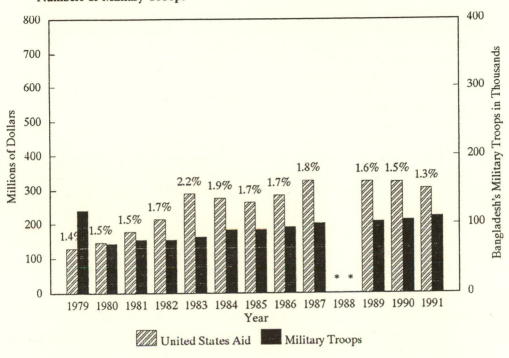

United States Aid ■ Military Troops

Source: U.S. Arms Control and Disarmament Agency, *World Military Expenditures and Arms Transfers,* Washington, D.C.: GPO, November 1991, p. 54. The figures for 1990 and 1991 are based on Huldt et al. *The Military Balance 1992–1993,* London: International Institute for Strategic Studies, 1992, p. 130.
*Figures for 1988 are unavailable.

The Royal Army began in the 1950s only after the Chinese takeover of nearby Tibet. Military training and supply are provided by India. There is a small internal security force as well. Total military forces may run to 12,000. The country appears very peaceful and serene.

MALDIVES

The 1,200 islands of the Republic of the Maldives make up 115 square miles. The total population may be as large as 225,000. The Maldives lie off the southwestern coast of India. The literacy rate is 93 percent. A republican form of government replaced the sultanate in 1968. A strong British military presence remained in the Maldives from 1956 to 1976. Sri Lankan mercenaries attacked the Maldives in November 1968. These Tamils were destroyed in one day.

Traditional Islamic law is the basis of the Maldivian legal system. Recent years have seen the beginning of a tourist industry with an increasing number of visitors arriving, mainly from Europe or Japan. There is a well-equipped international airport at Male, the capital (60,000 people).

The Republic of the Maldives has a diplomatic mission at the United Nations. The United States has a consulate at Male. There are no important military relations between the United States and the Maldives. In 1993 the United States may spend $70,000 in furthering officer education in the Maldivian armed forces. The Maldivian military is practically nonexistent except for the usual internal security forces.

There has been some U.S. aid to the Maldives under the Food for Peace legislation and other humanitarian acts. Perhaps as much as $30 million arrived in the 1980s, mainly for natural disaster aid.

NEPAL

Like Bhutan, Nepal has common frontiers only with China and India. Nepal is about the same size as Kansas. The near legendary capital, Kathmandu, boasts a population of 450,000 out of a country total of 19 million. Most of the population survive by farming and herding. Nepal is a full member of the United Nations. Her present government is a constitutional monarchy, begun in 1962. Nepal has road and air links with both Pakistan and India. Democratic reforms have been slowly coming to Nepal since 1945. There are still strong internal opposition parties.

India provides Nepal with strong economic help. Formal diplomatic relations began with China in 1955. Both the Soviet Union and the United States established embassies in 1959.

From 1950 to 1990, Nepal received $748 thousand in military sales contracts from the United States. Projections for 1993 are shown in Table 5.1. Note that the International Military Education and Training Fund money will pay for exactly fifteen students.[8] Perhaps as much as $350 million in total economic aid has arrived from the United States since 1951. About 150 to 175 Peace Corps volunteers work in Nepal each year.

Nepal's soldiers have a worldwide reputation as superior fighting men. This was gained through their service in the British Army for over a century. Nepal maintains about 30,000 to 40,000 men in her military forces. Her equipment is British. Her small air force of 200 to 300 men lacks combat aircraft. Nepal has peace-keeping troops with the U.N. forces along the Afghanistan–Pakistan frontier and in Lebanon.

Nepal's constitutional monarchy does not believe in paying out huge sums on military forces. Between 1979 and 1991, the percentage of Nepal's

Table 5.1
Projected U.S. Aid to Nepal (In U.S. Dollars)

	1993
International Military Education	200,000
Economic Development Assistance	17,500,000
Peace Corps	2,092,000
Totals	19,792,000

Source: FMS Control and Reports Division, Comptroller, DSAA, *Foreign Military Sales, Foreign Military Construction Sales and Military Assistance Facts, as of September 30, 1991,* Washington, D.C.: Data Management Division, Comptroller DSSA, 1992.

GNP spent on the entire military establishment rose from 0.9 percent (.009) to 1.2 percent (.012).[9] With a per capita annual income of around $160, Nepal has more pressing needs for her GNP, which rose by 41 percent during this same period.

NOTES

1. FMS Control and Reports Division, Comptroller, DSAA, *Foreign Military Sales, Foreign Military Construction Sales and Military Assistance Facts, as of September 30, 1991,* Washington, Data Management Division, Comptroller DSSA, 1992.

2. United States of America, *Congressional Presentation for Security Assistance Programs, Fiscal Year 1993,* Washington, GPO, Jointly Prepared by the Department of State and the Defense Security Agency, 1992.

3. *Foreign Military Sales, September 30, 1991.*

4. Ibid.

5. *Congressional Presentation, Fiscal Year 1993.*

6. *Foreign Military Sales, September 30, 1991.*

7. *Congressional Presentations, Fiscal Years 1992 and 1993.*

8. Ibid.

9. United States Arms Control and Disarmament Agency, *World Military Expenditures and Arms Transfers,* Washington, GPO, 1991, p. 74. The figures for 1990 and 1991 are based on Huldt et al. *The Military Balance 1992–1993,* London, International Institute for Strategic Studies, 1992, p. 135.

6

Southeast Asia

The world press tends to ignore parts of the world where there is little shooting going on. This is the present case in Southeast Asia. The Cambodian genocide of the 1980s was the last piece of shocking news to come out of this part of the world. Sprawling across a vast area of more than 3,000 miles from east to west and more than 2,000 miles from north to south, Southeast Asia comprises Myanmar (Burma), Thailand, Vietnam, Laos, Cambodia, Malaysia, Indonesia, Philippines, Brunei Darussalam, and Singapore.

Within these nine nations, there are virtually untapped rugged, trackless mountains, rich in mineral resources. There are dense jungles, fever-infested swamps, violent rivers, fertile inland plateaus, and river deltas. There are extremes of altitude, temperature, and climate. There are extremes of illiteracy, poverty, disease, and hunger. This part of the world is also poor. Some 456 million people live in this part of the world. Population and per capita income are shown in Figure 6.1 (p. 50).

Since the days of the clipper ships, Americans have been engaged in trade in this part of the world. Since 1945, American presidents have often viewed Southeast Asia through political trifocals. First, communism, especially Chinese communism, must not advance into this area. Second, the economic potential of the region needs realization. Last, the use of U.S. military forces in Southeast Asia is authorized when thought necessary.

The United States withdrew from its Philippine bases only in 1992. The American military presence remains, notably in Singapore and Thailand. U.S. support for any anti-Communist government or insurgency in this region continues to be very strong. Vietnam, North and South, have not been forgotten. The famous domino theory that once Vietnam fell to the Communists the rest of Southeast Asia would rapidly follow has been proven wrong. Yet it is argued that the continued presence of U.S. military aid and economic help in this area contained the further spread of communism after

Figure 6.1
Southeast Asia, Total Population and per Capita Income (In U.S. Dollars)

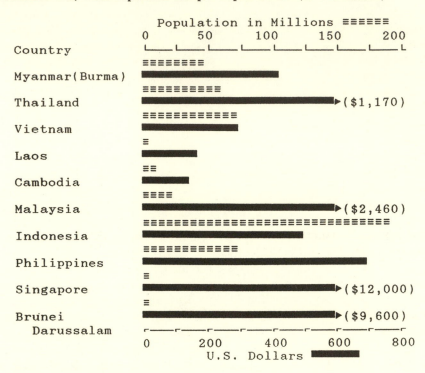

Note: U.S. 1990 per capita income was $21,800.

the fall of Hanoi. In very recent times, there has been a growing spirit of cooperation among many nations of this region. Certainly there are natural resources and human population in Southeast Asia to build another great industrial area on this planet. The political problems of any such unity movement, even if just on the economic level, make any such hope seem beyond the realm of current reality.

These are some of the interesting points to be looked at in our country-by-country approach to this region of the world.

MYANMAR (BURMA)

Myanmar, with a population of 42 million, is slightly smaller than the state of Texas. Common boundaries exist with China, Bangladesh, Thailand, and Laos. Laos is in the middle of the "Golden Triangle" drug traffic. Britain granted independence in 1948. The Anti-Fascist Peoples' Freedom League controlled the country until 1958. The local Communist threat was contained by 1958. A split in the ruling political party in 1958 brought a military takeover of the country. General U Ne Win set up a caretaker government which preserved at least the outward signs of a democracy. His political party won the free elections in 1960 by large majorities. After years of political bickering, a single party (Burma Socialist Program) was installed by the military in March 1974. General U Ne Win retired in 1981. He did not resign as chief of the only legal political party until 1988.

In July 1988, army troops opened fire on peaceful opposition political demonstrations. The number killed may have been more than 1,000. The demonstrations continued. By September 1988, the Burma Socialist Program had ceased to function. Despite the compromise efforts of the prestigious politician Dr. Maung Maung, the army took over completely in that same month. The army continued to quell demonstrators by killing as many of them as possible. The army abolished the civil government.

Myanmar has continuing problems with insurgents. It began with a revolt of local Communists in 1945. More recently, the drug production and sales came to complicate this problem. The Myanmar Army has far less success coping with the drug trade than with the Communists.

The United States and Myanmar usually maintain friendly relations. It was not until October 1988 that the United States stopped all forms of aid whether economic, humanitarian, or military. From 1950 to 1991, the United States signed $8.8 million worth of military sales agreements with Myanmar.[1]

Since 1979, Myanmar has invested in defense forces as shown in Figure 6.2 (p. 52). At present, the military establishment boasts nearly 300,000 troops. There are, in addition, large government paramilitary forces consisting of the People's Police Force (estimated 60,000) and the People's Militia (estimated 50,000).

Sustained military opposition against government forces comes from at least three main insurgent groupings. The Burma Communist party is still active despite its intraparty ethnic bickering. The National Democratic Front boasts some 20,000 trained troops. It exists mainly in border areas where its troops can scamper back and forth. There are several drug-related private armies that can often count on as many as 2,000 to 3,000 soldiers.

Fighting between the government and its rebel opponents remains heavy. The rebel opposition groups often fight each other. In all this bloodshed, Myanmar remains one of the poorest nations in the world.

THAILAND

Like Myanmar (Burma), Thailand faces internal rebel groups. The drug war goes on in this country as well. There are border difficulties with all her neighbors—Myanmar, Laos, and Cambodia. Only the frontier with Malaysia is usually quiet. Thailand, like Myanmar, is about the size of Texas.

Figure 6.2
Myanmar's Military Defense Expenditures (In Billions of U.S. Dollars as a Percentage of GNP)

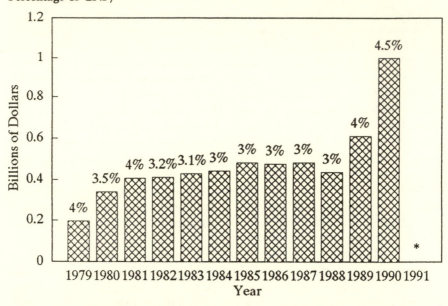

Source: U.S. Arms Control and Disarmament Agency, *World Military Expenditures and Arms Transfers,* Washington, D.C.: GPO, November 1991, p. 56. The figures for 1990 are based on Huldt et al. *The Military Balance 1992–1993,* London: International Institute for Strategic Studies, 1992, p. 134.
*Figures for 1991 are unavailable.

Thailand has a population of 55 million and a per person average income of $1,170. This is the second highest per person average income in Southeast Asia. By Southeastern Asian standards, the Thais are rich.

Thailand managed to keep her independence throughout the period of European imperialism. When a nonviolent revolution in 1932 saw the beginnings of the change from an absolute to a constitutional monarchy, the military was at its center. Some fourteen other military takeovers have occurred since 1932.

The Thai government also stresses continued independence as the basis for all internal and external arrangements. With the collapse of the government of South Vietnam after the defeat of U.S. forces, Thailand's attention is centered on the borders with Laos and Cambodia. The subsequent genocidal activities of the Khmer Rouge and the Vietnamese occupation of Cambodia in 1979 saw the Thai government faced with two problems.

The first was the defense of this frontier. This was accomplished by strengthened military forces in the region. The second was the refugee problem. Hundreds of thousands of Cambodians crossed the border fleeing for their lives. Both problems remain unsettled although the departure of the Vietnamese forces from Cambodia has helped.

The Thai military completely took over the government in a bloody event in 1976. Although they permitted a free election in 1988, they once again assumed command of the nation in February 1991.

The United States signed a treaty of friendship and commerce with Thailand in 1833. After 1945 Thailand developed very close military relationships with the United States. For example, both countries intend to end the drug traffic by force of arms. The United States also guarantees the independence of Thailand (1951).

From 1950 to 1991 the United States made $3 billion in military sales to Thailand.[2] U.S. aid for 1991, 1992, and 1993 is shown in Table 6.1. The United States maintains a military presence in Thailand. However, military advisors and assistance teams were prominent in Thailand from 1954 to 1991.

The Thais demand two years of military service of all men. Much of their equipment is American or British. Some 500,000 are in the Thai reserve units. Their navy is basically in the small warship class. There are about 25,000 marines. Thai military expenditures are shown in Figure 6.3 (p. 54). Even with near military rule, Thailand does not spend a large percentage of her gross national product on her armed forces.

VIETNAM

Vietnam was divided into two parts after the French military defeat in 1954. This is a country larger than North Carolina, Virginia, and South

Table 6.1
U.S. Aid to Thailand (In U.S. Dollars)

	1991	1992	1993
Military Financing	15,000,000		
International Military Education	2,400,000	2,500,000	2,250,000
Economic Support Fund	5,000,000	2,500,000	
Development Assistance	10,000,000	12,300,000	6,000,000
Food for Peace			2,610,000
Peace Corps	4,737,000	3,583,000	3,572,000
International Narcotics Control	4,000,000	5,000,000	4,000,000
Totals	41,137,000	25,883,000	18,432,000

Source: United States of America, *Congressional Presentation for Security Assistance Programs, Fiscal Years 1991–1993,* Washington, D.C.: GPO, 1991–1993.

Figure 6.3
Thailand's Military Defense Expenditures (In Billions of U.S. Dollars as a Percentage of GNP)

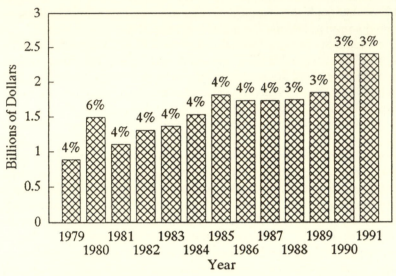

Source: U.S. Arms Control and Disarmament Agency, *World Military Expenditures and Arms Transfers,* Washington, D.C.: GPO, November 1991, p. 56. The figures for 1990 and 1991 are based on Heisbourg et al. *The Military Balance 1991–1992,* London: International Institute for Strategic Studies, 1991, p. 181, and Huldt et al. *The Military Balance 1992– 1993,* London: International Institute for Strategic Studies, 1992, p. 162.

Carolina. The population is on the order of 69 million. The government is a Communist people's republic. Universal suffrage exists. The Vietnamese Communist party is the only legal political group. Vietnam belongs to the usual international associations, including the United Nations. More than 90 percent of the population are Vietnamese. It is unusual in Southeast Asia for one ethnic group to have such an overpowering majority in any one country.

Ho Chi Minh founded the Vietnamese Communist party in Paris in 1920. From its beginnings, Ho intended a military revolution to bring communism to power in all of Vietnam. There was a very short period of cooperation between a U.S. military advisor team and Ho during the Japanese occupation from 1942 to 1945. In 1946, Ho's negotiations broke down with the French who had returned as white European colonial masters to all of Vietnam. The civil war began. This civil war did not end until 1975. At that time Vietnam again united, but under a native Communist government.

The years 1954–1971 saw U.S. military involvement gradually grow from a small military assistance group to 543,000 men in 1969. U.S. diplomatic and military policies in Vietnam throughout the administrations of presidents John F. Kennedy, Lyndon B. Johnson, and Richard Nixon did not keep any part of Vietnam within the "free world orbit."

The Vietnamese Communists received large amounts of military aid from both the Soviet Union and China during the years of struggle (1945–1971) against the two Western imperialistic powers—France and the United States. Since unification, there have been some democratically minded rebels operating in various parts of the countryside. Their numbers and natures are unknown to the outside world.

The Vietnam Army intervened in Cambodia in 1975. They ended the genocidal reign of the Khmer Rouge in 1978–1979. Vietnam–China relationship deteriorated in the 1980s. Some shots were exchanged along their common border.

With the end of the Soviet Union, Vietnam began to look for ways to establish more favorable relations with the United States. The POW-MIA issue still clouds this relationship. The United States still does not have diplomatic relationships with Vietnam. There have been several official and unofficial visits between these two nations in recent years.

The Vietnamese economy is deteriorating. There is no reliable information on how much the Vietnamese government spends on its military forces. With both Chinese and Soviet aid gone, the sum must be high. Vietnam's "Main Force" claims over 1,000,000 men, 90 percent of them in the army. Her equipment is mainly aging Chinese and Soviet second-class systems. Some military equipment abandoned by the United States is still in use. Her navy is in the small warship class.

Vietnam has huge paramilitary classes. The government is devoted to the concept of a true peoples's army. All must be ready to defend the homeland. More than 1 million receive some training in the Peoples's regional forces. Another 3 million parade as local forces. There also exists a tactical rear force of more than 600,000 veterans of the civil war. The Vietnamese Army maintains military advisor and construction units in both Cambodia and Laos.

LAOS

Laos is another Southeastern Asian country constructed from the ruins of the French colonial empire after 1945. The government is Communist. Laos has common frontiers with Vietnam, Cambodia, Thailand, and China. With a population of just over 4 million, Laos is the second poorest country in this region. The per person annual income is only $150, and the land area is somewhat smaller than Oregon.

Laos was occupied by the Japanese during World War II. After 1945, French colonial forces manipulated the royal Laotian government until 1953. Pro-Western governments managed to carry on in the midst of a three-way civil war until 1957. During the entire period after 1945, Communist rebels fought government forces in the wilderness areas. In 1972, a coalition government was formed that included the Lao People's Democratic party (Communist). The onrushing tide of communism in nearby Vietnam and Cambodia caused the collapse of the government in 1975. The Lao People's Democratic Republic came into existence in 1975.

The new people's government was military in nature. It began by taking widespread security measures against insurgent groups of all political colors. U.S. relations with Laos began a long slow decline in 1975, although diplomatic formalities have never been broken off. Two areas of conflict separate these two nations. As with Vietnam, the POW-MIA problem clouds all else. The problem of the drug trade has turned into a drug war in recent years. The United States tries to cooperate with any Southeast Asian government that fights the drug trade.

The United States still does not sell Laos military equipment. "The United States has not provided security assistance to Laos since 1975. Laos has been treated as a Communist country. . . . It will be necessary to make applicable legal determinations under the Foreign Assistance Act of 1961 prior to initiating military assistance."[3] The United States understands that the Laotian military is the key in all future negotiations.

The Laotian military forces may be as large as 60,000 men. Her air force has a few aging Soviet planes. Other equipment is also of Soviet manufacture, although some units still sport captured French and American armaments. Laos is landlocked. There are also home guard units more or less established in each village.

There are many rebel factions, each claiming to be the legal government of Laos. All these factions are very small. In total, they probably cannot count on 3,000 men. Some 5,000 to 6,000 Vietnamese military assistance and construction workers operate in Laos. Laos has not released official figures as to the levels of financial support for the armed forces in recent years.

CAMBODIA

Cambodian resistance groups received some $5 million from U.S. economic support funds between 1987 and 1992.[4] Cambodia is the third country in Southeast Asia to fall from the French colonial empire after 1945.

Cambodia is about the same size as Missouri. Estimates of population vary, coming from various countries and from U.S. agencies, from 5 million to 7.5 million. Cambodia has common frontiers with Vietnam, Thailand, and Laos.

Not until 1953 did French garrisons begin withdrawing. Cambodian independence dates from July 4, 1953. Warring political parties, led by such politicians as Prince Sihanouk, kept the population and the military divided. Cambodia declared her neutrality from the world in 1957. This led the Communist party of Kampuchea (Cambodia) to start a revolt outside the capital of Phnom Penh. The United States increased military support accordingly. The United States just as quickly abandoned Cambodia after pulling out of South Vietnam. The government collapsed in 1970.

In 1974 the new Communist Khmer Rouge government occupied the new country of Kampuchea. This government practiced genocide on a wide scale throughout the country. As many as 2 million people may have died. Hundreds of thousands of refugees fled into Thailand.

In mid-1978, the Vietnamese Army invaded Kampuchea. The Vietnamese intended to put an end to the Khmer Rouge military forces which had long harassed Vietnamese border areas. By 1979, the Vietnamese were successful. Pol Pot, the leader of the Khmer Rouge, was replaced as head of state. Although he continued to control the Khmer Rouge military forces, he was driven from the capital by the Vietnamese. He set up shop again in the jungle wilderness of Northern Cambodia.

The Vietnamese established a government in Phnom Pen that controls the capital and part of the country. The Khmer Rouge control the rest of the country. Exactly where the dividing lines are is unknown.

Cambodia once received economic help from the Soviet Union. Some humanitarian aid arrives from the United Nations. It may be as much as $56 million a year. Most of this money is funneled to the Cambodian refugees living in Thailand. Probably this humanitarian aid will dwindle accordingly.

The official Cambodian government claims an estimated 115,000 troops. Most military equipment is Russian or Vietnamese hand-me-downs. American Army trucks left over from previous conflicts are also common on Cambodian highways. The government's navy and air force is so small that their existence can be questioned. Some 25,000 men are counted in the government's provincial forces. The government also claims 35,000 district forces. Another 60,000 to 75,000 villagers are organized into home guard units.

This is a government at total war with the rebel groups operating in various parts of the countryside. The Khmer Rouge still claim 30,000 to 60,000 troops. The Kampuchea Liberty Forces say they control about 15,000. The supporters of Prince Sihanouk, the former leader, still have an estimated 30,000 men. What actually is going on at present is a four-sided civil war. Not much has changed in Cambodia since 1945. Statistics about the official government's support for its own military forces in relationship to the Cambodian gross national product are not available.

A U.N. Armistice Commission began operations in 1990. This U.N. unit has nearly 1,200 personnel. Their agenda called for free democratic elections. A coalition government representing all sides was negotiated. In 1992, the United States threatened to bar the Khmer Rouge from the new government, and the United Nations insisted that the Khmer Rouge conduct proper democratic elections in the parts of Cambodia under its control. In 1993 Norodom Sihanouk ratified the new constitution. The May elections saw the establishment of a coalition government under U.N. supervision.

The Khmer Rouge still control about 20 percent of the country with 10,000 men under arms.

MALAYSIA

Malaysia is about the size of New Mexico, a wealthy country by Southeast Asian standards with a per person average annual income of $2,400. There are 18 million people in this country. Geographically Asia, mainland Malaysia is bounded on two sides by water. Singapore is to the south. Thailand is to the north. Malaysia is divided by about 400 miles of the South China Sea. About one-1half the land area and 20 to 25 percent of her population is on the island of Borneo. Borneo is shared with Indonesia.

The Portuguese conquered part of this country in 1511. The Dutch arrived in 1641. They were replaced by the British between 1786 and 1795. By 1826 the British had full domination over what is now Asian mainland Malaysia. The Japanese Army occupied the entire country during World War II. The British left in 1948. Singapore, Sarawak, and Sabah joined the Federation of Malaysia in 1963. Singapore reclaimed her own independence in 1965. Malaysia has a constitutional monarchy.

Chinese Communist rebels began fighting the British in 1945. This rebellion grew very serious. In 1948 the newly independent Malaysia declared a state of emergency. It was 1960 before the Communist rebels were beaten. Very small Communist rebel bands still roam the southern mainland provinces and part of Sarawak.

Malaysia is a member of the nonaligned nations group in the United Nations. The government seeks to promote regional cooperation through the 1967-begun Association of South Asian Nations.

Relations with the United States are cordial. The United States in many ways treats Malaysia in the same manner as she does her NATO allies. There are many culture exchanges. The Fullbright awards program is in full swing. Malaysian graduate students attend many American universities. Peace Corps volunteers worked in Malaysia until 1983. They were no longer needed.

The United States favored Malaysia with $196 million in arms sales and construction from 1950 to 1991.[5] Malaysia's nonaligned status prevents her participation in most types of U.S. military aid.

The Malaysian military forces are approximately 130,000. There are some 42,000 in her active reserves. Although more than 11,000 strong, the Malaysian Navy remains in the small warship class. Her air force numbers some 12,000. Malaysian military equipment is mostly British, with some American materials mixed in.

Malaysia does not spend a large percentage of her gross national product on her military forces, as shown in Figure 6.4. The Malaysian Army fights Communist rebels British style. Small units search and destroy these bands when they strike out of their wilderness headquarters.

Figure 6.4
Malaysia's Military Defense Expenditures (In Billions of U.S. Dollars as a Percentage
of GNP)

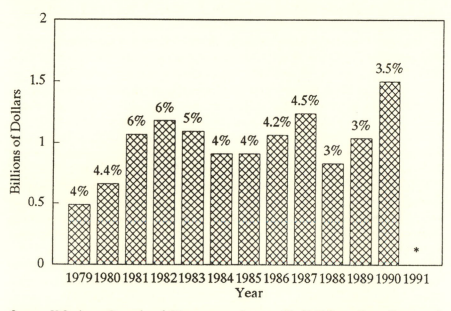

Source: U.S. Arms Control and Disarmament Agency, *World Military Expenditures and
Arms Transfers,* Washington, D.C.: GPO, November 1991, p. 72. The figures for 1990 are
based on Heisbourg et al. *The Military Balance 1991–1992,* London: International Institute
for Strategic Studies, 1991, p. 171.
*Figures for 1991 are unavailable.

INDONESIA

Indonesia has a population spread out over many islands. Java, Sumatra,
most of Borneo, the western half of New Guinea, Bali, and Timor are all
included. Indonesian is the official language, but there are more than 200
tribal dialects.

The Japanese occupied Indonesia during the World War II. The Dutch
returned to claim their colonial possessions in 1945 but left in 1949 after
four hard years of fighting. The western half of New Guinea remained
Dutch. The failure of negotiations over this mainly forest wilderness caused
the Indonesian government to seize Dutch property throughout the country.
This included the proven oil fields. The United States intervened as a friendly
power. A compromise arrived in 1962. Western New Guinea became part
of Indonesia in 1963. The New Guinea tribal chiefs voted to remain in their
new country in 1969.

The Indonesian Republic was established by rebels primarily led by
Sukarno. His career is filled with military activity. He led the rebellion

against the Dutch from 1945 to 1949. Parliament suspended him from the office of president in 1960. He was named president for life in 1963. Most of his military hardware and advisors came from the Soviet Union. He sent Indonesian troops on raiding missions in the North Borneo part of Malaysia in 1964 and 1965.

Yet, when the Indonesian Communist party staged a takeover in 1965, the army, led by General Suharto, smashed it. Sukarno died in this rebellion. Perhaps as many as 400,000 Communists lost their lives. The military continues in a strong position in the Indonesian government. Today Suharto is considered by many to be a determinant. His control over Indonesia's political system is almost dictatorial. Political liberty was lost in 1965.

The military continues to guarantee the government from both internal and external enemies. They continue to fight a small group of rebels on the eastern part of Timor with ever increasingly ferocity.

The foundation of the Indonesian defense forces is two years' selective service. There are nearly 300,000 men in the military forces at any one time. The Indonesian Navy remains in the small warship class. Their military equipment is a curious mixture of Russian, British, and American construction.

U.S. relationships with Indonesia have been friendly since General Suharto began his near military rule in 1965. Some $728 million in military sales went to Indonesia between 1950 and 1991.[6] At present, the U.S. Congress has reservations about further military aid because of the 1991 incidents on East Timor.

There is no doubt that General Suharto considers the rapid oil-based economic development to be more important than the military budget. Indonesian military spending levels are shown in Figure 6.5.

PHILIPPINES

The Philippine Islands are about the same size as Nevada. The population of 67 million is 83 percent Roman Catholic. Colonized by Spain in 1521, the Philippines became a colonial possession of the United States during the Spanish-American War (1898). The lives of the Filipinos are filled with almost unceasing internal civil war since the Philippine-American War of 1899–1902. The United States crushed the Philippines rebel forces of Aquinaldo.

Democracy and independence came at the same time in 1946. There was continuing rebel activity, especially on the islands of Mindanao and Luzon. The Japanese occupied the Philippines during the World War II. The Philippines received independence from the United States on July 4, 1946. The United States retained important naval and air bases in the Philippines under a renewable lease arrangement.

Independence was plagued by the Huk Communist revolt of 1945–1953. The Huks (Chinese-style Communists) fought the Japanese throughout the

Figure 6.5
Indonesia's Military Defense Expenditures (In Billions of U.S. Dollars as a
Percentage of GNP)

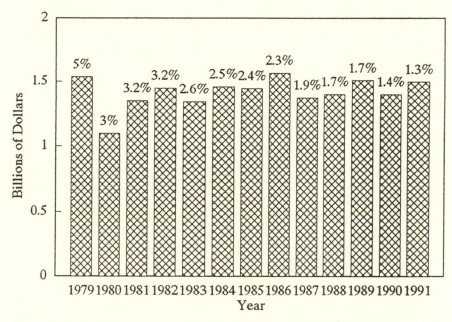

Source: U.S. Arms Control and Disarmament Agency, *World Military Expenditures and
Arms Transfers*, Washington, D.C.: GPO, November 1991, p. 66. The figures for 1990 and
1991 are based on Heisbourg et al. *The Military Balance 1991–1992*, London: International
Institute for Strategic Studies, 1991, p. 164, and Huldt et al. *The Military Balance 1992–
1993*, London: International Institute for Strategic Studies, 1992, p. 148.

war. In 1945 they expected inclusion in the peacetime government. This
opportunity was denied them by the United States. The end of the Huk
revolt did not pacify the countryside.

President Ferdinand Marcos declared martial law in 1972. He reasoned
that the growing bands of Communist rebels were a serious threat to continued democracy. Marcos crushed these rebels. He used the same search
and destroy methods that were employed in 1899–1902 and 1945–1953.
Marcos continued in power long after his government passed to a dictatorial
style. It is suspected that he helped plot the assassination of the major political opposition leader Aquino in 1983.

Under great pressure from the military presence of the United States,
Marcos permitted elections that were marked by open, widespread fraud in
1986. A quiet civil-led military takeover occurred. Marcos was forced to
flee. He sought safety in the United States. Aquino's widow, Corazón,
became president in 1986.

A new constitutional government began in 1987. Nationwide elections were held. President Aquino soon announced much-needed land reforms. This is the basic issue that all rebel groups have used to rally public support since 1900. An abortive military takeover was foiled by Philippine Army units in 1989.

A rather bitter argument developed over the renewal lease for the U.S. military bases in the Philippines. The Philippine government made a money demand that the American government considered wildly excessive. The Philippine government threatened to throw the United States out of the Philippines. Mt. Pinatubo settled this argument in 1991. This volcanic eruption forced the evacuation of Clark Air Force Base, the principal remaining U.S. military garrison in the Philippines.

Recently, after the death of her husband, Mrs. Marcos returned to the Philippines. She announced herself as a candidate for president in the forthcoming elections. Mrs. Marcos lost. Fidel Ramos is president with the apparent solid backing of the military. The last U.S. military units left the Philippines in 1992.

Land reform goes very slowly, as it has since 1898. Rebel groups continue in the jungles and mountains as they had long before 1898.

U.S. military aid to the Philippines amounted to $827.3 million between 1950 and 1990.[7] More recent U.S. security assistance is shown in Table 6.2. It is arguable that U.S. security assistance will continue to decline in the near future.

The Philippine government of Fidel Ramos (elected May 11, 1992) has some 110,000 actives and some 200,000 reservists. The army has some 70 percent of this total number. The navy remains in the small warship class. The Philippine Air Force is more than 16,000 strong but has fewer than 50

Table 6.2
U.S. Aid to the Philippines (In U.S. Dollars)

	1991	1992	1993
Military Financing	200,000,000	200,000,000	15,000,000
International Military Education	2,600,000	2,800,000	2,450,000
Economic Support Fund	160,000,000	120,000,000	45,000,000
Development Assistance	5,000,000	40,000,000	30,000,000
Food for Peace	32,113,000	33,428,000	33,092,000
Peace Corps	5,727,000	884,000	855,000
Totals	455,440,000	397,112,000	126,397,000

Source: United States of America, *Congressional Presentation for Security Assistance Programs, Fiscal Years 1991–1993,* Washington, D.C.: GPO, 1991–1993.

combat aircraft. Current equipment is almost exclusively of American manufacture.

Philippine support for the armed forces is shown in Figure 6.6.

SINGAPORE

Singapore is an island republic of 239 square miles located at the southern tip of the Malay Peninsula. The population of 3 million has the second highest per person average income in Southeast Asia, $12,000. Singapore's wealth is based on her shipping, manufacturing, and banking interests. Fully 90 percent of the population is literate. The government is a parliamentary democracy. Voting is universal and mandatory. The government is stable.

Singapore began as a commercial venture of Thomas Raffles in 1819. It remained a British colony until 1959. In that year, Singapore joined the British Commonwealth of Nations. After less than a two-year flirtation with the Federation of Malaysia, Singapore regained her independence in 1965.

Figure 6.6
Philippines' Military Defense Expenditures (In Millions of U.S. Dollars as a Percentage of GNP)

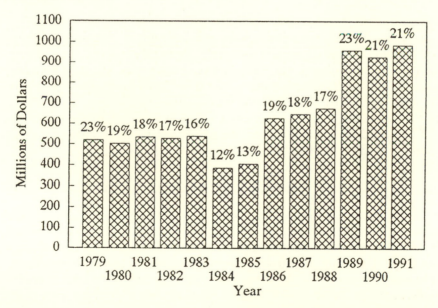

Source: U.S. Arms Control and Disarmament Agency, *World Military Expenditures and Arms Transfers,* Washington, D.C.: GPO, November 1991, p. 77. The figures for 1990 and 1991 are based on Huldt et al. *The Military Balance 1992–1993,* London: International Institute for Strategic Studies, 1992, p. 158.

A member of the nonaligned group in the United Nations, Singapore would like cordial relations with all countries and is a member of the Association of South East Asian Nations, begun in 1967. Relations with the United States are cordial. There are many student and teacher exchange programs between the two countries.

From 1950 to 1991, the United States negotiated $1.25 billion in arms sales and construction with Singapore.[8] More recently military aid takes the form of a small sum (about $15,000 annually) for the further military education of highly selected Singapore military and police personnel. There are ongoing negotiations with Singapore as a possible replacement base for U.S. fleet units that left the Philippines.

American present policy is expressed as follows:

Singapore is a staunch supporter of the continued presence of the United States in Asia and of our policies in the region. Singapore's location at the crossroads of major shipping and air routes gives it great importance for the fulfillment of U.S. interests. In 1991, deployments of USAF aircraft and additional USN ship units began under the terms of a Memorandum of Understanding concluded in November 1990, which increases U.S. access to the country's airfields and facilities. This access enhances our ability to fulfill commitments in Southeast Asia and the Indian Ocean. The United States pays no rent and has made no reimbursement for improvements to the facilities we use in Singapore.[9]

Singapore maintains a military force of about 60,000. A majority of these are draftees. Additional trained reserves of 275,000 are claimed. Most of their military equipment is British. Although the navy is of the small warship class, it is the strongest in Southeast Asia. There is an internal police force of 12,000. Singapore maintains military advisors in Angola, Bahrain, Kuwait, and Taiwan. New Zealand maintains a special forces unit in Singapore.

The armed forces received an average of 5 percent of Singapore gross national product from 1979 through 1991.

BRUNEI DARUSSALAM

Brunei, located on the northern coast of the island of Borneo, is about the size of Delaware; and the 375,000 inhabitants enjoy a per person average annual income of $9,600. Brunei sits on a large pool of oil, which accounts for 90 percent of her gross national product. The government is a sultanate. The law is framed by English Common Law. Brunei gained full independence in 1984. Britain retains large commercial interests and has great political influence in the country.

The sultan is the head and chief administrator of all parts of the government. Brunei maintains an all-voluntary military force of about 5,000 men. There are another 2,000 in the Royal Brunei Police.

There is a British Ghurka battalion permanently stationed in Brunei under the terms of their bilateral defense agreements. Brunei belongs to the United Nations and the Southeast Asia defense organization.

The first U.S. military presence goes back to a visit by the *USS Constitution* in 1845. Full diplomatic arrangements exist between the two countries.

American military influence in Brunei is very slight. Only $415,000 in military sales and construction were negotiated with Brunei from 1950 to 1991.[10] There are no plans at present for further U.S. military aid to Brunei.

Official U.S. government figures on the relationship between the money spent on the Brunei military and her gross national product are not available. Given the wealth of the sultanate, it must be a very small percentage.

NOTES

1. FMS Control and Reports Division, Comptroller, DSAA, *Foreign Military Sales, Foreign Military Construction Sales and Military Assistance Facts, as of September 30, 1990,* Washington, Data Management Division, Comptroller DSSA, 1991.

2. *Foreign Military Sales, September 30, 1991.*

3. United States of America, *Congressional Presentation for Security Assistance Programs, Fiscal Year 1993,* Washington, GPO, Jointly prepared by the Department of State and the Defense Security Agency, 1992.

4. *Foreign Military Sales, September 30, 1990.*

5. *Foreign Military Sales, September 30, 1991.*

6. Ibid.

7. *Foreign Military Sales, September 30, 1990.*

8. Ibid.

9. *Congressional Presentation, Fiscal Year 1993.*

10. *Foreign Military Sales, September 30, 1990.*

East Asia

This area of the world contains Japan and four Third World nations—China, Taiwan, North Korea, and South Korea. Japan remains the key to East Asia. Japan has been the key to East Asia since industrialization arrived early in the twentieth century. This area contains a population of at least 1,710,000,000, of whom 1,500,000,000 (about 88 percent) of this total population live in China. The Chinese have a per person annual average income of only $360. The Japanese enjoy an annual per person income of $17,100. This problem confronts any attempt by the governments with democratic institutions (Japan, South Korea, and Taiwan) to promote cooperation with the two governments dominated by their native Communist parties (China and North Korea). The economic gap is wide between the two political groupings and is also very dangerous.

This gap developed when Japan lost World War II and was occupied by a benevolent United States. General Douglas MacArthur became the military governor of Japan. Although he did not meddle with Japanese traditions or oust the emperor, MacArthur insisted that the Japanese return to the form of democratic government that preceded the military takeover in the 1930s. Japan became a constitutional monarchy with a political process that closely resembles that of the United States.

Using the protection of the American military garrisons, the Japanese, year by year, built up their capitalist economy until they became probably the foremost economic power in the world today. Perhaps still second to the United States, they have long surpassed the Germans. Japan was permitted to grow, gain strength, and then dominate much of the world industrial and trade markets as the worldwide economy emerged in the 1970–1990 period.

Japan still spends little on her self-defense forces, usually less than 6 percent per year of GNP. Until very recently, Japanese military forces could not serve overseas. Since Japan is a series of islands lying off the northeastern

Chinese, eastern South Korean, and eastern Russian Pacific coasts, her troops are always at home. During the Desert War in Kuwait, Japan sent many dollars but did not risk Japanese soldiers.

Taiwan is in much the same sort of favored position for some of the same reasons. She was protected by the American military until 1978. Today Taiwan has no direct American military support, but her capitalistic economy gives her the second highest per capita income in East Asia.

South Korea still has an American military garrison that looks across the armistice line into North Korea. The United States continues to offer its protection to South Korea much as it does to Japan.

All three of these nations have easy access to the world economy and especially to the large and very wealthy U.S. consumer-based internal market.

China and North Korea remained outside the U.S. sphere of economic influence and military protection after 1945. Both countries engaged the United States in the Korean War from 1950 to 1953. This is the precise reason their economic presents and possibly their economic futures contain far fewer economic gains than those of the Japanese, the Taiwanese, and the South Koreans.

There is a great indigenous military power in East Asia—the Chinese. There is a great visiting military power in East Asia—the United States. The interaction of these two great military powers is explained in the country-by-country approach that follows. Population and per capita income of these five countries are shown in Figure 7.1.

Figure 7.1
East Asia, Total Population and per Capita Income (In U.S. Dollars)

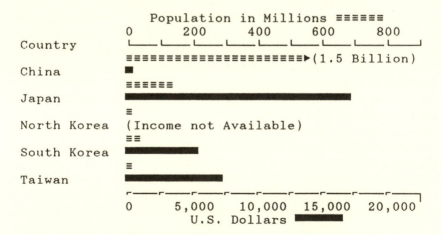

Note: U.S. 1990 per capita income was $21,800.

CHINA

China is slightly larger than the 48 lower United States. With a population of 1.5 billion and a per person average annual income of only $360, China is the key to the future economic growth of East Asia. China has an enormous potential consumer market and enormous, untapped natural resources. She is governed by the native Communist party.

Modern China was founded by Mao Zedong after the civil war in 1947. The nationalist followers of American-supported Chang Kai-Chek fled to Taiwan. Mao always felt that power grows out of the barrel of a gun. The Chinese peoples' liberation army has existed to support the native Communist party. As a result the peoples' liberation army is controlled by the Communist party, not the bureaucracy of the Chinese state. When the peoples' liberation army fights internally or externally, it wages the peoples' war. This army fights all kinds of wars, from local riot control through the spectrum of low-intensity conflicts to total war. The nearest brush with total war since 1947 was in the contest with the American-led U.N. forces in Korea from 1950 to 1953.

China signed a 30-year treaty of friendship with the Soviet Union in 1950. After Korea, relationships with the Soviet Union declined. In 1971, the U.N. General Assembly seated China in the place of Taiwan. President Nixon accepted an invitation to visit China in 1972. Full diplomatic relations were established in 1979.

The peoples' liberation army supported the Communist party as it led China through tough times. The "great leap forward" of 1958–1960 tried to increase the pace of economic development through the use of forced labor. Millions of Chinese were involved. Working-class resistance was so strong that the party abandoned the plan. In 1965, the great proletarian cultural revolution began. This was a high-level attempt to curb the growing pragmatism of the bureaucracy. A return to basic revolutionary principles was sought. This too was abandoned. In 1981, several high-ranking members of the Communist party were convicted of "committing crimes" during the cultural revolution.

Mao died in 1976. His widow and her leftist friends, purged from the party, led several failed takeover attempts. In 1979 heavy fighting occurred along the Vietnam border. War was narrowly averted.

China gradually moved toward more capitalist economic forms throughout the 1980s. This reform movement was crippled when the peoples' liberation army used full military force in 1989. A strike of students and workers in the capital, Beijing, was put down by elite tank and infantry units. Similar smaller movements in other parts of the country met the same fate. Perhaps as many as 7,000 died.

The party is colonizing the frontier provinces with surplus ethnic Chinese.

Manchuria, Inner Mongolia, Xinjiang, and Tibet are involved. Tibet has proven difficult since the peoples' liberation army arrived in 1951.

In 1992, the party congress announced further movement toward a form of capitalistic economy. China is due to complete the peaceful annexation of Hong Kong in 1997.

From 1984 to 1989, the United States arranged for some $305 million in arms and military sales construction with China. The current attitude of the United States toward China is expressed in the *Congressional Presentation for Security Assistance Programs, Fiscal Year 1993:*

U.S. Military Assistance to China remains suspended during a period of significant disagreement regarding human rights, weapons proliferation, and other issues. In mid-1989 Chinese leaders ordered a crackdown on many demonstrations, which led to the killing of unarmed people in Beijing and the subsequent repression of dissidents. Following the crackdown, the Administration adopted measures to express condemnation of the violence in China, including a suspension of all government-to-government sales and commercial exports of weapons to the PRC [Peoples' Republic of China]. In late 1989 and 1990, Congress passed legislation exacting a broad range of sanctions against China. (p. 133)

The peoples' liberation armed forces claim that three million draftees make up about one-half their numbers. Some women are among the draftees. The army accounts for two million. Although the navy is the largest in East Asia, it remains in the small warship class. The Chinese also have well-armed air force and naval air arm units. China contributes men to the U.N. peace-keeping activities in the Middle East and Kuwait. Military equipment is manufactured in China. The Chinese armaments industry is rapidly developing.

The ministry of public security controls nearly one million well-trained riot police. There are militia units said to contain another twelve million.

Despite these claims to very large readily available military units, China spends little on her military, as shown in Figure 7.2.

TAIWAN

The island of Taiwan is the richest of the Third World nations in East Asia. The population of 22 million shares a land area about the size of West Virginia. The government is dominated by the Chinese Nationalist party. Chang Kai-Chek brought this government to Taiwan when he fled from the Chinese mainland in 1947. Taiwan is best described as an industrial-military state.

Until 1978, U.S. military units blocked the sea and air approaches from the mainland to Taiwan. From 1947 to 1978, there was sporadic gunfire

Figure 7.2
China's Military Defense Expenditures (In Billions of U.S. Dollars as a Percentage
of GNP)

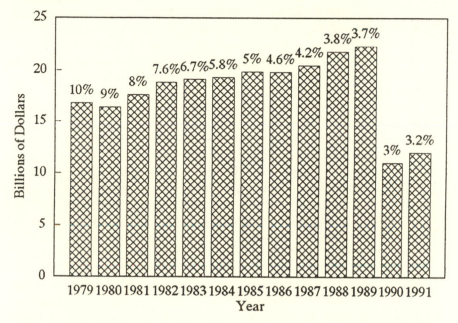

Source: U.S. Arms Control and Disarmament Agency, *World Military Expenditures and Arms Transfers,* Washington, D.C.: GPO, November 1991, p. 58. The figures for 1990 and 1991 are based on Huldt et al. *The Military Balance 1992–1993,* London: International Institute for Strategic Studies, 1992, pp. 143–144.

between the mainland and the Taiwan-held offshore islands of Quemoy and Matsu. Unofficial economic ties with the mainland began during the 1980s.

Under the military protection of the United States and with most-favored-nation economic treatment, Taiwan advanced rapidly. There was little internal difficulty.

From 1950 to 1991, the United States sold Taiwan $8.6 billion worth of military hardware and construction contracts.[1] The United States still sells armaments and military construction contracts to Taiwan. Without formal diplomatic relations, all such sales are for cash. A decision of President George Bush to sell Taiwan advanced American fighter aircraft during the presidential election of 1992 caused some political discontent in the United States.

Taiwan maintains nearly 500,000 men in her armed forces. All males are liable for two years' military service. The equipment is almost exclusively American or of local manufacture. Taiwan has a small warship class navy. She has a small internal paramilitary force.

Taiwan spends a small portion of her gross national product on her military. It amounted to 7 percent in 1979 and declined to 5.4 percent by 1989. It is doubtful that Taiwan will freely join the mainland or that China will try to conquer the island. Certainly current world politics would not permit the latter.

NORTH KOREA

North Korea, a nation about the size of Mississippi, occupies about one-half the Korean Peninsula, and has a population of 24 million. North Koreans enjoy a standard of living much higher than that of the Chinese but much lower than that of Japanese or Taiwanese. The government is a Communist state headed by the leader of the Communist party.

North Korea was created in 1945 by an agreement between the United States and the Soviet Union that divided their zones of occupation along the 38th parallel. A seemingly democratic state emerged in the south. North Korea was Communist from the moment the Japanese garrison withdrew. North Korea was originally a client state of the Soviet Union.

The Soviets trained and equipped the North Korean Army, which invaded South Korea in 1950. Quick response by the American garrison in Japan enabled the South Koreans to hold on until U.S. aid could arrive. The Inchon landings in 1950 turned the tide. The U.N. forces (mostly American) beat the North Koreans all the way back to Yalu River, the boundary with China.

Despite Chinese warnings, the U.N. forces continued to attack. In late 1950, large numbers of volunteers from the Chinese peoples' liberation army joined the fight. The battle lines changed frequently until late spring 1951. After that, most of the fighting was along the stabilized front of the 38th parallel.

Although armistice negotiations began in 1951, it was not until 1953 that the shooting stopped. A military armistice commission composed of officers from both sides still supervises the agreement. There have been frequent minor armistice violations all along the 38th parallel since 1953. The United States still maintains a substantial garrison in South Korea. The year 1971 saw beginnings of several negotiations aimed at political unification of the peninsula. None has as yet seen success.

U.S. policy toward North Korea remains hostile. The United States insists that only a united Korean people can decide the entire nation's destiny.

North Korea claims a total of more than one million in her armed forces, and a ready reserve of 600,000 plus a five-million-man militia. Equipment is a mixture of Russian and Chinese with some equipment of North Korean design and manufacture. The North Korean Navy remains a small warship fleet.

North Korea is a military-dominated Communist state devoted to the expansion of communism throughout the world. Long has North Korea served as a funnel for military aid from the Soviet Union to other nations in the Third World. During 1983, North Korea sent military aid, which often included some troops, to the following revolutionary movements in Africa: the Palestine Liberation Organization, People's Front of the Liberation of Africa, Zimbabwe African National Liberation Army, and the Mozambique People's Liberation Army. She also aided revolutionary groups in the following countries: Kenya, Costa Rica, Mexico, Argentina, Brazil, Bolivia, and Paraguay.[2]

North Korea spent a steady 20 percent of her gross national product on her military forces from 1979 to 1991. The total expenditures went from $4.2 billion in 1979 to $8 billion in 1991. Her GNP increased 31 percent during these same years. North Korea's munitions industry explains her high level of prosperity, for a nation of the Third World. Recently North Korea departed from all international arms control agreements. It is reported that North Korea has begun a crash program to produce nuclear arms.

SOUTH KOREA

South Korea occupies about one-half the Korean Peninsula and is about the size of Indiana. With a population of about 45 million, the average per person annual income is nearly twice that of North Korea. The government is a republic that is sometimes even democratic. Like North Korea, South Korea became independent when the Japanese withdrew in 1945. The beginning of modern economic and political development was ruined by the conflict of 1950–1953 (see North Korea). Syngman Rhee was the first of a long line of strongman presidents. He ran the country until student riots forced his resignation in 1960. A military takeover installed Major General Park Chung Hee as head of state. Civilian rule returned in 1963. Park then retired, only to be elected president in 1967, 1971, and 1978. He was assassinated in 1979.

The army again took control. Further student demonstrations began in 1980. They were met by South Korean Army special forces units. At least 200 were killed. Others went to military prisons. Martial law ended in 1981.

The civilian government returned to control until 1989. Then the military began a tough crackdown on all leftist elements. Some 1,500 people were placed in military prisons.

Democracy gained some speed in 1990 with the formation of the party for peace and democracy. Local elections were held in 1990 for the first time in thirty years. Yet the South Korean Army remains the ever-watchful guarantor of the nation's independence from internal as well as external enemies.

Negotiating efforts with North Korea for the unification of the peninsula all failed in 1991 and 1992. The two Koreas did sign an agreement in 1991 that provided for a step-by-step approach to end the war that began in 1950.

The United States guarantees the independence of the Republic of South Korea from foreign enemies and Communist-type internal enemies. Some 40,000 American troops stand guard in South Korea. Without massive military aid from the United States, South Korea would have ceased to exist by 1952.

South Korea maintains her armed forces at about the 700,000 level. Equipment is American and includes F-16 aircraft. A large navy is in the small warship class. Civilian reserves are over 3 million.

From 1950 to 1991, the United States made more than $6 billion in military sales and military construction sales to South Korea.[3]

The 1993 U.S. opinion of the Korean situation is expressed in the *Congressional Presentation for Security Assistance Programs:*

The two accords between South and North Korea signed in late 1991 have the potential force to enhance stability on the Korean peninsula. Their full and rapid implementation, especially in alleviating the threat of a North Korean nuclear program, will be the key to a more peaceful Korea. In the meantime, however, renewed hostilities on the peninsula remain the most likely threat to peace in Northeast Asia. North Korea's million-many army and military equipment advantage over the South make it well-positioned for an attack that could still come with little or no warning. (p. 217)

South Korea has maintained her military forces in the 600,000 range since 1979. She routinely spent 4 to 5 percent of her gross national product for her military budget. Her GNP increased by 29 percent from 1979 to 1991.

South Korea has the advantage of U.S. military protection and favored-nation economic entry into the U.S. consumer economy.

NOTES

1. FMS Control and Reports Division, Comptroller, DSAA, *Foreign Military Sales, Foreign Military Construction Sales and Military Assistance Facts, as of September 30, 1991,* Washington, Data Management Division, Comptroller DSSA, 1992.

2. Mark L. Urban, *International Defense Review* 7 (1983); 931.

3. *Foreign Military Sales, September 30, 1991.*

8

North Africa

Africa is at present one of the most unfortunate parts of the world, a region of lost opportunities. North Africa saw true independence regained only after 1945 and the creation of eleven countries. They share the misery of a common, often drought-riddled part of the world. They share the misery of constantly changing governments, often run by military strongmen. Their populations have exploded since 1945.

One single common factor ties these nations together—the Moslem religion. Yet religion takes a back seat to the drive of army-backed politicians for political power. The close working relationship between the local military in North Africa and each government of these eleven nations is a major reason that the situation is dismal.

Foreign military sales by former colonial powers such as France and Britain have not helped to stabilize these governments. The military interventionist tactics of both the Soviet Union and the United States further destabilized the entire region.

This is a vast area of the world. It contains varied populations and per capita incomes as shown in Figure 8.1 (p. 76).

The wealth of these countries varies from a high of $5,500 average per person annual income in Libya to $130 in Ethiopia. There is little famine in Algeria, Libya, Morocco, or Tunisia. Millions are under the constant threat of starvation in Ethiopia and Somalia. Even U.N. military intervention to distribute food relief has done little to stabilize Somalia.

Governments are shaky in all countries. The military is the only stabilizing force in this part of the world. The military often make and unmake national governments. The lot of the great majority of the people in this part of the world is misery, if not starvation. Here, as in Asia, the military represent the actual power of the state. Government is often expressed in a combination of guns and food.

Figure 8.1
North Africa, Total Population and per Capita Income (In U.S. Dollars)

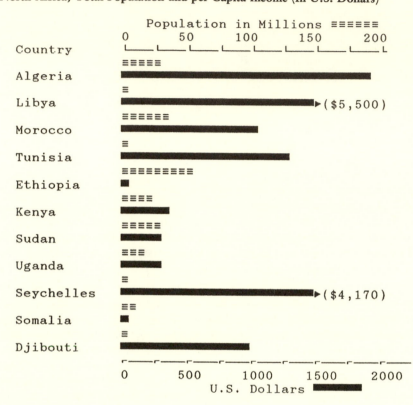

Note: U.S. 1990 per capita income was $21,800.

Foreign military intervention has been constant since 1945. The former colonial powers such as France and Britain continue to exercise great influence through their economic and military assistance programs.

The Cold War saw the United States and the Soviet Union trying to outbid each other for support in many of these nations by providing military advisors, hardware, and money. Today the United States carries on a similar guns-and-food strategy in parts of North Africa.

ALGERIA

Algeria is almost one-third the size of the 48 contiguous states. A population of 26 million, expected to double within fifteen years, has a per person average annual income of $2,170, the second largest in North Africa. The population is split between 4 million largely nomadic Berber tribesmen who live in the desert interior and some 22 million who live along the Mediterranean coast. There is little reason to expect normal relations between these two groups. Military patrols in the desert remain large and constant.

Algeria won independence from France in 1962. Most of the French colonists returned to France. Independence came after a long and bloody eight-year revolt. The constitution permits only one political party.

Ahmed Ben Bella became president in 1962. A bloodless military takeover replaced him in 1965. Eleven years of military rule followed. Colonel Houari Boumedienne became president in 1976. On his death in 1978, Colonel Chadli Bendjedid became president. He resigned in 1992. A five-member High Commission of State took power. When its president, Mohammed Boudiaf, was assassinated on June 29, 1992, Ali Kafi assumed power.

In 1967, Algeria declared war on Israel. Ties were broken with the United States. Algeria received military aid from the Soviet Union. From 1967 to 1987, the Soviet Union supplied Algeria with $3.5 billion in arms. West Germany, France, and Britain also sell military equipment to Algeria.

In 1985, the United States announced that Algeria was again eligible for military arms contracts and aid. Algeria has yet to take advantage of this offer.

The United States remains watchful:

Following disturbances in 1988, the government made a commitment to hold democratic multiparty elections and move toward a free market economy. After the first round of elections, the Islamic Salvation Front appeared poised to win control of the National Assembly. On January 11, 1992, President Bendjedid resigned and the second round of elections was canceled in an apparent attempt to prevent the accession to power of the Islamic Salvation Front which favored establishment of an Islamic system of government. These events plunged Algeria's political scene into confusion and potential instability for the foreseeable future.[1]

Algerian armed forces total about 175,000 supported by a maximum of 150,000 trained army reservists. The equipment is nearly all of Soviet manufacture. The growing Algerian Navy remains in the small warship class. Algeria's Air Force is large for North Africa. There are 10 fighter-bomber squadrons. Internal security police number 45,000. This defense force remains the key to Algeria's internal political future. Algerian armed forces also stand guard against possible trouble with Morocco and Libya.

In recent years, Algeria has spent on her armed forces relatively modest portions of her gross national product. Between 1979 and 1989, these sums varied from 4 to 5 percent while Algeria's GNP rose by 48 percent.

LIBYA

Libya is larger than Alaska. Because of oil riches, the 4.5 million Libyans enjoy the largest per person average annual income in North Africa, $5,500.

Few of the people live in the vast southern desert. Libyan civilization clings to the shores of the Mediterranean. Libya was an Italian colony before 1945. King Idris I ruled from 1945 to 1969. Oil was discovered. The military took over in 1969. The military organized the revolutionary command council. The Arab Republic of Libya came into being. Colonel Mu'ammar al-Quadhafi became the head of state. He continues to control Libya. A series of "5 year plans" did not bring prosperity to Libya.

Quadhafi promotes Arab unity under his domination. He intends to eliminate Israel. Quadhafi supports international terrorism. In 1984 and 1985 alone, some 30 acts of terrorism were attributed to his support. Among Quadhafi's direct military interventions were support for Idi Amin, the Ugandan dictator, in 1979 and the 1980 and 1983 invasions of Chad. Libyan and French troops have clashed repeatedly in Chad over the years.

Quadhafi proclaims that the strong always rule. He says that there is no need for money in the socialist state. He maintains that the only true religion is his own brand of Islam.

Libya bought its arms from the Soviet Union. At least $15 billion was spent on such arms from 1969 to 1989.

The United States is a determined enemy of Quadhafi. In 1986, the U.S. Air Force fought an 11-minute war with Quadhafi. This was caused by a series of Libyan-based terrorist attacks against U.S. forces in West Germany. All U.S. military sales to Libya ceased by 1980.

Quadhafi maintains 85,000 in his armed forces. There is a system of selective service. The equipment is all Soviet. There is a large air force of Soviet-built fighter-bombers. There are some 7,500 men in various paramilitary units. All forces are under Quadhafi's personal control.

Quadhafi routinely spends 13 to 20 percent of Libya's gross national product on his military. Libya's GNP declined by 13 percent from 1979 to 1989. Libya is best described as an Islamic police state. The population seems content with its high standard of living.

MOROCCO

Morocco is the size of Oregon and Washington, with 27 million people who have an average annual income of $1,000. The government is a constitutional monarchy. There are numerous political parties. Morocco has universal suffrage.

The French began occupying parts of Morocco in 1833. Spain began in 1860. The Moroccan struggle to maintain independence occupied the French, British, Spanish, Germans, and Americans before World War I. Morocco became a French protectorate in 1911. Not until 1921 was Morocco pacified.

During World War II, Moroccan forces fought against the Germans. In 1956, the French agreed that the protectorate had ended. By 1962, both

Spain and France recognized Moroccan independence. Spain withdrew from the Spanish Sahara in 1969.

The death of King Mohammed V in 1961 began a thirteen-year period of political instability. In 1965, King Hussan II declared a state of emergency. The military supported the king. This lasted until 1970. The present constitution was adopted in 1970. Army cadets tried a military takeover in 1971. This revolt was crushed by troop units loyal to the king. An assassination attempt on the life of the king failed in 1972.

In 1976, the last Spanish garrisons left the Spanish Sahara. Hassan II pushed his claim to all of the Spanish Sahara. The region is rich in phosphates. Hassan II's troops were met with guerrilla resistance of the Polisario front. This liberation movement has the financial and military support of Algeria. Libya initially sent support. Fighting still continues with various bursts of intensity. By U.N. action, the Spanish Sahara became a legal part of Morocco in 1992. Morocco supported the U.N. in the Gulf War against Iraq.

The United States supports the Moroccan government. During the period 1950–1991, the United States negotiated $1.3 billion in military sales and construction with Morocco.[2] In more recent years, American military aid to Morocco has been heavy, as shown in Table 8.1.

Morocco maintains 200,000 men in her armed forces. Equipment is American and French. Morocco practices conscription. The Moroccan Navy is very small, armed mainly with coastal defense vessels. The air force has four fighter-bomber squadrons. There are 10,000 well-trained police and a royal guard of 2,000. There are a varying number of desert tribesmen ready to fight for the king.

Table 8.1
U.S. Aid to Morocco (In U.S. Dollars)

	1991	1992	1993
Military Financing	40,000,000	40,000,000	40,000,000
International Military Education	1,150,000	1,150,000	1,150,000
Economic Support Fund	12,000,000	12,000,000	12,000,000
Development Assistance	12,500,000	23,000,000	25,225,000
Food for Peace	38,452,000	36,759,000	20,000,000
Peace Corps	3,361,000	1,383,000	1,713,000
Total	107,463,000	114,292,000	100,088,000

Source: United States of America, *Congressional Presentation for Security Assistance Programs, Fiscal Years 1991–1993*, Washington, D.C.: GPO, 1991–1993.

Morocco does not spend a large part of her gross national product on her military. She averaged 5.5 percent from 1979 to 1991. During this same period, Morocco's GNP increased by 44 percent.

TUNISIA

Tunisia is about the size of Missouri. The 8.5 million people enjoy an annual average income of $1,300. A constitutional form of government is dominated by several political parties. Universal adult voting is practiced. France established herself as the protector of Tunisia in 1881. Tunisia was part of the North African battleground in World War II. German and Allied forces fought over much of the country. In the face of increasingly popular demands for independence, France left Tunisia in 1956. The last French troops did not leave the naval base at Bizerte until 1962. Despite occasional problems, France remains Tunisia's largest supplier of military items.

The Destourian Socialist party has been in power since 1956. Labor unrest caused by widespread economic problems led to domestic violence in the 1970s and the 1980s. The army, ever loyal to President Habib Bourguiba, kept the peace. The government has blocked repeated attempts of the Islamic movement to gain political power. General Zine el-Abidine is the current president. The army remains the foundation on which the state rests. A dispute over their oil-rich border areas often mars relations with Libya.

Tunisia tends to support the Palestine Liberation Front. She also supported the U.S. 11-minute war with Libya in 1986. Tunisia's total armed forces number 40,000, 70 percent of them short-term draftees. The navy is very small. Her air force has about 55 aircraft of American manufacture. Other military equipment is purchased from Italy, France, Britain, and the United States.

Between 1950 and 1991, the United States sold Tunisia $626 million in military equipment and construction.[3] In more recent years the United States has furnished aid as shown in Table 8.2.

Tunisia is another North African country that does not spend a large portion of GNP on the military. In 1979, it amounted to 5 percent; by 1991, it was 3 percent. During these years, Tunisia's GNP increased by 45 percent.

ETHIOPIA

Ethiopia is about the size of Texas. A population of 53 million people shares the smallest average annual income in this part of Africa, $130. Ethiopia's history since 1945 is plagued with civil war, military takeovers, foreign intervention, fire, plague, drought, and starvation for millions. Except for worldwide humanitarian aid, millions of Ethiopians would have starved since 1988.

Table 8.2
U.S. Aid to Tunisia (In U.S. Dollars)

	1991	1992	1993
Military Financing	30,000,000	10,000,000	10,000,000
International Military Education	1,450,000	1,250,000	1,250,000
Economic Support Fund	10,900,000	3,000,000	10,000,000
Food for Peace	15,000,000	10,000,000	5,000,000
Peace Corps	2,152,000	1,008,000	1,014,000
Total	59,502,000	25,258,000	27,264,000

Source: United States of America, *Congressional Presentation for Security Assistance Programs, Fiscal Years 1991–1993,* Washington, D.C.: GPO, 1991–1993.

The current troubles began during the reign of the last emperor, Haile Selassie I. A long drought, beginning in 1982, brought on the deaths of hundreds of thousands from starvation. Strikes and student demonstrations, often led by native Communists, brought on a military takeover in 1974. Haile Selassie I was run out of the country.

The military rulers established a one-party socialist state. They began land reforms. Opposition was violent and widespread. One bloody revolt followed another throughout the 1980s. Ties with the United States were broken. In 1977, the Soviet Union became the principal military friend of Ethiopia. Soviet advisors and Cuban troops arrived. They defeated invading Somali forces in 1988.

Another drought began in 1984 and it continued into the 1990s. Within Ethiopia proper, the Ethiopian People's Democratic Front began a major revolt against the Communist government in 1991. They soon forced the government to leave the country. They announced plans for a democratic coalition government. This withdrawal led to the loss of the province of Eritrea in 1991. Eritrea became an independent nation in 1993. Ethiopia is now a landlocked nation.

In the midst of this turmoil, the greater part of the Ethiopian population continues to face the threat of starvation. Withdrawing food supplies from the entire population of the rebellious province of Eritrea was only one form of official ethnic warfare being waged.

The United States continues to maintain a watchful stance:

In May 1991, the dictatorial . . . regime fell and was replaced by a broadly-based traditional government which has committed itself to developing Ethiopia into a democracy with respect for human rights. . . . The proposed Fiscal Year [1993] International Military Education and Training Program would fund an orientation tour to U.S. military training facilities for a small group of key Ethiopian military leaders and professional military education courses for additional students.[4]

Since the revolution of 1991, no new national armed forces have been organized. Perhaps as many as 70,000 armed rebels rule the country. Reasonable current support figures for Ethiopia's revolutionary forces are not available.

ERITREA

Eritrea is the latest African nation to gain independence since 1945. An Italian colony from 1890, Eritrea became a part of Ethiopia at the end of World War II. The new country is a slice of northern Ethiopia lying along the Red Sea between Djibouti and Sudan. No final determination of her boundary with Ethiopia has been made. The capital, Asmara, has about 300,000 people out of 3.5 million. The Moslem and Christian religions dominate. English is the major foreign language taught in the public schools. The estimated literacy rate is 62 percent.

After thirty years of civil war as a province, the Eritrean People's Liberation Front defeated the Ethiopian Army in 1991 capturing the capital Asmara. Eritrea received her independence in 1993. A transitional government began, consisting of a National Assembly, the Council of Government, and a judicial body. The transitional constitution guarantees multipolitical parties, basic human rights, and respect for law and order. The interim president is Issayas Afewerke, leader of the successful military revolution against Ethiopia.

Well over one-half of the population relies on foreign aid food shipments. The infrastructure of the country is being rebuilt. The port of Massawa is back in operation. Telephone lines are back in service.

The new government faces the prospect of one million refugees returning from abroad. The present national budget depends on large amounts of foreign aid. Italy will probably be a large provider; the World Bank, the United States, and the European Community have promised assistance. Foreign investment is welcomed. Eritrea is a member of the United Nations and the Organization of African Unity.

Soldiers of the Eritrean People's Liberation Front have agreed to work for the country for two years without pay. The soldiers also provide internal security throughout the country. Soldiers of the Eritrean People's Liberation Front form the basis for the Army of Independent Eritrea. The Eritrean Navy is almost all of the former Ethiopian small warship navy which no longer has any bases. China has recently furnished two twin turboprop transport aircraft to begin the Eritrean Air Force. A civil war has begun between the Afars near the Djibouti border and government troops. The total armed forces are estimated between 60,000 and 85,000. Military equipment is mainly Russian.

KENYA

Kenya is slightly smaller than Texas with a population of 26 million and an average annual income of $380.

Kenya was a British colony until 1964. Independence came after a bloody black-against-white rebellion lasting four years. This Mau Mau rebellion was led by Jomo Kenyatta. Kenyatta was the first president. Many Europeans and Asians voluntarily left Kenya.

The Kenya African National Union political party has ruled Kenya since independence. This single political party is so filled with dissident groups that democracy is practiced in Kenya. Officeholders often lose elections to opposition groups. Yet a presidential order has the force of law. Such orders are not challenged.

Since independence, there has been steady progress in agriculture and industry. Only in 1974 and 1975 was the system shaken by charges of corruption and oppression. Normally the country remains at peace. The Kenyan military guarantee the continuation of the government.

The British maintain a military closeness with Kenya. Joint military exercises are often held with the British. U.S. forces use Kenya's sea and air bases. Kenya also buys some military equipment and accepts training programs from Britain, the United States, France, West Germany, Canada, and Pakistan.

From 1950 to 1991, the United States sold Kenya $255 million in military equipment and sales.[5] More recent planned American aid is shown in Table 8.3 (p. 84).

Kenya maintains a very small self-defense force of 25,000. Equipment for the army is mostly British. Kenya's small air force has American equipment. The Kenyan Navy numbers only 1,200. It is more of small coast guard than a navy.

From 1979 to 1991, Kenya's spending on military forces declined from 4.7 percent to 2.6 percent of GNP while that figure climbed by 34 percent.

Kenya's external security is guaranteed by Britain and the United States.

SUDAN

Sudan is about one-third the size of the lower 48 states, with a population of 27 million and an average per person annual income of $350. The 1956 constitution was replaced by a military dictatorship in 1985. Sudan gained independence from the British and the Egyptians in 1956. An ethnic-based civil war in the south began in 1955. It is still going on.

Table 8.3
U.S. Aid to Kenya (In U.S. Dollars)

	1991	1992	1993
Military Financing	8,000,000	4,000,000	
International Military Education	1,175,000	1,100,000	1,000,000
Economic Support Fund	7,000,000		
Development Assistance	26,000,000	26,000,000	17,200,000
Food for Peace	7,707,000	8,018,000	2,271,000
Peace Corps	3,176,000	2,416,000	2,565,000
Total	53,058,000	41,534,000	20,036,000

Source: United States of America, *Congressional Presentation for Security Assistance Programs, Fiscal Years 1991–1993,* Washington, D.C.: GPO, 1991–1993.

The National Unionist party dominated the first government. Economic difficulties led to a military takeover in 1958 when General Ibrahim Abboud became the dictator. Widespread riots and strikes in 1964 forced the military to step aside. Between 1965 and 1969, several civil governments failed to cope with the growing ethnic and economic problems. In 1969, another military takeover brought Colonel Gaafar Muhhammed Nimeiri to power. In 1971, the local Communists came to power for a few days. The military restored Nimeiri to power. When another revolt was crushed in 1976, Nimeiri's government offered amnesty.

In 1983 Nimeiri incorporated traditional Islamic punishments into the law code. This led to national controversy and a state of emergency in 1984. The state of emergency ended in late 1984.

A long drought in the south produced serious food shortages in 1985. Another military takeover ousted Nimeiri in 1985. General Suwar el Dahab took power. The military soon stepped aside. Elections were held in 1986. A coalition government resulted, headed by Sadiq al Mahdi.

The economy continued to worsen. Bread riots began in 1988. The civil war in the south gained strength. In late 1988, the coalition government dissolved. The remaining political parties swung more toward Islamic fundamentalism. Colonel Omar al-Bashir led a successful military revolt in 1989. Instability in the south continued throughout the 1980s. Only in 1992 did government forces make real headway against the animalistic southern tribes. Fighting continues. Sudan has accepted equipment from China and military advisors from Iran.

Sudan has been plagued with drought almost every year since independence. The situation deteriorated by 1991 to the point that only massive internal food aid prevents widespread starvation. Some seven million lives are threatened by this famine.

Sudan broke her diplomatic ties with the United States in 1967 over the Arab–Israeli war. Diplomatic relations began again in 1972. Assassination of an American relief officer in 1973 caused further difficulties. It was not until 1976 that the United States resumed full relations. Further problems involved the shooting of a U.S. embassy employee in 1986. From 1950 to 1986, the on-again off-again relationship with Sudan saw the United States furnish $18.2 million in military aid and construction sales to the Sudan.[6] In recent years,

The Sudanese military regime traditionally has favored a moderate pro-Western Sudan. However, human rights abuses by the current military regime have been the cause of repeated expressions of concern by the United States. We suspended all military aid in 1989 because of our concerns with government actions associated with the civil war.

Military assistance is currently prohibited by Section 513 of the Foreign Operations Appropriations Act of 1989, which forbids such assistance when the military overthrow a democratically-elected government. The current government, while professing neutrality in the Gulf War, is demonstratively pro-Iraq and increasingly critical of the US role in the Middle East.[7]

Sudan maintains an armed force of 72,000. The navy consists of a few river patrol craft. The army has 66,000 men. It has British equipment. The Sudanese Air Force is small. The rebel army in the south (Sudanese Peoples' Liberation Army) claims 66,000 men. They are without modern arms. These rebels operate along the Sudan–Ethiopian border.

Statistics concerning the amount of the gross national product spent on the military vary widely. Sudan continues to the plagued with two great problems. The ethnic based civil war in the south continues. The drought-induced country-wide starvation continues to grow ever more serious.

UGANDA

Uganda is about the size of Oregon. A population of 19 million has an average per person annual income of $300. A military government rules the country. The constitution was suspended in 1985. The British gave Uganda independence in 1962. An argument over the supremacy of the central government versus a loose federation of ethnic tribes plunged the country into a civil war. It is still going on.

In 1966, Milton Obote assumed all government powers. A military revolt in 1971 led by general Idi Amin Dada crushed the government. The next eight years of military rule produced rapidly economic decline. Idi Amin practiced genocide on several tribal groups. As many as 300,000 may have lost their lives.

In 1978, the Tanzanian Army repulsed an invasion attempt by Idi Amin. With the help of disaffected elements, the Tanzanian military conquered Uganda. In 1979, Idi Amin fled the country.

The Uganda National Liberation Front assumed control, and 1980 saw the military once again assume power. Fighting with the various tribal groups continued.

The current government was established in 1986 on the promise that a democratic system would come about in four years. There are still insurgent elements among several tribes.

The United States has maintained diplomatic ties with Uganda, but except for humanitarian aid, has provided very little assistance. "Despite its stated commitment to human rights, periodic abuses by the army continue, especially during efforts to eradicate lingering insurgencies. We have repeatedly stressed to the government the importance of ending these abuses and prosecuting those responsible, and the government has undertaken to do so."[8]

Uganda has an army estimated at 20,000. The national resistance army became the national army after the 1986 revolt. Tanzanian military advisors do most of the military training. There is no navy. The air force is part of the army.

Information is not available concerning defense spending relative to the gross national product.

SEYCHELLES

The 171-square-mile islands Republic of the Seychelles lies in the Indian Ocean off the northern tip of Madagascar and southeast of Kenya. The population is 70,000. Most of the people live on Mahe Island. They have an annual per person income of $4,170. The Seychelles are the one country in North Africa where the population is over 98 percent Christian. The ethnic mix is French and English. Both languages, along with Creole, are used by the government. The government is a single-party republic (Seychelles People's Progressive Front).

Britain granted independence in 1976 only after a fully democratic government was established. There has been some internal difficulty. A military takeover occurred in 1977. The country knew rule by decree until 1979. A new constitution turned the country into a one-party state in 1979. Mercenaries tried to overthrow the government in 1981, and the army mutinied in 1982. Both revolts were crushed by loyal troops and Tanzanian forces within days.

From 1950 to 1991, the United States sold $263,000 worth of military equipment to the Seychelles.[9] In recent years (1991–1993) the United States has furnished some $9.9 million in economic assistance and another $1 million for Peace Corps funding.[10] There is a U.S. Air Force tracking station on Mahe Island.

The Seychelles maintains a small self-defense force of 1,500 men. The navy and the air force practically do not exist. There is a people's militia of about 1,000. A Tanzanian Army battalion has been stationed on Mahe for several years.

Figures concerning the level of support for the military forces are not available.

SOMALIA

Somalia and Ethiopia are currently North Africa's two most unfortunate nations. In normal times, Somalia's estimated seven million people enjoy a per person average annual income of only $170. It is doubtful that it is that high in 1993. Some 98 percent of the people are Somalis. Ethnicity is not a problem.

The Somali Republic began in 1960 with the union of former British and Italian Somaliland. In 1969, a bloodless military takeover installed Major General Mohamed Barre as leader. Political parties were abolished. In 1970, the country became the Somali Democratic Republic.

In 1971, Somali troops took advantage of Ethiopia's civil war. They invaded Ogaden province where a majority of the population was Somali. With the help of Soviet military aid and Cuban troops, Ethiopia drove out the Somalis by 1978. The United States withdrew from Somalia.

Severe drought conditions began in 1984. Only massive international relief kept the Somalis from starving for the rest of the 1980s. Recently the drought conditions, coupled with continued border clashes with the Ethiopians, have seen the virtual collapse of the Somali government.

Officially, Somalia maintains a militia force of 43,000 and paramilitary units of another 30,000. More than likely this is an only-on-paper defense force. The latest news reports from Somalia tell the story of a lawless country with a completely collapsed economy smitten further by galloping famine.

In late 1992, the famine situation worsened. Rival Somali gangs prevented U.N. Food for Peace shipments from reaching the refugee camps. Led by an offer of sizable military forces by the United States, the United Nations hopes to end the political–military anarchy that dominates the country. In December 1992, the United Nations authorized a peace-keeping mission of some 28,000 troops. These units, led by the United States, received instructions to see to it that the relief food supplies reached Somalia's starving population. Supply routes are open in most of Somalia. Warlord rivalry with U.N. forces continues at a high level. It is estimated that another one million Somalis will starve to death if law and order collapses again.

DJIBOUTI

Djibouti is the size of New Hampshire. Its 550,000 people have a per person average annual income of $1,000. France granted Djibouti independence in 1977. The French keep 4,000 troops in Djibouti in case the country is attacked by Ethiopia or Somalia. Djibouti is afflicted with the same drought conditions as the rest of the Horn of Africa. France maintains Djibouti's economy.

Djibouti maintains a small military establishment of 1,500 men. The United States opened an embassy in 1980. American military aid has been virtually nonexistent. The United States has furnished humanitarian aid under the Food for Peace program since the long drought began in 1984.

NOTES

1. United States of America, *Congressional Presentation for Security Assistance Programs, Fiscal Year 1993,* Washington, GPO, Jointly prepared by the Department of State and the Defense Security Agency, 1992.

2. FMS Control and Reports Division, Comptroller, DSAA, *Foreign Military Sales, Foreign Military Construction Sales and Military Assistance Facts, as of September 30, 1991,* Washington, Data Management Division, Comptroller DSSA, 1992.

3. Ibid.

4. *Congressional Presentation, Fiscal Year 1993,* p. 166.

5. *Foreign Military Sales, September 30, 1991.*

6. *Foreign Military Sales, September 30, 1990.*

7. *Congressional Presentation, Fiscal Year 1992,* p. 277. Sudan is not mentioned in the Fiscal Year 1993 program.

8. *Congressional Presentation, Fiscal Year 1993,* p. 326.

9. *Foreign Military Sales, September 30, 1991.*

10. *Congressional Presentation, Fiscal Years 1991–1993.*

□ □ **9**

Central Africa

Many of the early predictions about the fate of the newly liberated nations throughout Africa tended to reduce the potential political role of the military. This proved to be a mistake. Before the departure of the colonial powers, such as Britain, Belgium, and France, many European officers expected to stay on to lead the new armies. The rapid addition and promotion of black officers, however, often from the enlisted ranks, had a disastrous effect on the internal stability of these armies. As the officers from the former colonial powers began to leave, a type of discipline, based on the subordination of the military to the civil side of the state, collapsed. This is more or less the case throughout the many nations that have gained independence in Africa since 1945.

The six countries in Central Africa, far removed from the apartheid problems of the south and the fierce Moslem hatred of Israel and multiple Moslem sectarian problems of the north, offer proof on both sides of the following question. In the absence of great external influences such as a worldwide religion (Arabs versus Jews) or a strong racist policy of a nearby white power (Republic of South Africa), have black officers loyally served their civil governments? A second question also needs an answer. How often and how quickly have the former colonial powers intervened in this region?

This configuration of Central Africa contains six nations: Burundi, Central African Republic, Chad, Rwanda, Tanzania, and Malawi. This is a slice of Africa that stretches from the southern border of Libya to Mozambique and Zambia. This is the heartland of Africa. It is the part of Africa that has made the least splash on television and in the newspapers since independence. It is the part of Africa written about least in books and magazine articles. Have these nations simply become the lost tribes of Africa? Have they slowly become a series of success stories for the nations of the Third World? Are their political–military histories different from those of North, West, and South Africa?

The people in this part of the world on the average are poor. The annual per person average income reaches a high at $440 and drops to a low of $175. Only Tanzania has a relatively large population. All maintain regular military forces of varying sizes (see Figure 9.1).

BURUNDI

Burundi is about the size of Maryland. A population of 6 million has a per person average annual income of only $220. Burundi borders Zaire, Rwanda, and Tanzania. The populace is 65 percent Roman Catholic and 35 percent tribal religions. The literacy rate is less than 50 percent. The history of Burundi since independence turns on brutal warfare between the Tutsi and Hutu tribal groups.

This tribal competition existed for centuries before the white Western European imperialistic powers arrived. In the nineteenth century, the Germans made Burundi part of German East Africa. The Belgians assumed control after World War I. Both European nations left the local government intact. The Tutsi continued to rule the Hutu.

In the 1950s, a movement began among the Tutsi to liberalize the restraints placed on the Hutu. Burundi gained independence in 1962. The Union for National Progress continued the reform movement. This movement collapsed

Figure 9.1
Central Africa, Total Population and per Capita Income (In U.S. Dollars)

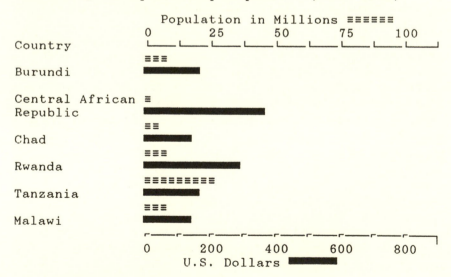

Note: U.S. 1990 per capita income was $21,800.

in 1965. Hutu politicians from all political parties won an overwhelming majority in both houses of the national legislature. King Mwambutsa IV sent them home.

Hutu army officers staged a military takeover. Civil war, based on tribal lines, began when Tutsi army troops crushed this uprising. A Tutsi army officer, Michel Micombero, took power in 1966. Some 5,000 Hutus died. The new government continues to maintain Tutsi control of the country.

Hutus were purged from all levels of government in 1969. A Hutu uprising led to their widespread massacre. Genocide became the practice of the Tutsi government. Between 100,000 and 500,000 Hutu died.

In 1974 Burundi became a one-party state. Micombero stepped down in 1969. Colonel Jean Baptiste Bagaza replaced him. Power continues in the hands of the Tutsi elite who control the army.

In 1985 Bagaza began persecution of the Christian churches. In 1987 the military seized control. Major Pierre Buyoya came to power. The persecution of Christian churches stopped.

Hutus killed a few Tutsi in 1988. The army massacred about 30,000 Hutus. There are many Hutu refugees in neighboring countries. After the 1988 killings, a second reform movement began. The Buyoya government has promised constitutional reforms and increased human rights.

Buyoya maintains a total military force of 7,500. The military gets only about 3 percent of the gross national product. Burundi military equipment is mostly British, with a few American planes.

United States opinion on the current situation in Burundi is that "Burundi is moving rapidly toward democratic reform and constitutional government. . . . The Burundi military's acceptance of these reforms has been one of the key factors in President Buyoya's ability to bring stability and a more democratic government to his country. These developments offer hope for ethnic reconciliation and resulting human rights improvements."[1]

CENTRAL AFRICAN REPUBLIC

The Central African Republic is a landlocked nation that borders Congo, Zaire, Sudan, Chad, and Cameroon. A population of 3 million has a per person average annual income of $440. The country is slightly smaller than Texas.

France granted independence in 1960. The present constitution began in 1986. Barthelemy Boganda was the first president. He died in an airplane crash just before final independence. His nephew, David Dacko, became president. Worsening economic conditions led to a general strike in 1965. Colonel Jean Bedel Bohassa led a military takeover in 1966. He assumed all power as president. In 1976, he became Emperor Bohassa I.

The country suffered under his rule. He personally participated in the beating deaths of some school children who expressed opposition to his regime. He was much like Idi Amin of Uganda, but the scale of his inhumanity did not run into the tens of thousands of victims.

French military intervention led to David Dacko's return to power in 1979. Bohassa was sentenced to life in prison. A military takeover brought General Andre Kolingba to power in 1981. The military started a return-to-democracy trend in 1985. This trend is slow but steady.

The Central African Republic is within the French-controlled Franc Zone in Africa. France guarantees the continued existence of the Central African Republic's government.

The United States maintains friendly relations with the Central African Republic, but sold only $483,000 in military sales and construction to the country from 1950 to 1991.[2] In recent years, American military aid remains limited to training a handful of army officers under the International Military and Training Education Program. France continues as the principal source of military aid and training.

The Central African Republic's military forces total 6,500. Another 3,000 make up the national military police. The military forces in 1989 received only 1.7 percent of the gross national product.

CHAD

Chad is a largely desert country about the size of Texas, Oklahoma, and New Mexico. The 5.5 million people have an average per person annual income of $190. Chad borders Niger, Libya, Sudan, Central African Republic, Cameroon, and Nigeria. The French granted independence in 1960. Chad has remained a member of the French African economic arrangement. French troops guarantee her independence.

Chad's first president was Francois Tomballaye. The first constitution survived until 1982. It was replaced by the "Fundamental Act of the Republic." A civil war began in 1985 as a tax revolt. The Moslem majority in the north rose against the government in N'Dijamena in the south. French troops supported the government. In 1975 the army staged a takeover. General Felix Malloum became the head of state. In 1979, the Moslem forces from the north invaded the south.

At this point, all civil government collapsed. Several conferences established a national union transitional government. In 1980, the fighting resumed. The Moslems in the north received military aid and troops from Libya. Quadhafi sent 7,000 troops into Chad. French troops withdrew in 1980.

Libya then invaded Chad in 1981. The Libyans withdrew under fierce pressure from France and the United States. They returned in 1982. French and Zairian troops defeated the Libyan forces.

From 1983 to 1987, Chad was divided between governments established in the north and the south. In 1987 Chadian forces, using new equipment furnished by the United States, defeated Libyan troops.

Quadhafi announced that he would support the government in the south, now led by Hisene Habre. Habre's government collapsed in 1990. A new national charter began in 1991. Idriss Deby became president. There are constant reports of fighting between the army and rebel forces.

Chad has some 17,000 men under arms. There are 5,700 men in the national military police. The rebel forces (Democratic Council of the Revolution) may number 1,000. Libya trains and supplies the rebel forces. The French maintain a 1,200-man garrison in Chad.

The United States continues to support the established government in the south. American aid in recent years is shown in Table 9.1.

Figures concerning Chad's support level for military forces are not available. Until resolution of both the civil war and the problem with Colonel Quadhafi of Libya, Chad will remain one of the lost tribes of Central Africa.

RWANDA

Rwanda is about the size of Maryland. This country borders Burundi, Tanzania, Uganda, and Zaire. The 8 million people have a per person average annual income of $310. Rwanda's population is 85 percent Hutu and 14 percent Tutsi. Belgium granted independence in 1962.

Serious fighting between the Hutu and Tutsi tribes began in 1959. Some 200,000 Tutsis fled. Gregoire Kayibanda, leader of the party of the Hutu

Table 9.1
U.S. Aid to Chad (In U.S. Dollars)

	1991	1992	1993
Military Financing	2,000,000	2,000,000	2,000,000
International Military Education	300,000	380,000	400,000
Economic Support Fund	6,000,000		
Development Assistance	6,000,000	15,000,000	11,700,000
Food for Peace	2,315,000	1,400,000	
Peace Corps	1,619,000	1,518,000	1,582,000
Total	18,234,000	20,298,000	15,682,000

Source: United States of America, *Congressional Presentation for Security Assistance Programs, Fiscal Years 1991–1993*, Washington, D.C.: GPO, 1991–1993.

emancipation movement, became the first president. He tried to negotiate with the Tutsis. He established diplomatic relations with more than 40 countries, including the United States.

Despite some progress, the government began purging dissident elements by 1968. Major General Juvenal Habyarimana led a military takeover in 1973. All civil authority ended. His new national revolutionary movement for development tried to pick up the original program of Kayibanda. The civil war continued. Habyarimana was elected president in 1978, 1983, and 1988.

Rwanda has large mineral deposits of tin and tungsten. The government has embarked on an unpaid program of community projects. Roads, bridges, schools, hospitals, communications, and the like are maintained by a system of unpaid work programs. All able-bodied men participate.

From 1950 to 1991 Rwanda received $1.9 million in military sales and construction contracts from the United States.[3] More recently, the United States has declared some satisfaction with Rwandan progress toward democracy and the proper recognition of human rights. For the present, the United States will offer military aid only in the form of training for a few officers under the International Military Education and Training Program.[4]

Rwanda faces a continuing civil war. Tutsi forces enter the country from neighboring Uganda. There may be as many as 300 to 500 rebels in the field. Some fighting occurs every year.

The Rwandan government maintains a military force of 5,500 men. There is a national police force of 1,500. Most of the military equipment comes from Belgium.

Current figures reflecting Rwanda's level of support for her military forces are not available.

TANZANIA

Tanzania is a little smaller than Texas and New Mexico. Its 26 million people have a per capita average annual income of $120. Tanzania borders Kenya, Uganda, Rwanda, Burundi, Zaire, Zambia, Malawi, and Mozambique. There is a long coastline on the Indian Ocean. Tanzania is split almost evenly among Muslims, Christians, and tribal cults. There is a long history of ethnic peace.

Tanzania received independence from Britain in 1961. The government is a one-political-party socialist republic with military overtones.

Julius K. Nyerere founded the Tanganyika African National Union in 1954. He became the prime minister under the democratic constitution. He was elected president in 1961. Zanzibar joined the new republic in 1964.

In the 1970s, the government began moving its urban and rural unemployed into a series of new agrarian villages. Brutal coercive measures were used when people hesitated to obey. Agriculture production dropped 50 percent. This was the beginning of the government's attempt to establish state control of all aspects of the national economy. It failed. The infrastructure deteriorated. Manufacturing declined by 60 percent in the 1980s.

Since 1988, the government has gradually abandoned the concept of state socialism for a more open market economy. Recent inflation rates have been as high as 25 percent. Tanzania remains an object lesson in failed state socialism. Economic depression hinders all progress toward democracy and human rights at present.

The United States maintains friendly relations with Tanzania. What aid Tanzania receives from the United States comes via such organizations as the World Bank and the United Nations. At present, the United States does not contemplate any military aid to Tanzania beyond training a few army officers.

The Tanzanian armed forces claim 48,000. Some 22,000 of these are two-year draftees. The navy is a tiny coast guard. The air force is also very small. There are 1,500 national police. Tanzania claims a citizen's militia of more than 100,000.

Tanzania spends about 3 percent of GNP on military forces. Only the continuing economic crisis keeps Tanzania from becoming a leading African state. Her military is not a problem to her neighbors or to herself. Tanzania is the least lost of the Central African lost tribes.

MALAWI

Malawi is a landlocked nation. Neighbors are Zambia, Tanzania, and Mozambique. Malawi is an absolute monarchy. Dr. Ngwazi Hastings Kamuzu Banda is president for life. Malawi is about the size of Pennsylvania. A population of 9 million has a per person average annual income of $175. Malawi received independence from the British in 1964. Banda purged his government of dissidents in 1964. Those who oppose him often disappear.

Until 1979, the economy boomed. Manufacturing arrived in the 1980s. It soon accounted for 15 percent of the gross national product. The more recent economic crisis has deepened as worldwide demands for goods slackened. Depleted farmland has become a problem.

The effects of Mozambique's civil war have been unkind to Malawi's economy. RENAMO rebels operate along the frontier with Mozambique. Such activity cuts Malawi's rail access to the sea. In 1986, Malawi agreed to let the RENAMO rebels use her territory. Malawi troops have tried to police the rail connection with Mozambique.

The United States does not give military aid to Malawi. Although Malawi severely restricts the personal freedom of her citizens, the Malawian military forces are not guilty of human rights abuses.

Malawi maintains an army of 7,500. She keeps 800 troops employed along the Mozambique frontier. There is also a 500-man national police force. Support for the military has declined from 5 percent in 1979 to 2 percent in 1991 of GNP. In the same period, the GNP increased by about 50 percent.

NOTES

1. United States of America, *Congressional Presentation for Security Assistance Programs, Fiscal Year 1993,* Washington, GPO, Jointly prepared by the Department of State and the Defense Security Agency, 1992.

2. FMS Control and Reports Division, Comptroller, DSAA, *Foreign Military Sales, Foreign Military Construction Sales and Military Assistance Facts, as of September 30, 1991,* Washington, Data Management Division, Comptroller DSSA, 1992.

3. Ibid.

4. *Congressional Presentation, Fiscal Year 1993.*

□ □ **10**

East and West Africa

There are no longer two superpowers competing for African support. The United States' current deficit, now running at nearly $400 billion annually, will have some impact on support levels in the near future. While American interest remains in the few African nations rich in oil, most of the 25 nations in West Africa have little to attract capitalistic self-interest.

East and West Africa are still important to the United States for several reasons. These 25 nations play an often decisive role in international meetings and conferences. The region has other natural resources besides oil that are beginning to run short. There are large deposits of copper, iron, bauxite, uranium, cobalt, manganese, gold, and diamonds.

Africa needs capital investment. These nations willingly trade their natural resources for advanced industrial technology. Parts of this area are strategically important. The tanker routes from the oil-rich fields of the Middle East pass through the offshore waters of many of these nations. Continuing tribal and internation rivalries are producing instability in many economies and political systems.

Intervention by the United States will continue for the immediate future. These 25 nations have a particular significance for Americans of African descent who take a deep interest in various parts of the region. The United States will continue to promote its guiding principle in African affairs. The United States will promote political stability, economic reform, and democracy. American military aid rests on this policy.

These nations show many of the terrible aspects of tribal and religious diversity that plague both North and Central Africa. In this area, the European colonial administrations left the local problems much as they had found them on their arrival (see Figure 10.1 on p. 98).

Figure 10.1
East and West Africa, Total Population and per Capita Income (In U.S. Dollars)

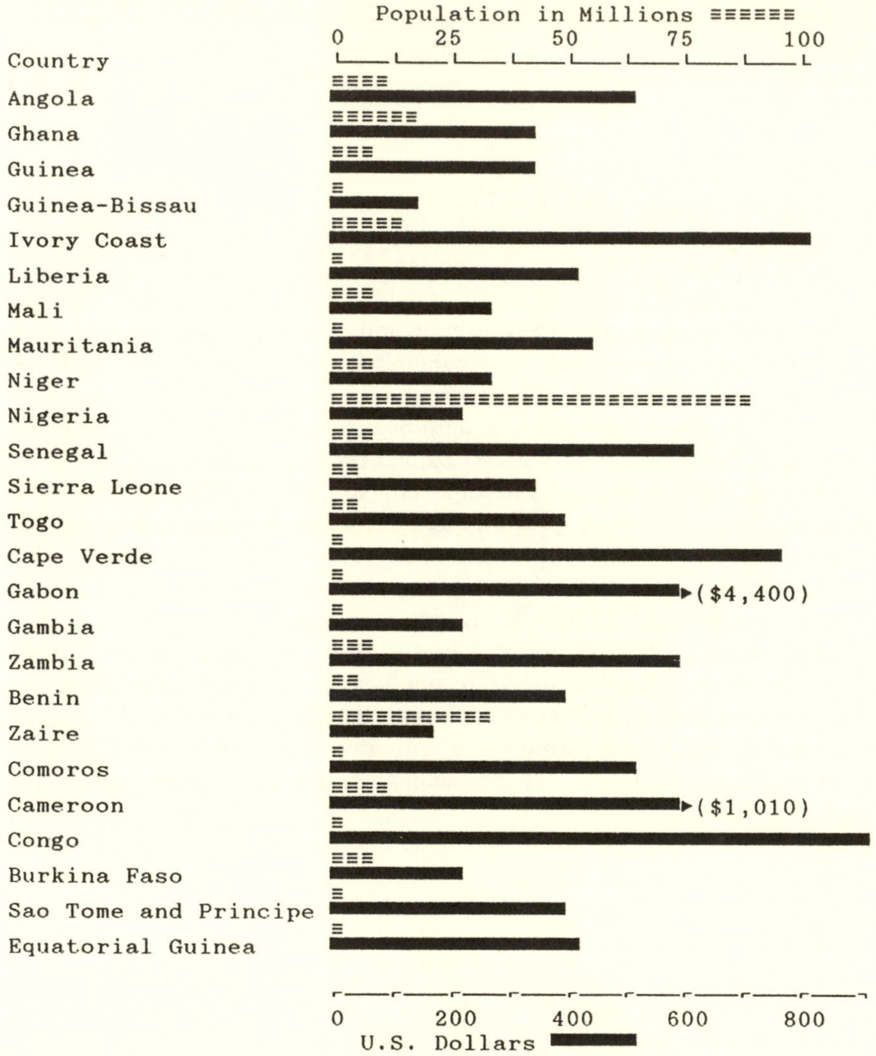

Population in Millions ≡≡≡≡≡≡

```
Country        0      25      50      75      100

Angola
Ghana
Guinea
Guinea-Bissau
Ivory Coast
Liberia
Mali
Mauritania
Niger
Nigeria
Senegal
Sierra Leone
Togo
Cape Verde
Gabon                                    ►($4,400)
Gambia
Zambia
Benin
Zaire
Comoros
Cameroon                                 ►($1,010)
Congo
Burkina Faso
Sao Tome and Principe
Equatorial Guinea

               0      200     400     600     800
               U.S. Dollars ▬▬▬▬▬
```

Note: U.S. 1990 per capita income was $21,800.

ANGOLA

Angola is about the size of Texas. With 9 million people and a per person average annual income of $620, Angola borders Zaire, Zambia, and Namibia. She is a Marxist people's republic governed by the Popular Movement for the Liberation of Angola–Labor Party.

Angola was a Portuguese colony until independence in 1975. Black rebels began two separate wars for independence in 1961. These first rebel efforts fell before Portuguese military might. The National Union for the Total Independence of Angola began a third revolutionary movement in the 1960s which met with little success.

The overthrow of Portugal's home government by the socialists in 1974 brought about immediate independence for Angola. In 1975 the three rebel groups worked out the Alvor Accord. They divided the country between them. Armed clashes became common.

Each group had foreign military aid. The Popular Movement for the Liberation of Angola received aid from Cuba, the Soviet Union, Nigeria, Sweden, and Denmark. The two anti-Marxist groups merged into the National Front for the Liberation of Angola. This new group received military aid from China, France, Britain, Romania, North Korea, Zaire, South Africa, and the United States.

More than 400,000 Portuguese settlers went home. The number of black dead is unknown. By 1977, the People's Republic of Angola was in control. It was recognized by the United Nations. The United States did not grant diplomatic recognition.

The victory of the Marxist People's Republic did not end the civil war. South Africa continued to support the rebel opposition group. Cuban troops began to arrive to support the Marxist government. They soon numbered more than 50,000. South Africa withdrew her forces after losing on the battlefield in 1989. Cuban forces began to withdraw in 1991.

The civil war continues. The United States continues to give military aid to the antigovernment rebels. Both sides declared their wish for a negotiated settlement. A peace accord was signed in 1991. An uneasy truce exists that is often broken. Nearly 1,000 U.N. troops and observers serve in Angola. Shooting was common in the capital as late as 1993. At present, the United States offers only a small officers training program to the Angolan government.

The Angolan government maintains armed forces at the 100,000 level, 25 percent of them draftees. Another 10 percent are activated reservists. There are still several hundred Soviet military advisors in Angola. Angolan military equipment is mainly Russian. Angola maintains an infantry battalion in Sao Tome and Principe.

The rebel opposition may have as many as 30,000 troops. They should merge with the government's military forces as total unification proceeds.

There are 450 U.N. observers in the country watching over the cease-fire and merger arrangements.

Statistics are not available concerning the government's military funding. All sources agree that the Angolan economy is a total wreck.

GHANA

Ghana is about the size of Illinois and Indiana. A population of 15 million has an average annual per capita income of $380. With a coast along the Atlantic Ocean, the county borders Togo, Burkina Faso, and Ivory Coast. Ghana has an authoritarian government. There are no political parties. Universal suffrage is practiced. The British gave Ghana a constitutional government in 1954. Kwame Nkrumah led the Convention People's Party to victory in the first elections. Britain granted final independence in 1957.

Nkrumah began building a modern industrialized socialist state. When criticized, Nkrumah used the Prevention Detention Act. Anyone could be jailed without trial for five years.

In 1966, the army took over, and Nkrumah was dismissed. Army leaders formed the National Liberation Council. They agreed to a return to constitutional civil government, and Ghana returned to civilian rule in 1969. Kofi A. Busia led the Progress party to victory in the elections.

Economic decline forced Busia's government into currency devaluation in 1971. In 1972 the army took over. Colonel I. K. Acheampong now led the National Redemption Council. In 1975 the Supreme Military Council, led now by General I. K. Acheampong, seized power.

Continuing economic decline saw Lt. General Frederick Akuffo came to power in 1979. His government fell in a bloody military takeover led by junior officers. Lt. Jerry Rawlings came to power. Several senior officers were shot. Special tribunals tried and disposed of hundreds more.

The Rawlings group declared the Third Republic in 1979. President Limann led the new democratic government. In 1981, Lt. Rawlings led another military takeover. He dissolved the constitution and established the Provisional National Defense Council. This is a military dictatorship. Ghanaians live under a cost-conscious military regime.

Relations between the United States and Ghana are strained. The United States objects to the lack of democratic institutions in the Ghanian government. The only military aid Ghana receives from the United States is enough money to educate a few army officers every year.

Ghana maintains 12,000 men in her armed forces. She has 10,000 soldiers and 4 patrol boats in her navy. Her air force has less than 20 combat planes. Her troops serve in peace-keeping missions in Liberia, along the Afghanistan–Pakistan border, in Kuwait, and in Lebanon. These peace-keeping forces total nearly 2,600 men. A people's militia claims 6,000 men.

Between 1979 and 1991, Ghana spent less than 1 percent of GNP on her military. The GNP rose 49 percent during this same period.

GUINEA

Guinea is about the size of Oregon. Its 7.5 million people have an average per person annual income of $380. Guinea has common frontiers with Guinea-Bissau, Senegal, Mali, Ivory Coast, Liberia, and Sierra Leone. The government is a military dictatorship. There is one newspaper.

After World War II, Ahmed Sekou Toure emerged as the black leader. In 1947, he founded the Democratic party of Guinea which broke with the native Communists in 1950. In 1957 Toure won a key election. Guinea rejected membership in the new French Franc community of African nations. Toure died in 1984.

The army stepped in, claiming a wish to set up a democracy. Colonel Lausana Conte assumed power. Dissident military forces failed in an attempt to seize power in 1985.

Conte is committed to a severe structural adjustment program. This includes a free market economy. The socialist state ceased to exist. Rising prices and unemployment led to serious rioting in 1988. The army crushed this movement. Power is supposed to return to an elected civilian government in 1994.

Guinea is a nonaligned nation. She enjoys good relations with the United States. At present, U.S. military aid is limited to training a few army officers each year.

The armed forces have 10,000 men. Draftees account for 80 percent of this total. Military equipment is a mixture of French and Soviet manufacture. The navy is a coast guard. The tiny air force claims no more than 15 combat airplanes.

Figures describing the support level for the military forces are not available.

GUINEA-BISSAU

Guinea-Bissau is about the size of Indiana. It lies on the Atlantic coast and borders Senegal and Guinea. The 1 million people have a per person average annual income of $160. Portugal granted independence in 1974. The government is a republic established in 1984.

Amilcar Cabral organized the African Party for the Independence of Guinea and Cape Verde in 1956. He began a rebellion in 1966. Portugal sent in 30,000 troops. They could not crush the rebels. By 1972 the rebels controlled most of the country. When the Portuguese left, a shaky democracy was established.

A military takeover in 1980 gave Joao Bernardo Vieira absolute power.

The government discovered a military takeover plot in 1985. Six plot leaders were shot. Others are still in jail. The government enjoys the support of the vast majority of the population.

Guinea-Bissau is most famous for its 1988 toxic waste contract. Britain, Switzerland, and the United States dump toxic waste in Guinea-Bissau. This contract is up for renewal in 1993.

Guinea-Bissau has 10,000 men in its armed forces. Its air force has perhaps three combat-ready planes. The navy is a very small coast guard. There is a national police force of 2,500. Guinea-Bissau has observers in Angola as part of the U.N. peace-keeping operation.

U.S. military aid is limited to training a few army officers each year. Historically, Guinea-Bissau spends no more that 3 percent of her GNP on her military forces.

IVORY COAST

Ivory Coast, about the size of New Mexico, borders Ghana, Mali, Liberia, and Guinea. Her 13 million people have a per person average annual income of $820. France granted independence in 1960.

Houphouet-Boigny became president in 1960, and 1990 saw his reelection as president at the age of 85. He maintained close ties with France. French troops remain in the country. His death in late 1993 brought threats of revolution.

The United States supports the government of Ivory Coast. U.S. military aid is limited to training a few army officers every year.

Ivory Coast has 7,500 men in the armed forces. The navy is a coast guard. The air force has less than ten combat aircraft. There are perhaps 8,000 men in the various paramilitary units. Military equipment is French. France maintains a marine infantry regiment in Ivory Coast. France guarantees the existence of the government.

Ivory Coast annually spends between 1 and 2 percent of its GNP to support the military.

LIBERIA

Liberia, about the same size as Pennsylvania, borders Ivory Coast, Guinea, and Sierra Leone. The government is a constitutional republic. There are several political parties.

Liberia was Africa's first republic. The American Colonization Society began sending blacks back to Africa in 1822. In 1847, Liberia became a republic with a U.S.-type constitution.

President William R. Toblert, Jr., lost power in 1980 as the result of a military takeover. Sergeant Samuel K. Doe seized power. A period of martial law followed. A new constitution brought elections in 1985. Doe was elected president in a widely contested election.

General Thomas Quiwonkpa led a military takeover in 1985. Some 12,000 died. Doe installed a dictatorship. In 1985 the rebels formed the National Patriotic Front of Liberia. They declared war on the government.

By 1990, 10,000 died and 200,000 fled the country. In 1990 a West African peace-keeping force of 7,500 from Gambia, Ghana, Guinea, Nigeria, and Sierra Leone arrived to restore order. The rebels captured and killed Doe. A cease-fire followed in 1991. It was soon broken. In 1993 Liberia is gripped by the civil war.

The United States maintains diplomatic relations with Liberia. All American citizens were pulled out of Liberia. American military aid declined by 75 percent from 1985 to 1988. The decline continued in 1989 and 1991. By 1992 all military aid to Liberia had ceased except for the training of a few army officers.

There are no organized armed forces in Liberia. There are no reliable figures about the rebels. What law and order exists is maintained by the West African peace-keeping forces.

MALI

Mali is about the size of Texas and California. A landlocked nation, Mali borders Ivory Coast, Burkina Faso, Niger, Algeria, Mauritania, Senegal, and Guinea. Her population of 8 million has a per person average annual income of $250. The military control Mali.

France granted independence in 1960. Mali remains in the French Franc African community. Bad harvests following prolonged droughts plague the nation. In 1989, Mali agreed to start democratic reforms in return for increased economic assistance.

The military overthrew the government in 1991. The army promised to build a democracy. Alpha Oumar Konare was sworn in as president after elections held in 1992.

U.S. military aid to Mali is limited to training a few army officers each year.

Mali maintains a military of 7,500. Her military equipment is French. Her navy consists of several river patrol boats. Her air force has no combat planes. There are 8,000 in various paramilitary units. The Turages, in the extreme desert north, are in revolt. Their number and equipment are unknown. About 2 percent of the GNP goes to support the military.

MAURITANIA

Mauritania, a little smaller than Alaska, lies on the Atlantic coast and borders Western Sahara, Mali, and Senegal. Her 2 million people have a per person average annual income of $460. The military forces govern Mauritania.

France granted independence in 1960. President Moktar Daddah dominated the country until 1978. He moved the country toward its white Arab heritage. Attempts were made to reorient the blacks in the south. Mauritania became a nonaligned nation.

The military seized power in 1978. Lt. Col. Mohamed Khouna Ould Haidalla became chief of state. A long drought began in the 1980s. Lt. Col. Maayouia Ould Sid'Ahmed Taya took control in 1984. Some local elections occurred in 1986.

Racial tensions generated by the government's white Arab policy arose. The black half of the population in the south became restless. Black troops tried to take over in 1987. They were crushed. Racial tensions between the black government of Senegal and the white government of Mauritania remain at a fever pitch. Mass deportations of minorities began in both countries.

Trouble also existed along the frontier with Western Sahara. Mauritania annexed the southern half of Western Sahara in 1976. The Saharans began a guerilla resistance. Some 8,000 Moroccan troops and the French Air Force intervened. Not until 1980 did Mauritania give up her claim to Western Sahara. There is a U.N. mission of some 300 troops and officials along the border with Western Sahara.

Although the United States maintains friendly relations with Mauritania, at present there is no plan to provide military aid. The military government in Mauritania is allied with Iraq.

Mauritania maintains 12,000 in her military. Her navy consists of fewer than ten coast guard patrol boats. Her air force has fewer than ten combat aircraft. Another 6,000 men are in various paramilitary units. There are not any important internal or external threats to the ruling military.

Support for the military declined from 12 percent of GNP in 1979 to 4 percent in 1991. The GNP increased by 47 percent during this same period.

NIGER

Niger, a landlocked nation, is almost twice the size of Texas. Neighbors are Chad, Libya, Algeria, Mali, Burkina Faso, and Benin. Her population of 8 million has a per person average annual income of $290. She is ruled by a military government.

France granted independence in 1960. Hamani Diori served as president. He was reelected in 1965 and 1970. The military crushed the constitutional government in 1974. Niger's economic progress depends on the world uranium market. The slump in this market, plus the drought conditions of the 1980s, led to the present economic crisis. Niger remains a member of France's Franc North African community. France maintains military advisors in Niger. Threats from Libya or Turage Arabs in the north are always present.

Niger is a member of the nonaligned nations. The United States maintains friendly relations with Niger and grants sums over $25 million a year in the form of economic assistance and Peace Corps funding. American military aid is limited to training a few army officers every year. Niger supported the United Nations in the Gulf War.

Niger maintains a military establishment of 3,500 men. Her air force has only transport planes. There are 4,500 men in various internal security organizations. Niger is not threatened by internal or external foes. She spends an average of 1 percent of her GNP on her military. Niger's GNP increased by 38 percent from 1979 to 1991.

NIGERIA

Nigeria is about the size of Arizona, California, and Nevada. It lies on the Atlantic coast, and its neighbors are Cameroon, Chad, Niger, and Benin. Nigeria's 88 million people have a per person average annual income of $230. The military rule Nigeria. Britain granted independence in 1960.

Nigeria has ethnic problems. Her population is divided between warring tribes. In 1966 Ibo army officers overthrew the government. They established a federal military government. A second military takeover in 1966 saw the killing of thousands of Ibos. Hundreds of thousands of Ibos returned to their homeland in southeastern Nigeria.

In 1976 Lt. Col. Emeka Ojukwu declared Ibo independence as the Republic of Biafra. A genocidal civil war lasted for three years. Perhaps hundreds of thousands of Ibos died. Gen. Murtala Muhammed seized power in 1975. He was killed in 1976. Lt. Gen. Olusegun Obasanjo became head of state. He installed the Second Republic in 1977. Alhaji Shehu Shagari was elected president in 1978 and 1983. The economic crisis began as the price of oil fell on the world markets.

In 1983 the military seized control. Maj. Gen. Muhammadu Buhari pledged to bring better management to the government. He promised to return to civilian rule when economic conditions permitted.

In 1985 Maj. Gen. Ibrahim Babangida took power. He promised many reforms. He promised a return to civilian rule, first by 1990 and then by 1992. An attempted military takeover against him failed in 1990. Seventy of the plotters were shot after trial by secret military courts.

U.S. relations with Nigeria are friendly. Several Nigerian heads of state have visited Washington. Many thousands of Nigerians are educated in the United States. From 1950 to 1990, the United States sold Nigeria $65.9 million in military equipment and construction.[1]

Currently the United States adopts the position that "although Nigeria remains under military rule, its president . . . has set a timetable for return to civilian government. While there are serious human rights violations, the government is seeking to improve its record."[2]

Nigeria has an army of 85,000. The navy is in the small warship class, and a 10,000-man air force has nearly 100 combat planes. Nigerian internal police forces number 15,000. Nearly 6,000 troops are in peace-keeping missions. A few are in Angola and Kuwait. More than 5,000 are in Liberia. Some 900 are in Sierra Leone.

Nigeria spent 24 percent of GNP on the military in 1979 and less than 1 percent in 1991. The GNP increased by 40 percent in this same period. The Nigerian government is cutting the size of the armed forces.

SENEGAL

Senegal is about the size of South Dakota. With an Atlantic coastline, it borders Guinea-Bissau, Guinea, Mali, and Mauritania. Her 8 million people have a per person average annual income of $615. Senegal is a republic. France granted independence in 1960.

Senegal began independence as part of the Mali Federation, which broke up within a few months. Leopold Sedar Senghor became Senegal's first president. In 1962 Prime Minister Mamadou Dia led a military takeover. It failed. Dia spent 12 years in prison.

Abdou Diouf became president in 1981. Senegal suffers from the declining world economy of the 1980s. There are longstanding border disputes with Mauritania. In 1989 this problem led to a massacre of Senegalese in Mauritania. Revenge killing of Mauritanians took place in Senegal. Relations with Mauritania are still tense.

Senegal's relations with the United States are friendly. From 1950 to 1991, the United States sold Senegal $2.7 million in military equipment and construction.[3] Senegal participates in international peace-keeping operations in Zaire, Lebanon, and the Gulf region. She has troops in Liberia.[4]

In recent years the United States has provided aid to Senegal as shown in Table 10.1.

Senegal maintains 10,000 men under arms. The 9,000-man army is mostly draftees. Her navy is a small coast guard. The air force has fewer than ten combat planes. France maintains 1,500 troops in Senegal. France guarantees the existence of Senegal.

Senegal averages spending on her military forces of 3 percent of GNP. Between 1979 and 1989 Senegal's GNP increased by 50 percent.

SIERRA LEONE

Sierra Leone is about the size of South Carolina. It lies along the Atlantic coast and borders Liberia and Guinea. Her 4.25 million people have a per person average annual income of $200. Sierra Leone is a republic. Britain granted independence in 1978.

Sir Milton Margai's Sierra Leone Independence Party led the anti-British

Table 10.1
U.S. Aid to Senegal (In U.S. Dollars)

	1991	1992	1993
Military Financing	1,000,000	1,000,000	500,000
International Military Education	525,000	525,000	605,000
Economic Support Fund	5,000,000	3,000,000	
Development Assistance	19,000,000	20,300,000	18,000,000
Food for Peace	5,000,000	8,200,000	13,245,000
Peace Corps	2,596,000	2,542,000	2,959,000
Totals	33,121,000	35,267,000	35,309,000

Source: United States of America, Congressional Presentation for Security Assistance Programs, Fiscal Years 1991–1993, Washington, D.C.: GPO, 1991–1993.

movement. Sir Milton served as prime minister until his death in 1964. Sir Albert Margai set up a one-party government in 1964. Opposition from the All People's Congress stopped him. In 1967 the All People's Congress won the elections. Siaka Stevens became the prime minister. Brig. Gen. David Lansana arrested Stevens. A group of army officers then arrested Lansana. They formed the national reformation council. Brig. A. T. Juxon-Smith took power. He was overthrown in the sergeant's revolt of 1968. Stevens again became the prime minister.

In 1970, a state of emergency was proclaimed. In 1971 and 1974, military takeover plots were uncovered. The leaders were shot and violence began. In 1977, the elections brought charges of fraud. A rigged election in 1978 supported Stevens. In 1985 Stevens resigned. Maj. Gen. Joseph Momoh came to power.

Sierra Leone is a nonaligned nation. Several thousand Sierra Leone students are in the United States. Relations between Sierra Leone and the United States are cordial. Sierra Leone amended her constitution in 1991 to provide for more democracy. American military aid is limited to training a few army officers each year. Most of Sierra Leone's military support comes from Britain.

Sierra Leone has a peace-keeping force in Liberia. These 800 men are a serious drain on the Sierra Leonean economy. Most of the rest of the 3,200-man army is trying to oust a Liberian guerrilla force of 800. Sierra Leone has no air force. Her navy is a very small coast guard. Some 800 Nigerian troops stay in Sierra Leone. Nigeria assumed responsibility for the continuance of Sierra Leone.

Sierra Leone spends less than 1 percent of GNP on her military. Her rate of growth is uncertain. Continued corruption in her government, plus the world economy decline, worry this nation's leaders.

TOGO

Togo is slightly smaller than West Virginia. It lies on the Atlantic coast and borders Benin, Burkina Faso, and Ghana. France granted independence in 1960. A population of 4 million has a per capita income of $390.

In 1963 the army murdered Togo's first president, Sylvanus Olympio. Nicholas Grunitsky became president. A plot to overthrow the government in 1966 did not succeed. In 1969 Col. Gnassingbe Eyadema took power. He began a one-man rule in a one-political-party state. He is the only candidate for president in each election. He wins with 99.7 percent of the vote every time.

A group of dissidents tried to overthrow Eyadema in both 1976 and 1986. They failed. French troops intervened to save the government in 1986. France guarantees the continued existence of the government.

Togo is a pro-Western country with good relations with the United States. The United States sends economic aid to Togo. American military aid is limited to training a few officers each year.

Togo has 5,500 troops. Equipment is French. The navy has five patrol boats. The air force has fewer than 20 combat planes. The national police count another 1,000. Togo spends an average of 3 percent of GNP on military forces. The GNP increased 53 percent between 1979 and 1991.

CAPE VERDE

The Cape Verde Islands are about the same size as Rhode Island. They lie in the Atlantic Ocean off the coasts of Mauritania and Senegal. The 3.75 million people have a per capita average annual income of $760. Cape Verde has a constitution. Portugal granted independence in 1975.

At that time, the Cape Verde Islands were part of Guinea-Bissau. Cape Verde declared her independence from Guinea-Bissau in 1981.

The Cape Verde Islands are overpopulated. There are serious food shortages. Drinking water is often in short supply. The one-party government continued until the elections of 1991. Antonio Mascarenhas Monteiro was elected president in the first free elections in 1991.

The United States provides humanitarian and economic assistance to Cape Verde. American military aid is limited to educating a few army officers each year.

The Cape Verde Islands maintain 1,500 men in the military forces. The navy has several coast guard boats. The air force has no combat planes.

Statistics concerning the amount of money spent on these 1,500 are not available.

GABON

Gabon is about the size of Colorado. Lying on the Atlantic coast, it borders Congo, Cameroon, and Equatorial Guinea. Her 1 million people enjoy the highest standard of living in this part of Africa. The per capita average annual income is $4,400. The government is dominated by the Democratic Party of Gabon. The army supports the government. France granted independence in 1960.

The economy is based on the export of natural resources, especially oil. France's Elf Petroleum dominates the economy.

Leon M'Ba was elected president in 1961. Political instability brought a military revolt in 1964. French troops ended the revolt. They are still in Gabon. M'Ba died in 1967. Omar Bongo became president, elected in 1975, 1979, and 1986 to 7-year terms.

In 1968 President Bongo established the one-political-party state. The government attempts to overcome various tribal disputes that still trouble the state. The leading opposition group is the Movement for National Recovery. Strikes and political unrest in 1990 led to a promise of multiparty elections. French troops intervened again in 1990 after several members of the new Progress Party were shot. The French hinted that the multiparty elections were necessary. These elections produced a multiparty national assembly in 1991.

Gabon maintains good relations with the United States. American aid arrives in the form of Peace Corps volunteers. American military aid is limited to training a few army officers each year.

The army has 3,500 men. The navy is in the small warship class. The air force has about 20 combat planes. There are another 5,000 men in various paramilitary units. The equipment is French. France maintains nearly 1,000 troops in Gabon. France guarantees the existence of the government.

From 1979 to 1991, Gabon spent between 2 and 5 percent of GNP annually on her military. During this same period, GNP increased by 41 percent.

GAMBIA

Gambia, somewhat smaller than Connecticut, is surrounded on three sides by Senegal. The Atlantic Ocean is on the fourth. A population of 900,000 has a per capita average annual income of $230. Gambia has a constitutional government. There are several political parties. Britain granted independence in 1965. Gambia became a republic in 1970. She did not have any military forces until 1981.

Sir Dawda Kairaba became president in 1970. In 1981 Libyan-backed dissidents revolted. Many died before Senegalese troops crushed the rebels. Gambia signed a mutual defense treaty with Senegal. Senegal continues to guarantee the Gambian government.

Gambia's economy is based on agricultural products. The droughts of the 1980s and the slowing world economy hurt the Gambian economy.

Gambia is a member of the nonaligned nations. The United States provides aid to Gambia with the Food for Peace Program. There are Peace Corps volunteers in Gambia. American military aid is limited to training a few army officers in some years.

Gambia's armed forces total 1,000. Another 700 are in various paramilitary units. Gambia has 150 serving in Liberia. Her equipment is British and her troops often participate in joint exercises with the British.

Statistics on Gambia's military spending are not available.

ZAMBIA

Zambia is a landlocked nation slightly larger than Texas. She has boundaries with Angola, Tanzania, Zimbabwe, Mozambique, Namibia, Malawi, and Zaire. Her 5 million people have a per capita average annual income of $580. Zambia was Northern Rhodesia under British colonial rule. Independence came in 1964.

Kenneth Kaunda became president and held power until 1991. Until 1975, cobalt and copper exports fed an expanding economy. Kaunda's one-party state flourished. The depressed prices of both cobalt and copper after 1975 led to deepening economic distress. Money was borrowed from foreign countries to keep the government going. The Soviet Union was very helpful. By 1990, the collapse of the Soviet Union and the growing economic depression caused dangerous political tensions. Kaunda agreed to hold open multiparty elections.

Frederick Chiluba headed the Movement for Multiparty Democracy in 1990. He defeated Kaunda in the presidential election of 1991. This movement toward democracy saw several nations, including the United States, cancel Zambia's debts.

Kaunda's government had a no-contact policy with the United States. The Soviet Union provided military aid. Relations between Chiluba and the United States are improving. American military aid planning is limited to training a few army officers.

The Zambian Army supported Kaunda's government. It supports Chiluba's government. The military has a force of 19,000. The air force has about 80 Russian-made combat planes. There are another 1,500 men in various paramilitary units. Equipment is British and Russian.

Current statistics on Zambian military spending are not available.

BENIN

Benin is slightly smaller than Pennsylvania. It lies on the Atlantic coast and borders Nigeria, Niger, Burkina Faso, and Togo. The 5 million people have a per capita average annual income of $400. France granted Benin independence under the name of Dahomey in 1960. The name was changed to Benin in 1975.

There were a series of military revolts after independence. In 1972, Col. Ahmed Kerekou took power. He established a Marxist-Leninist state. In 1989, after the collapse of the Soviets, Kerekou announced an end to the Marxist-Leninist state. He was defeated by Nicephore Soglo in the 1991 free elections.

Opposition to the Soglo government comes from the Communist Party of Dahomey. The United States is watching Benin carefully. Planned American military aid is only for the training of a few army officers in future years.

Benin's military forces supported the Marxist-Leninist government. They now support President Soglo. They number 4,500. The navy has perhaps three patrol boats. The air force has no combat aircraft. There are 2,500 men in various security forces. The people's militia claims 2,000.

Benin spent about 2 percent of GNP on her military between 1979 and 1991. Her GNP increased by 59 percent in this same period.

ZAIRE

Zaire is about the size of the United States east of the Mississippi. It lies on the Atlantic coast and borders Angola, Zambia, Tanzania, Burundi, Rwanda, Uganda, Sudan, Central African Republic, and Congo. The 35 million people have a per person average annual income of $180. Belgium granted independence in 1960.

The constitutional government lasted seven days. The army mutinied. Belgian troops arrived to protect white settlers. Moise Tshombe declared Katanga Province a separate nation.

A U.N. peace-keeping force arrived. Prime Minister Lumumba welcomed aid from the Soviet Union. Lumumba was dismissed. Col. Joseph Mobutu seized power. Lumumba died. Mobutu gave power to civilians led by Kasavubu. A number of provincial-based political groups claimed power.

By 1961 the country was again unified, except for Katanga Province. Tshombe agreed to a single government in 1963. U.N. troops remained until 1964.

Tribal revolts began in 1964. Tshombe became prime minister. Government forces made progress against the rebels. Belgian troops and the U.S. Air Force arrived. By 1966, only a few rebels remained.

In 1965 Tshombe was replaced by Evariste Kimba. Political unrest led to a military takeover. Lt. Gen. Mobutu seized power. He declared himself president and still is.

Some military units revolted in 1966. Mobutu crushed them. A second military challenge in 1967 failed. For ten years, Zaire enjoyed peace.

In 1977, Katanga dissidents invaded Zaire from Angola. Moroccan troops arrived. The government attacked. The rebels fled after several weeks of hard fighting.

In 1978, the same group tried again. French Foreign Legion and Belgian troops arrived. The United States provided air transportation. Thousands died. Peace returned in 1980.

Serious economic conditions and government corruption grew in the 1980s. President Mobutu announced an end to one-party government in 1990. A conference on multiparty government began in 1991. Mobutu announced that he would remain in office until resolution of political differences.

Zaire is a nonaligned nation. Relations with the United States were close until 1992. Between 1950 and 1991, the United States sold Zaire $144.7 million in military equipment and construction.[5] As late as 1992, Zaire was to receive $3.3 million in military aid and nearly $327 million in economic assistance.[6] The United States waits for the outcome of the Zaire conference on multiparty government.

Zaire maintains 50,000 in her military forces. The army's equipment is of Soviet manufacture. Her air force has Soviet planes. There are 1,500 men in various paramilitary units.

Current figures on Zaire's support of her military forces are not available.

COMOROS

The Comoros Islands are one-half the size of Delaware. They lie in the Indian Ocean off the coasts of Mozambique and Tanzania and off Madagascar. The 500,000 people have a per capita average annual income of $530.

Comoros declared unilateral independence from France in 1975. One island, Mayotte, remained with France. Ahmed Abdullah became president. A group of mercenaries installed Ali Soilih in power. He brought in state socialism. Youth gangs began a reign of terror. The government nearly disappeared.

In 1978, another band of mercenaries led by Bob Denard arrived. Denard overthrew Soilih. He restored Abdullah to the presidency. Close ties existed with the extreme right in France and South Africa. Military aid passed from South Africa through the Comoros to RENAMO rebels in Mozambique. In 1982, Comoros became a one-party state.

The military tried to seize power in 1985 and in 1987. In 1987, Abdullah tried to replace Denard. A French security unit assisted. Instead, Abdullah was murdered. Said Djohar became interim president. He gained French support to oust Denard. Denard fled to South Africa.

Elections in 1990 gave the presidency to Djohar. In 1991, talks began to form a multiparty political system. Little progress has occurred.

The United States does not give military aid to Comoros.

Comoros maintains a standing military establishment of 2,000 men. France has a naval base and Foreign Legion troops on Mayotte. The Comoros Islands are tied to France by a defense treaty.

Information on military spending is not available.

CAMEROON

Cameroon is about the size of California. Lying on the Atlantic coast, Cameroon borders Equatorial Guinea, Gabon, Congo, Central African Republic, Chad, and Nigeria. The 11.5 million people enjoy the second highest per capita average annual income in West Africa, $1,010. There is a one-political-party government.

After World War II, British and French mandates in this area became U.N. trusteeships. The United Nations granted full independence in 1972. The military tried to take over in 1984. They failed. Many died or were jailed. In 1990, political unrest began again. Government troops even opened fire on school children during a peaceful protest.

Government stability allows for the development of transportation, cocoa plantations, and oil products.

Relations with the United States are good. Many students study in the United States. The United States does not furnish military aid to Cameroon.

Cameroon is closely allied with France. Cameroon maintains 12,000 troops. All equipment is French. The navy is a small coast guard. The air force has fewer than 20 combat planes.

Cameroon spends an average of 1.5 percent of GNP on the military. Her GNP is growing at the rate of 4 percent a year.

CONGO

Congo is about the size of New Mexico. Lying on the Atlantic coast, Congo borders Zaire, Central African Republic, Cameroon, and Gabon. The 2.5 million people have a per capita average annual income of $930. France granted independence in 1960.

Fulbert Youlou was the first president. In 1963, organized labor deposed Youlou. The military took charge. Massamba-Debat was elected president. The army took power in 1968. Maj. Marien Ngouabi assumed power. He set up a Marxist people's republic. In 1977, Ngouabi was assassinated. Col. Joachim Yhomby-Opango became president. In 1990, the government appointed a commission to return the Congo to a multiparty political system. In 1991 a multiparty constitution was proclaimed.

Congo is a nonaligned nation. Relations with the United States are good. Congo played a key role in the evacuation of U.S. citizens from Zaire in 1991. The United States continues to watch Congo develop from a Marxist to a democratic state. At present, the United States does not give military aid to Congo beyond training a few army officers in some years.

The military force totals 11,000. All equipment is Soviet made. The navy is a small coast guard. The air force has about 30 Soviet-built war planes. Congo aids the peace-keeping forces in Angola. There are an additional 13,000 troops in various internal security organizations.

Information concerning money spent on the military is not available.

BURKINA FASO

Burkina Faso, a landlocked state about the size of Colorado, borders Benin, Niger, Mali, Ivory Coast, Ghana, and Togo. The 9 million people have a per capita average annual income of $205. Her government is a popular front composed of five Marxist and socialist political parties. France granted independence in 1960.

Maurice Yameogo was the first president. Yameogo banned all political parties but his own Voltaic Democratic Union. In 1966, the military intervened. Lt. Col. Aboukar Sangoule Lamizana took power. The military overthrew Lamizana in 1980. Col. Saye Zebro took over. He was replaced by Maj. Dr. Jean Baptiste Ouedraogo in 1982.

Another military takeover came in 1984. Capt. Thomas Sankara began his rule. Sankara was assassinated in 1987. Blaise Compaore became head of state. Compaore talked of a more liberal political system after the collapse of the Soviet Union. Military rule ended in 1991. President Blaise Compaore won the free election in 1991. He retains the support of the military.

The United States maintains good relations with Burkina Faso. American aid has been limited to participation in emergency food assistance. American military aid has trained only 30 army officers over the years.

Burkina Faso's military forces number 9,000. The equipment is a mixture of French and Soviet manufacture. She has fewer than ten combat planes. Information on military spending is not available.

SAO TOME AND PRINCIPE

Sao Tome and Principe are two islands in the Atlantic Ocean about the size of Indianapolis. They lie off the coast of West Africa. Nearby mainland nations are Nigeria, Cameroon, Equatorial Guinea, and Gabon. Their 130,000 people have a per capita income of $384. The government is controlled by the Marxist Movement for the Liberation of Sao Tome and Principe. Portugal granted independence in 1975.

Manuel Pinto da Costa was the president until 1991. He maintained close relations with East Germany. Miguel Trovoada became president in the free elections of 1991. Close ties are being established with Portugal.

The United States maintains good relations with Sao Tome and Principe. American military aid is limited to the training of a very few army officers.

The size of the military forces is not known. There is no budget information from Sao Tome and Principe.

EQUATORIAL GUINEA

Equatorial Guinea is about the size of Maryland. Lying on the Atlantic coast, it borders Gabon and Cameroon. The population of 400,000 has a per capita average annual income of $430. The capital, Malabro, is on an island off the Cameroon coast. The government is controlled by the Democratic Party for Equatorial Guinea. Spain granted independence in 1968.

Franciscio Macias Nguema became president. He created a one-party state. It is thought that he was insane. His actions led to a one-third drop in the population. Religions were suppressed. Education stopped. The economy collapsed. Foreigners ran for their lives.

In 1979, the army rose in revolt. Macias was shot. Lt. Col. Teodoro Obiang Nguema Mbasogo took power. Very little progress was made in the economy. Close relations are maintained with Morocco and Spain. Both countries provide economic and military aid.

The United States maintains correct relations with Equatorial Guinea. American military aid is limited to training several army officers in some years.

Equatorial Guinea maintains 1,500 troops. The navy is a tiny coast guard. The air force has no combat planes. Internal security forces claim another 2,000. Morocco maintains 400 troops near the capital. Information about military spending is not available.

NOTES

1. FMS Control and Reports Division, Comptroller, DSAA, *Foreign Military Sales, Foreign Military Construction Sales and Military Assistance Facts, as of September 30, 1991*, Washington, Data Management Division, Comptroller DSSA, 1992.

2. United States of America, *Congressional Presentation for Security Assistance Programs, Fiscal Year 1993*, Washington, GPO, Jointly prepared by the Department of State and the Defense Security Agency, 1992, p. 261.

3. *Foreign Military Sales, September 30, 1991*.

4. *Congressional Presentation, Fiscal Years 1991–1993*.

5. *Foreign Military Sales, September 30, 1991*.

6. *Congressional Presentation, Fiscal Years 1991–1993*.

11

Southern Africa

All issues—local, national, and international—in Southern Africa are bound to a single political concept. Apartheid, as recently practiced by the white minority government of the Republic of South Africa, dominates all aspects of this richest part of the African continent. The Republic of South Africa is not a Third World nation. It is a wealthy, industrialized state. It exists for the benefit of the white minority who dominate a disadvantaged black majority many times their size. The eight black nations of Botswana, Lesotho, Mozambique, Zimbabwe, Namibia, Mauritius, Madagascar, and Swaziland must await the outcome of the black versus white contest in the Republic of South Africa before they can finish emerging from their own colonial past.

Changes seem to be in the air everywhere in Southern Africa. Political certainty is a thing of the past. The black man is on the move. The old white colonial-motivated minorities are in full retreat from political power. It seems that the African National Congress will win in the Republic of South Africa.

Even the black military governments of the postindependence period seem shaky. The collapse of the Soviet Union has left some black dictators on shaky ground at home, as their ready supply of economic and military aid has vanished. Long-entrenched dictators have disappeared. In Namibia, a new university will soon challenge the establishment. Yet, in Zimbabwe the government has imposed sanctions on its new university. There appears some hope for peace in Mozambique. Botswana's single political party practices democracy. Britain is carefully forming a multiracial army in Namibia.

The end of the Cold War brought about many of these changes in Southern Africa. The end of the Cold War caused the white minority government of the Republic of South Africa to rethink the political device called apartheid. The hope for Southern Africa still lies in one question: what is to be the fate of the Republic of South Africa?

Any real progress in Southern Africa depends on the ability of the blacks and whites in the Republic of South Africa to continue their negotiations. Not only must the negotiations continue, they must also resolve the questions of bringing the black majority to full political power and preserving the rights of the white minority at the same time. This has never worked out well in any other part of the African continent since 1945. Wherever a new nation was faced with tribal rivalries, religious rivalries, or black–white rivalries, the future has been military rule, seizures of power by dictators, genocidal strife, drought, and pestilence.

This has been the pattern in North Africa, Central Africa, and East and West Africa. None of the states in the rest of Africa has solved the human relations problems of the various elements of their populations. Until the Republic of South Africa resolves its black versus white dilemma, all the rest of Southern Africa is in a holding pattern.

The Republic of South Africa interfered in the territories of its black neighbors constantly during the 1980s. In 1981, South African military forces began operations in Angola and Mozambique to combat terrorist groups that were operating in South Africa. In 1986, South African forces attacked Zimbabwe, Botswana, and Zambia, again searching for terrorists that operated within South Africa.

These major border crossings by South African troops largely ceased in 1987 when black railway workers began a series of long strikes which led the white government to give almost unlimited emergency powers to its military forces. Many confrontations, especially in the reserves set aside for black tribes, led to gunfire.

In 1988, more than two million black workers went on strike. The fatigued South African government began to change its political stripes. Frederick W. de Klerk came to power. In 1990 the African National Congress returned from exile. Its leader, Nelson Mandela, now freely operates throughout the Republic of South Africa. In 1991, de Klerk announced plans to end all racial separation laws.

Negotiations are under way between the de Klerk government and the African National Congress. Riots and shootings continue throughout the Republic of South Africa. The issue of black versus white is far from settled. All the other nations in Southern Africa watch and wait as events unfold.

The black versus white problem must be settled in the Republic of South Africa before its resolution in the rest of Southern Africa. The Republic of South Africa maintains very large military forces based on universal white male conscription. She maintains 75,000 in her current forces. She accepts selected black volunteers. Nearly 750,000 white reservists back them up. The equipment is mainly British, but South Africa now manufactures a large percentage of her own armaments.

For example, both the navy and the air force are reequipped with arms made in the Republic of South Africa. There are also nearly 100,000 men in the Republic of South Africa's security police. These police are well armed.

Except for worldwide political opposition, South Africa could have long ago swept aside the puny military efforts of the other nations in this region and made all of Southern Africa her own.

The existence of this enormous economic and military complex built by the white minority in the Republic of South Africa is why the rest of the world goes slowly in demanding the end of white minority rule. Apparently all sides fear a possible shootout between the blacks and the whites.

Southern Africa is the richest part of Africa. It teems with educated blacks as well as whites. It is underpopulated. Its mineral wealth is enormous. It possesses a trained work force of whites and blacks. It is more than able to feed its population. It has developed an elaborate network of railways and highways.

This is the part of Africa with the most hope for the future. It is also the part of Africa where patience on both sides appears to be quickly running out. There is no doubt that a majority of the Republic of South African whites want to integrate the blacks into their society.

They have voted so. It is a question of how to bring this about without getting black domination by way of the ballot box. It is doubtful that the white governing minority will accept a world turned upside down where the blacks are the haves and they, the whites, are the have nots.

Figure 11.1 on page 120 shows population and per capita income in the nine nations of Southern Africa.

BOTSWANA

Botswana, about the size of Texas, borders the Republic of South Africa, Zimbabwe, Zambia, and Namibia. The 1.5 million people have a per capita average annual income of $1,975. Botswana is a parliamentary democracy with universal adult suffrage. Britain granted independence in 1965.

The expanding economy is based on the mining industry. Debeers Botswana Mining and Bamangwato Concession, Ltd. are both large diamond-mining companies. Botswana produces more high-quality diamonds than any other country in the world. Copper mining is also important. Botswana is economically tied to the Republic of South Africa. The economy will falter if imports from the Republic of South Africa are cut off. Botswana has an expanding capitalist society.

Botswana is opposed to the Republic of South Africa policy of apartheid. The African National Congress was welcome here during its long exile. Officially Botswana remains a neutral nation. She remains free of serious internal strife.

The United States is a strong supporter of Botswana. During the years of great drought (1986–1989), the United States gave Botswana $338 million in food aid.[1] Other forms of American aid are large and continuous, as shown in Table 11.1 (p. 120).

Botswana maintains 5,000 men in her military forces. The equipment is

Figure 11.1
Southern Africa, Total Population and per Capita Income (In U.S. Dollars)

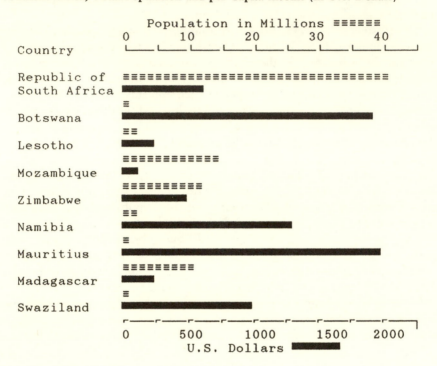

Note: U.S. 1990 per capita income was $21,800.

Table 11.1
U.S. Aid to Botswana (In U.S. Dollars)

	1991	1992	1993
Military Financing	1,000,000	1,000,000	
International Military Education	375,000	400,000	375,000
Food for Peace	7,000,000	7,000,000	6,300,000
Peace Corps	4,046,000	3,198,000	3,169,000
Totals	12,421,000	11,598,000	9,919,000

Source: United States of America, *Congressional Presentation for Security Assistance Programs, Fiscal Years 1991–1993,* Washington, D.C.: GPO, 1991–1993.

British. Her air force has fewer than 15 British-made combat planes. She also has an internal security force of about 1,000. President Quett K. J. Masire is also commander-in-chief of the armed forces.

Because of the declining world market for diamonds, Botswana began severe budget cuts in 1991. Historically, Botswana's military spending increases and decreases with the nature of the Republic of South Africa's racial problems.[2] The Republic of South Africa remains a lingering problem. Botswana will continue to welcome refugees from racial oppression from anywhere. During the 1980s, South African terrorists often attacked across the frontier. Botswana tightened her border security. These attacks largely stopped by 1990.

Military spending in U.S. dollars and as a percentage of GNP for 1979–1990 is shown in Figure 11.2. GNP increased by 78 percent during this period.

Figure 11.2
Botswana's Military Defense Expenditures (In Millions of U.S. Dollars as a Percentage of GNP)

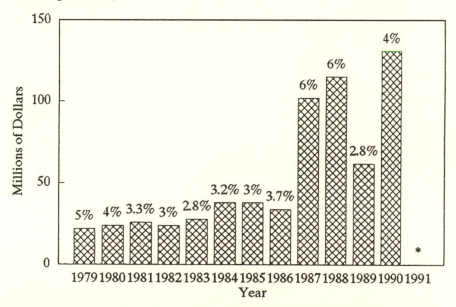

Source: U.S. Arms Control and Disarmament Agency, *World Military Expenditures and Arms Transfers,* Washington, D.C.: GPO, November 1991, p. 55. The figures for 1990 are based on Huldt et al. *The Military Balance 1992–1993,* London: International Institute for Strategic Studies, 1992, p. 192.
*Figures for 1991 are unavailable.

LESOTHO

The Kingdom of Lesotho, about the size of Maryland, is completely surrounded by the Republic of South Africa. The 2 million people have a per capita average annual income of $240. Britain granted independence in 1966. Lesotho is a military state. Lesotho does not suffer from tribal divisions that plague many African states.

The Basutoland National Party came to power with independence. It lost the elections of 1970. Prime Minister Leabua Jonathan declared a state of emergency. Elections in 1985 were cancelled. In 1986, the military ousted Jonathan. Maj. Gen. J. M. Lekhanya took control.

The Republic of South Africa blockaded Lesotho in 1986. South African Army units established a perimeter around Lesotho. Lesotho was giving sanctuary to rebel groups working to overthrow the South African government. A military takeover followed. The rebels were expelled.

In 1990, King Moshoeshoe was exiled by the military government. He remains a rallying point for dissident groups. Lesotho is ruled by a self-appointed military council. The normal civil administration continues to flourish. Lekhanya promised elections in 1992.

Lesotho's economy is tied to that of the Republic of South Africa. Her diamonds, water, and livestock have but one market. She depends entirely on South Africa as a source of employment for her population. Lesotho is opposed to South African racial policies.

The United States maintains close relations with Lesotho. Just before the collapse of the Soviet Union, Lesotho began overtures to Eastern European countries, North Korea, and China. American military aid consists only of training a very few army officers in some years. The United States does not interfere in the arrangements between Lesotho and the Republic of South Africa.

Lesotho has a tiny armed force of 2,000 men. Her equipment is South African. This army functions as an internal defense force whose main mission is to defend the military government. The Republic of South Africa guarantees Lesotho's continued independence.

Statistics on Lesotho's military expenditures are not available. Some estimates have Lesotho spending 10 percent of her annual budget on the military.

MOZAMBIQUE

Mozambique, twice the size of California, lies in the Indian Ocean and borders Tanzania, Malawi, Zambia, Zimbabwe, Swaziland, the Republic of South Africa, and the Mozambique Channel. The 15 million people have a per capita average annual income of $110. Her government is a Marxist one-party state. Civil war began in 1975. The economy is in ruins. A severe drought ruined agriculture in the 1980s. There has been famine and heavy loss of life.

The Front for the Liberation of Mozambique, established in 1962, led Mozambique to independence after a ten-year guerrilla war against the Portuguese. The new government quickly turned to Marxism. By 1976, money and military aid from white Rhodesia and the Republic of South Africa were intensifying a civil war. In 1977, Mozambique formally adopted Marxism-Leninism as its guiding political philosophy. A 20-year pact began with the Soviet Union.

The opposition, now named the Mozambique National Resistance (RENAMO), stepped up operations. RENAMO waged brutal campaigns against government supporters and the entire physical infrastructure.

To ease this pressure, Mozambique signed a nonaggression treaty with the Republic of South Africa. In 1984, Mozambique agreed to expel members of the African National Congress. South Africa promised to stop military aid to RENAMO. Mozambique did not keep her part of the bargain. Neither did South Africa.

In 1986, Joaquim Chissano became president. He began negotiations with RENAMO. He began to pull away from the Communist nations. President F. W. de Klerk of the Republic of South Africa visited in 1989. Chissano visited Washington in 1990.

Chissano is leading Mozambique from Communism to pragmatism. A four-year cease-fire began in 1990. It is often broken. South Africa continues support for RENAMO. Mozambique does not approve of South Africa's racial policies. There is talk of free elections.

Mozambique received massive military aid from the Communist nations until 1990. Economic aid arrived from the non-Communist countries. The United States is the largest provider of humanitarian aid. From 1987 to 1989, the United States gave $338.8 million in emergency food aid.[3] The United States does not give military aid to Mozambique.

Mozambique maintains an army of 60,000 men. The equipment is Soviet. The navy has a few Soviet-made patrol boats and the air force has fewer than fifty Soviet-made combat planes. The RENAMO rebels are perhaps 20,000 in number. Zimbabwe maintains 4,000 men in Mozambique to protect her own frontiers. Malawi has 1,000 troops in Mozambique for the same reason. There are still Russian and North Korean military officers leading Mozambique troop units.

Mozambican expenditures on military forces from 1979 to 1990 are shown in Figure 11.3 (p. 142). During this same period, the GNP grew 25 percent.

ZIMBABWE

Zimbabwe, a landlocked nation about the size of Montana, borders Mozambique, Zambia, Botswana, and the Republic of South Africa. The 11 million people have a per capita average annual income of $540. The government is a British-style parliamentary democracy. Britain granted independence in 1980.

Figure 11.3
Mozambique's Military Defense Expenditures (In Millions of U.S. Dollars as a
Percentage of GNP)

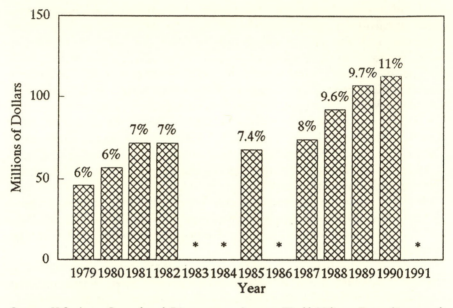

Source: U.S. Arms Control and Disarmament Agency, *World Military Expenditures and
Arms Transfers,* Washington, D.C.: GPO, November 1991, p. 74. The figures for 1990 are
based on Huldt et al. *The Military Balance 1992–1993,* London: International Institute for
Strategic Studies, 1992, p. 204.
*Figures for 1983, 1984, 1986, and 1991 are unavailable.

Zimbabwe was a British colony known as Southern Rhodesia from 1888.
Northern Rhodesia and Nyasaland became Zambia and Malawi in 1964.

In 1964, Prime Minister Winston Field was replaced by Ian Smith. He led
the all-white Rhodesian Popular Front party to electorial victory in 1965.
Smith then unilaterally declared independence from Britain. In 1965, the
U.N. Security Council imposed economic sanctions on Rhodesia. Black
rebels took to the bush in 1967. They received aid from the Marxist movement in Mozambique.

After Portugal granted independence to Angola and Mozambique in
1976, Smith began to negotiate. The white Rhodesians agreed to black
majority rule. The blacks won the elections in 1979. Bishop Abel Muzorewa
became the first black prime minister. This did not end the guerrilla war. A
cease-fire began in late 1979. The U.N. Security Council lifted the economic sanctions.

Special elections, supervised by the British, were held in 1980. Robert
Mugabe's Zimbabwe African National Union won an absolute majority.

Zimbabwe became a nonaligned nation. Mugabe promised a raceless peaceful nation. Zimbabwe opposes apartheid, but it does not furnish haven for anti-South African rebels.

Political splits soon developed. The opposition leader, Joshua Nknoma, and other dissidents began a civil war. Parts of Zimbabwe have been under martial law.

The opposition Zimbabwe Unity Movement lost the elections in 1990. Mugabe claims his government now has a mandate to form a one-party Marxist state. There is growing unrest among university students and union members. New opposition political parties are forming.

Britain maintains a British military training team in Zimbabwe. The United States maintains proper relations with Zimbabwe. American military aid is limited to training a few officers from time to time.

Zimbabwe maintains a racially mixed force of 55,000 men. All military equipment is British. The air force has about 60 combat planes. There is a national police force of about 15,000. Special police count 3,000 more. A national militia claims 20,000. Zimbabwe has 5,000 to 10,000 troops in Mozambique fighting the RENAMO. She has observers with the U.N. peace-keeping forces in Angola.

Zimbabwean support for military forces from 1979 to 1990 is shown in Figure 11.4 (p. 126). During this same period, the GNP increased by 60 percent.

NAMIBIA

Namibia, about the size of Texas and Louisiana, borders Angola, Zambia, Zimbabwe, Botswana, and the Republic of South Africa. Her 1.5 million people have a per capita average annual income of $1,300. Her government is a republic with several political parties and universal adult suffrage.

Namibia became a German protectorate in 1888, known as German Southwest Africa. South Africa conquered Namibia during World War I. After World War II, the Republic of South Africa refused to permit the formation of a U.N. trusteeship.

In 1966, the Communist-dominated Southwest Africa People's Organization (SWAPO) began a civil war aimed at independence. Despite U.N. peace-keeping attempts, this conflict continued until 1990. Some 40,000 died. At times, Cuban troops acting as Angolan units were in Namibia. At times, South African units invaded Angola. Finally the United Nations granted complete independence in 1990. Namibia now has at least 40 political parties. Perhaps the 24-year civil war is over.

Namibian independence was a U.S. goal from 1980. The United States cooperated with the U.N. peace-keeping forces. American military aid to Namibia is limited to training a few army officers every year.

The British are supervising the formation of the Namibian Army. So far, about 6,000 of the needed 10,000 are trained. The air force still exists only

Figure 11.4
Zimbabwe's Military Defense Expenditures (In Millions of U.S. Dollars as a
Percentage of GNP)

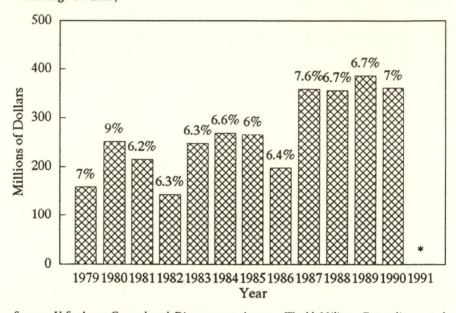

Source: U.S. Arms Control and Disarmament Agency, *World Military Expenditures and
Arms Transfers*, Washington, D.C.: GPO, November 1991, p. 87. The figures for 1990 are
based on Huldt et al. *The Military Balance 1992–1993*, London: International Institute for
Strategic Studies, 1992, p. 214.
*Figures for 1991 are unavailable.

on paper. The British are establishing the Namibian Army one unit at a
time. They are recruiting men from both the white-led Southwest Africa
Territorial Force and the black People's Liberation Army of Namibia.

There is no information on support levels for the new army.

MAURITIUS

Mauritius is an island to the east of central Madagascar. Ocean isolation
separates her from the black versus white problems of the other nations in
Southern Africa. The 1.2 million people have a per capita average annual
income of $1,950. The government is a British-type parliamentary democ-
racy. Britain granted independence in 1968. Mauritius's economic prosperity is based on the world price of sugar. The population is of mixed racial
inheritance.

The Mauritius Labor party was formed by the Hindu majority. It won the
election in 1947. The Mauritius Labor party dominated the government
until 1982. Sir Seewoosagur Ramgoolam became the first prime minister.

British troops crushed minor dissident groups. In 1982 Aneerood Jugnauth's Socialist party won the elections. He became prime minister. The Socialist party also won the 1987 elections.

Mauritius's economy, based mainly on the sugar crop, is very vulnerable to world economic forces. The gradually falling price of sugar in the 1980s has led to widespread economic difficulties. At present, there are attempts to bring in light industry, including modern textiles production.

The United States is pleased with Mauritius. The government was very cooperative during the Gulf War. The thriving Western-style democracy pleases the United States. American military aid is limited to the training of several security force officers in some years.

Mauritius does not have an army. She has a 4,500-man security police force. England, France, and India all maintain military missions on Mauritius. All three guarantee Mauritian independence. Communist activity on Madagascar is closely watched. Mauritius is the best example of peace and prosperity that can exist in an African multiracist society.

Mauritius spends an average of 1.5 percent to 2 percent of GNP on her security forces. From 1979 to 1991, GNP rose by 61 percent.

MADAGASCAR

Madagascar is an island nation about twice the size of Montana lying off the southeast coast of Mozambique. The other near African neighbors are Comoros and the Republic of South Africa. The 12 million people have a per capita average annual income of $200.

Madagascar has a 1975 constitution. The Marxist-Leninist oriented Vanguard of the Malagasy Republic is the only political party. Her leading trading partners are France, the United States, and Japan. She imports food and oil. Her main suppliers are France, the former Soviet Union, Germany, Qatar, and the United States.

France established a protectorate over Madagascar in 1885. French troops destroyed the native government in 1895–1896. Malagasy volunteers fought for France during World War I. The British occupied the island in 1942. The Free French arrived in 1943.

Madagascar received her independence amid the domestic tranquility after 1945. The post-1945 experience was not the same as that of Algeria. France granted independence in 1960.

Philibert Tsiranana became president for the second time in 1972. He soon resigned amid massive antigovernment, Communist-led civil unrest. General Gabriel Ramanantson led the military to power. He soon resigned. Lt. Col. Richard Ratismandrava became head of state. He was soon assassinated. Maj. Gen. Gilles Andriamahazo formed a military government. Open rebellion was suppressed.

Admiral Didier Ratsiraka led an interim government. In 1975 he was elected president by a large majority. He established the Marxist-Leninist Democratic Republic of Madagascar. His National Democratic Front is the only legal political party.

In 1979 the military government arrested opposition leaders, expelled foreigners, and broke strikes. Ratsiraka was reelected in 1982. By 1986 Madagascar was firmly under the control of the National Democratic Front.

Madagascar abandoned its close ties with France. Agreements were sought with the Soviet Union, North Korea, and various members of the Communist Eastern European block. The recent collapse of these new friends brought the call for new elections. Contested elections in 1990 gave a clear victory to the military government. Most restrictions on political opposition were dropped. There are still occasional riots and strikes. The military remain in control. Her Marxist orientation has stopped all normal relations with the Republic of South Africa. Madagascar exists in virtual economic and political isolation from the rest of Southern Africa.

The military government expelled some U.S. diplomats in 1971. It closed a NASA tracking station in 1975. Two U.S. oil companies were thrown out in 1976. It was not until 1989 that relations began to improve. The United States began to provide economic aid under the Food for Peace Program in 1988. U.S. policy is expressed as follows:

Madagascar currently is moving away from its failed socialist policies toward a market based economy and has made steps toward an open democracy with multiple political parties. U.S. policy is to encourage this, as well as to assist in the protection of the environment and the Malagasy Army's civic assistance role.[4]

U.S. military aid is limited to training a few army officers.

Madagascar has 21,000 troops, mostly draftees. The navy is a small coast guard, and the air force has fewer than 15 combat planes. An 8,000-man internal security force is the key to national politics. A nonaligned nation, Madagascar tends to use her military only at home. Soviet military advisors were welcome in the 1980s. Madagascar's military equipment is made in the U.S.S.R.

Information on Madagascar's support level for her military is not available.

SWAZILAND

Swaziland, about the size of New Jersey, borders Mozambique and the Republic of South Africa. Her 800,000 people have a per capita average annual income of $900. Swaziland is a monarchy. Britain granted independence in 1968.

Under the constitution, political parties are forbidden. Parliament's role is limited to debate and advice. The king is an absolute monarch.

The only external difficulty since independence was a little trouble along the frontier with Mozambique in the mid-1980s. The only major challenge facing the government is its relationship with the Republic of South Africa. King Mswati III keeps a delicate balance in his own country between those who support apartheid and those who condemn it. A nonaggression pact with the Republic of South Africa permits close cooperation between the security police of the two nations.

Swaziland is dependent on South African investment and good will for its continued existence. Good relations are maintained with the United States. American military aid consists of training a few army officers in some years.

The British maintain a military mission. Swaziland has a self-defense force of 3,500 men. An average 1 to 1.5 percent of GNP goes to the military. GNP increases by 5 to 6 percent a year.

NOTES

1. United States Department of Commerce, *Foreign Economic Trends and Their Implications for the United States, Botswana, September 1990,* Washington, GPO, 1990.

2. United States Arms Control and Disarmament Agency, *World Military Expenditures and Arms Transfers,* Washington, GPO, 1991, p. 55. The figures for 1990 are based on Bo Huldt, editor and his staff, *The Military Balance, 1992–1993,* London, International Institute for Strategic Studies, 1992, p. 192.

3. United States Department of Commerce, *Foreign Economic Trends and Their Implications for the United States, Mozambique, August, 1991,* Washington, GPO, 1991.

4. United States of America, *Congressional Presentation for Security Assistance Programs, Fiscal Year 1993,* Washington, GPO, Jointly Prepared by the Department of State and the Defense Security Agency, 1992, p. 232.

12

The Caribbean

The American view of the Caribbean has varied considerably in the nineteenth and twentieth centuries. This reflects basic changes in the relations between the United States and the other Caribbean nations.

Any attempt to identify U.S. strategic interests is complicated by the fact that at any given moment there may be several competing ideologies at work within the Caribbean basin. At times, the inner workings of the various Caribbean nations may coincide with the majority view in the United States. At other times, they diverge and tend to produce conflict between the United States and its nearest Latin American neighbors. Further complications then arise as the United States continually reassesses the types and numbers of military forces in the Caribbean. The protection of American interests and native democracies is of first importance.

The Caribbean strategic concept held by most Americans is that this region is an American lake. This vision, which is still the primary military strategy of the United States, sees our Latin American mission primarily in the Caribbean Sea. This is based on the overwhelming importance of this area to the United States. Eight of the Latin American nations lie in the Caribbean. The Caribbean is the main area of American and Latin American interface. Many U.S. trade routes go through the Caribbean. Control of the Panama Canal allows U.S. naval and ground forces to shift rapidly from the Pacific Ocean to the Atlantic.

Many Americans think that U.S. Latin American policy is really Caribbean policy. Until the drug wars during the Reagan administration were declared, most Americans paid little attention to the rest of Latin America. Argentina and Peru are a long way off. Colombia now has importance because of the drug wars. The Panama of Noriega made us mad. Even El Salvador seemed like a fight between two swarms of mosquitoes, hardly worth our time.

What was really vexing after 1945 were Castro in Cuba and the threat of the Soviets in Grenada. The Caribbean basin represents the southern military flank of the United States. During the Bush administration, the United States again defined the Caribbean as the area of Latin America with the highest security priority.

This was done for the following reasons. The Caribbean nations provide some important raw materials that are in short supply in the United States. A majority of our oil imports use the Caribbean shipping lanes. The military bases in this region are a critical link in the defense plans of the United States. The Caribbean is a very poor region. It is politically unstable at the present time. Local revolutions and military takeovers were commonplace in the 1980s. More are likely to follow in the 1990s.

This political instability reflects badly on the solidarity of the United States–led Western Hemisphere alliance system. The United States must be able to guarantee regional political stability or face direct challenges to U.S. preeminence in this region. Although Soviet influence is mostly dead, the Chinese and the North Koreans continue to spread their own brands of Marxism–Maoism throughout this region. To mention only one item, refineries owned by Caribbean countries furnish more than one-half of U.S. petroleum products. Mexico literally lies just over our southern border. The Mexican government is unstable as we go into the 1990s. Nearly 50 percent of our bauxite imports come from Jamaica. Other strategic materials coming from the Caribbean basin are silver, zinc, gypsum, antimony, mercury, bismuth, selenium, barium, rhenium, and lead. The United States must control the sea trading lanes in the Caribbean basin. To do this, the United States must maintain friendly governments in the nations that control these sea lanes. These nations are eight in number. Figure 12.1 gives population and income figures.

Latin America has been likened to the thigh and leg of the United States. In this case, the Caribbean basin is the kneecap of American world economic and military posture. Should the close relationship between the United States and the eight Caribbean basin nations go sour, the United States will lose the mobility to flex its thigh and leg muscles. In recent years, American foreign policy has begun to forge a firmer set of economic ties with both Canada and Mexico. This is supposedly the first step to bringing all the lands and peoples from the Arctic to the Antarctic into one economic or free trade union. This is also one of the first steps in the American plan to bring about a New World Order based on global free trade in which capitalism will cure the economic ills and abuses of the current system.

If this is to be done, then the economic ills of the Caribbean need solving first. Food, clothing, shelter, and basic medical care must be provided to all the people of this region. The basic problem in doing this is that far too much of the wealth in each of these Caribbean nations is held in the hands of a very small percentage of the people. Some redistribution of the wealth

Figure 12.1
The Caribbean, Total Population and per Capita Income (In U.S. Dollars)

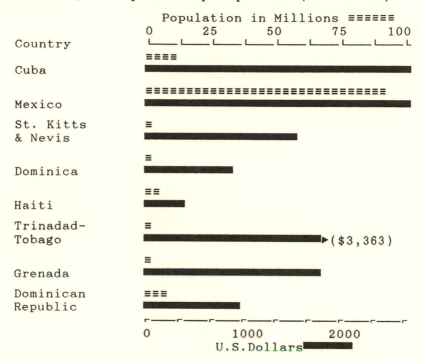

Note: U.S. 1990 per capita income was $21,800.

will be necessary. It is doubtful if the wealthy few will voluntary give up their economic privileged status. In this case local governments, backed by the United States, must force them to share with their less well off fellow citizens. Every rebel group in the Caribbean basin purports to be ready to redivide the wealth among the many. The United States often supports the status quo government, which is kept in power by the wealth of the privileged few.

Each of these eight nations needs to be examined for possible dissident groups that adversely effect American interests. It is to be remembered that American foreign, economic, and military policy differs from country to country in the Caribbean region. Americans are very pragmatic as they view the Latin American political landscape in the early 1990s.

CUBA

Cuba is an island nation about the size of Pennsylvania just off the southern tip of Florida. Other close neighbors are the Bahamas, Haiti, Jamaica, and the Yucatan Peninsula of Mexico. The 11 million people have a per capita average annual income of $2,644. The government is Marxist-Leninist. Fidel Castro is the head of state. Prior to 1989, Cuba's major markets were the Soviet Union, the Communist East European block nations, and China. The Cuban economy is displaying signs of weakness now. There is no sign of any large dissident revolutionary movement.

The United States acquired Cuba in the Spanish-American War of 1898 and granted independence in 1902. Cuba began independence with a democratic government. In 1903 the United States leased Guantanamo Navy base at the eastern tip of Cuba. The lease ends only with mutual consent.

General Gerardo Machado became president in 1924. Beginning in 1929, the Great Depression hurt the Cuban sugar-based economy. The army overthrew the government in 1933. Sergeant Fulgencio Batista assumed power. Batista and the army ruled Cuba. He ended the last vestiges of democratic government in 1952.

In 1953 a rebel group led by Fidel Castro Ruz attacked the important army barracks at Santiago de Cuba. Many of the rebels died. Castro went to jail. Batista pardoned the survivors in 1955.

Castro went to Mexico where he trained between 80 and 100 men. They landed in Oriental Province in 1956. Batista's force killed or captured many, and Castro fled into the mountains with the few left.

With Communist support, Castro built his numbers into the thousands. He cooperated with several non-Communist dissident groups. Batista fled Cuba in 1959. Castro was the popular hero. He became the new head of state. He promised to return democracy to Cuba.

Anticommunist leaders landed in jail. Hundreds of thousands of Cubans fled to the United States. In 1961 Castro proclaimed his Marxist-Leninist government. Land and business were nationalized. The legislature was abolished. Human rights were abandoned.

Castro proclaimed a constitution in 1976. The national assembly of the People's Government began meeting. Cuba is organized like the former Soviet Union.

The Cuban economy continued to exist only because of massive Soviet military and economic aid until recent political changes in the Soviet Union and Eastern Europe caused the end of this support. The Cuban economy, still based on sugar, is in trouble. The world sugar price continues at very low levels.

The United States broke off diplomatic relations with Cuba in 1961. Cuban foreign policy spreads the cause of communism by interfering in non-Communist nations. Argentina, Chile, Venezuela, Panama, Peru, Colombia, and Grenada have Cuban trained and led revolutionary movements. Cuban troops openly intervene in Ethiopia, Somalia, and Angola.

In 1961 the United States at first supported and then abandoned some 1,500 anti-Castro Cubans landing at the Bay of Pigs. In 1962, the United

States and the Soviet Union nearly began a nuclear war over Soviet missiles in Cuba. In exchange for the removal of the Soviet missiles, the United States agreed not to bother Castro.

Cuba and the United States began talking again in 1977. The United States does not give economic or military aid to Cuba.

Cuba maintains 185,000 men and women in the military forces. Some 85,000 are conscripts. Another 20,000 are in the first line of reserves. There are 150,000 reservists subject to call up. The navy is in the small warship class. The air force has nearly 150 combat-ready planes. There is a youth land army of 120,000, a civil defense force of 75,000, and a territorial militia of 1,500,000. A state security police force counts 17,500. Equipment is Soviet. Some of the newest equipment is Chinese.

The former Soviet Union still maintains nearly 4,500 military advisors in Cuba. They are being withdrawn. The United States maintains 4,500 troops at Guantanamo Bay Navy base.

Castro remains popular with the Cuban people. Foreign businessmen are invited to make capital investments in Cuba.

Cuba spent 7 percent of her gross national product on the military in 1979 and 4 percent in 1991. Her GNP increased 53 percent during these same years.

MEXICO

Mexico is larger than Alaska. It spans the southern tail of the continent from the Pacific Ocean to the Gulf of Mexico with the United States to the north and Belize and Guatemala to the south. The 89 million people have a per capita average annual income of $2,680. Mexico is a federal republic. Her present constitution dates from 1917. There are many political parties. All Mexicans over 18 can vote. The Institutional Revolutionary party gained power in 1921.

Mexico gained her independence from Spain in 1820. During the 1800s, a series of repressive governments held power. Mexico lost a war with the United States in 1847–1849. She gave the United States territory that now includes, among others, the states of New Mexico, Arizona, and California. The United States supported Benetio Juarez in his efforts to oust the French puppet Maximillano Habsburg just after the American Civil War. American economic penetration of Mexico began about this same time.

By 1900, American companies had large investments in Mexico, particularly in mining and oil. The Mexican revolution, begun in 1910, saw many lost American economic interests. During this revolution, President Woodrow Wilson of the United States sent General John J. Pershing into Mexico on a failed military expedition to capture Pancho Villa. Mexico normally does not support American military intervention anywhere in Latin America.

Mexico has a quiet, law-abiding population. Mexican dissident political revolutionaries are poorly organized. President Salinas de Gortari began a six-year term in 1988. Mexico's problems are economic. Inflation reached 160 percent in 1987. Wage and price controls are used. Inflation in 1990 was 24 percent.

In 1989 the government began divesting itself of state-owned industries. Mexico works to bring her schedule of debt payments on line. Relations with the United States are usually friendly. There is a 2,000-mile border. Cooperation exists in trade, finance, narcotics control, the environment, and culture, among others. The growing number of illegal Mexicans working in the United States causes friction. Mexico was included in President Bush's free trade treaty with Canada. The key to Mexico's immediate future lies in the state of the economy. Mexico cooperates with the United States in the war on drugs.

Mexico received $189.7 million in arms sales from the United States from 1950 to 1991.[1] Recently the United States has provided Mexico with aid, as shown in Table 12.1.

Mexico has 180,000 in the armed forces, 60,000 of them draftees. Some 350,000 are claimed for the reserves. The navy is in the small warship class, and the air force has about 115 combat planes. Equipment is mostly of American design. There is a rural defense militia of about 15,000. The Mexican military guarantees the existence of the present government. There is little if any organized rebel revolutionary opposition at present.

Mexico spends on the average about 5 percent of GNP on the military. Between 1979 and 1991, Mexico's GNP increased by 50 percent.

Table 12.1
U.S. Aid to Mexico (In U.S. Dollars)

	1989	1990	1991	1992
International Military Education	200,000	200,000	400,000	400,000
Economic Growth Fund				100,000
Development Assistance	11,400,000	9,500,000	14,000,000	16,100,000
Food for Peace	26,500,000	22,800,000	22,700,000	23,100,000
Drug Prevention	15,000,000	15,000,000	19,300,000	26,000,000
Totals	53,100,000	47,500,000	56,400,000	65,700,000

Source: United States of America, *U.S. Department of State Dispatch,* March 2, 1992, Washington, D.C.: GPO.

ST. KITTS AND NEVIS

St. Kitts and Nevis are two islands in the western Caribbean. Their closest neighbors are the U.S. Virgin Islands, Antigua and Barbuda, and French Guadeloupe. They total 101 square miles. Their 40,000 people have a per capital average annual income of $1,600. Britain granted independence in 1983. Government is a British-type parliamentary democracy.

The economy depends on the world price of sugar. These islands do not use tourists to balance bad sugar-crop years. There is an antitourism sentiment that dates from the repressive administration of Robert Bradshaw. He was the first prime minister when the island achieved self-government as an associate state of the United Kingdom in 1967. Bradshaw, a black nationalist, discouraged tourism. He tried to nationalize all land holdings.

The current prime minister is Dr. Kenneth Alphonse Simmonds. He tries to lure tourists to the islands. He secured a loan of $5 million from the Caribbean Development Bank.

The United States maintains friendly relations with St. Kitts and Nevis. These islands are strategically located in the Leeward Islands near shipping lanes of major importance to the United States. From 1985 to 1991, the United States sold these islands $4.8 million in military equipment and construction.[2] In recent years, the United States gave no military aid to St. Kitts and Nevis.

St. Kitts and Nevis does not maintain military forces. Her very small police force keeps law and order. Britain guarantees the defense of the islands.

DOMINICA

Dominica is a 290-square-mile island in the Windward Islands. French Guadeloupe is 30 miles to the north. French Martinique is 30 miles to the south. The 85,000 people have a per capita average annual income of $976. Britain granted independence in 1978. Government is a British-style parliamentary democracy.

Political discontent led to the formation of a temporary government in 1979. Democratic elections in 1980 gave victory to the ruling Dominica Freedom party. The alert police foiled dissident takeover attempts in 1980 and 1981.

Dominica took a leading role in demanding U.S. intervention in Grenada in 1983. Relations with the United States are friendly. From 1986 to 1991 the United States sold Dominica $3.9 million in military equipment and construction.[3] The United States has no plans for military aid to Dominica in 1993.

Dominica's armed forces consist of a special service unit of 100 men. There are also 325 men in the regular police force. A tiny coast guard patrols the island waters with one boat. Equipment is American. About 5 percent of the GNP is spent on the military. Britain guarantees the defense of the island.

HAITI

Haiti, about the size of Maryland, shares an island with the Dominican Republic. Other close neighbors are the islands of Puerto Rico, Cuba, and Jamaica. The 6 million people have a per person average annual income of $440. Haiti gained her independence from France in 1804. The provisional government is dominated by the military. No honest election has taken place since independence.

In 1791, Toussaint l'Ouverture led a black revolt against the French. By 1804 the defeated French withdrew from Haiti. In 1848, the Dominican Republic broke away. From 1848 to 1915, Haiti had 15 different military dictators.

In 1915, the U.S. military intervened to protect American citizens and property. The United States occupation lasted until 1934.

Francois Duvalier was elected president in 1957. He assumed total power for life in 1964. On his death, his son Jean Claude Duvalier took control.

Drought brought prolonged famine in 1975–1977. Hurricane Alice further damaged the economy in 1980. A severe economic depression began. Jean Claude Duvalier fled before a military takeover in 1986. He left for France in a U.S. Air Force plane.

General Henri Namphy assumed power. In 1987 a new constitution was approved. Leslie Manigat won the presidential election in 1988. Fraud was open and widespread. General Namphy again took control.

Namphy was overthrown in a military takeover in 1988. A revolt inspired by Jean Claude Duvalier began in 1991. The military crushed these rebels. Jean Bertrand Aristide became president in 1990 amid widespread charges of fraud. In late 1991, the military ran Aristide out of the country. The Organization of American States imposed diplomatic and economic sanctions on Haiti. General Raoul Cedras took control.

Marc Bazin became prime minister in 1992. The hope was that Aristide and Bazin would work out a compromise. Thousands of Haitians have taken to small boats. They are landing in the United States by the thousands. U.S. immigration is sending them back to Haiti. Some U.S. courts are letting them stay. Relations between the Cedras government and the United States show little improvement.

Between 1950 and 1991, the United States sold Haiti $4.1 million in military equipment and construction.[4] In 1993 the U.S. government plans on aid to Haiti are shown in Table 12.2.

Haiti is the poorest nation in the Caribbean basin. She maintains a standing military force of 7,500. Equipment is mostly American. These troops control an ever-restless population. There is a small terrorist secret police

Table 12.2
U.S. Aid to Haiti (In U.S. Dollars)

	1993
International Military Education	430,000
Economic Support Fund	15,000,000
Development Assistance	22,000,000
Food for Peace	12,600,000
Totals	50,030,000

Source: United States of America, *Congressional Presentation for Security Assistance Programs, Fiscal Year 1993,* Washington, D.C.: GPO.

organization. Haiti spends in excess of 10 percent of her annual budgets on her military. Haiti is a military state, always on the verge of revolution.

TRINIDAD-TOBAGO

Trinidad and Tobago are two islands just off the coast of Venezuela. They are about the size of Rhode Island. The population of 1.3 million has a per capita average annual income of $3,363. Britain granted independence in 1962. Government is a British-style parliamentary democracy.

Dr. Eric Williams founded the People's National Movement in 1956. He was prime minister from 1962 until his death in 1981.

In 1981 the National Alliance for Reconstruction won the elections. A. N. R. Robinson became prime minister. Hard economic times started with the end of the oil boom in 1981. In 1990, local Moslem extremists captured the parliament building and the TV station. These rebels surrendered after a six-day siege.

Trinidad-Tobago is a nonaligned nation. The United States is the main trading partner. Very cordial relations are maintained with the United States. The last American military installations on the islands dating from World War II were returned in 1980. In 1993 the United States plans to aid Trinidad-Tobago under the military assistance program as shown in Table 12.3 (p. 240).

Trinidad-Tobago has 2,750 men in her armed forces. There is a small coast guard. The air force has no combat planes. There are 4,000 men in the police force. Most of the equipment is American.

In 1979, Trinidad-Tobago spent less than 1 percent of GNP on her military. In 1991, she spent nearly 2 percent. In this same period, GNP increased by only 14 percent.

Table 12.3
U.S. Aid to Trinidad-Tobago (In U.S. Dollars)

	1993
Foreign Military Financing	500,000
International Military Education	75,000
Totals	575,000

Source: United States of America, *Congressional Presentation for Security Assistance Programs, Fiscal Year 1993,* Washington, D.C.: GPO.

GRENADA

Grenada is an island nation about the size of Washington, D.C., lying to the north of Trinidad-Tobago. The 90,000 people have a per capita average annual income of $1,900. Britain granted independence in 1974. Government is a parliamentary democracy.

Sir Eric Gairy was the first prime minister. In 1979, the New Joint Endeavor for Welfare, Education, and Liberation movement (JEWEL) took over. Prime Minister Maurice Bishop established the Marxist-Leninist People's Revolutionary Government. Close ties developed with Cuba, the Soviet Union, and other Communist countries. Many Cuban advisors and construction workers arrived. They began to build an airport large enough to service Soviet bomber squadrons.

In 1983, a power struggle resulted in the execution of Prime Minister Maurice Bishop. The People's Revolutionary Army seized power. Civil order broke down. Other Caribbean nations, notably Dominica, asked the United States to restore law and order.

The United States invaded Grenada. The Marxist leaders Bernard Coard and General Hudson Austin were arrested. Hundreds of Cuban volunteers were taken prisoner.

President Reagan gave three reasons for U.S. military intervention. He would protect the 1,000 American citizens on Grenada. He wished to forestall further political chaos. He wanted to restore the constitutional government of Grenada. Not to be forgotten is the construction of a world-class airfield capable of servicing the Soviet bomber aircraft.

New elections in 1984 saw Henry Blaize of the New National Party become prime minister. U.S. troops left Grenada in 1986.

Between 1984 and 1991 the United States sold Grenada $8.1 million in military equipment and construction.[5] There are no plans for further military aid for 1993.

Grenada maintains some 6,500 police. Her spending level in support of these police is not known. Their equipment is American. The United States guarantees the independence of Grenada.

THE DOMINICAN REPUBLIC

The Dominican Republic, about the size of New Hampshire and Vermont, shares an island with Haiti. Puerto Rico is the other near neighbor. Her 7.5 million people have a per capita average annual income of $680. The Dominican Republic proclaimed independence from Haiti in 1844. Government is a representative democracy established in 1966.

In 1861 the Dominican Republic voluntarily returned to Spanish rule. In 1865 a revolution reestablished independence. A long civil war began in 1901. In 1905 U.S. forces seized the capital, Santo Domingo, for nonpayment of debts. In 1916, the U.S. Marines took over the entire country. They left in 1924.

Free elections established a democratic government. In 1930, the commander of the army, Rafael L. Trujillo, seized power. He established a military dictatorship. His rule saw great economic development. Human rights became nonexistent. He massacred the Haitian minority.

In 1960, the Organization of American States voted diplomatic sanctions against the Dominican Republic. Trujillo had plotted the assassination of Venezuela's President Romulo Betancourt. Trujillo died in 1961.

In 1962 Juan Bosch was elected president. The military overthrew Bosch in 1963. Elements loyal to Bosch began a civil war in 1965. The United States intervened to protect its citizens and their property. Communist organizers seized control of the anti-Bosch forces.

U.S. troops policed the elections of 1966. Joaquin Balaguer defeated Bosch. U.S. forces withdrew.

Balaguer was reelected in 1970 and 1974. He lost in 1978 to Antonio Guzman. Salvador Jorge Blanco became president by the elections of 1982. Growing economic difficulties led to serious unrest. Rioting began in 1984. Balaguer won the presidency in 1986. The economic crisis deepens each year with the continued low price of sugar on the world market. The Dominican Republic is allied closely with the United States and the other members of the Organization of American States. The Dominican government never courted the Soviet Union or its allies. Some 1 million Dominicans live in the United States. From 1950 to 1991, the United States sold the Dominican Republic $29.6 million in military equipment and sales.[6] Aid from 1991 to 1993 is shown in Table 12.4 on page 142.

The Dominican Republic maintains 25,000 men under arms. The navy is in the small warship class. The air force can fly ten combat planes. Equipment is American. There are some 16,000 men in the national police. Military service is voluntary.

Table 12.4
U.S. Aid to the Dominican Republic (In U.S. Dollars)

	1991	1992	1993
Military Financing	1,000,000	2,000,000	500,000
International Military Education	900,000	900,000	700,000
Economic Support Fund	12,000,000	5,000,000	5,000,000
Development Assistance	11,335,000	13,000,000	17,220,000
Food for Peace	23,827,000	14,306,000	14,858,000
Peace Corps	3,315,000	2,213,000	2,336,000
Totals	52,377,000	37,419,000	40,614,000

Source: United States of America, *Congressional Presentation for Security Assistance Programs, Fiscal Years 1991–1993*, Washington, D.C.: GPO, 1991–1993.

The 1979 support level for the military was 1.8 percent of GNP. This declined to less than 1 percent by 1991. During this same period, GNP increased by 53 percent.

NOTES

1. FMS Control and Reports Division, Comptroller, DSAA, *Foreign Military Sales, Foreign Military Construction Sales and Military Assistance Facts, as of September 30, 1991*, Washington, Data Management Division, Comptroller DSSA, 1992.
2. Ibid.
3. Ibid.
4. Ibid.
5. Ibid.
6. Ibid.

13

Central America

Central America begins at the southern border of Mexico and continues to the northern border of Colombia. Costa Rica, El Salvador, Guatemala, Honduras, Panama, Nicaragua, and Belize make up this region. The United States sees its role in this area as one of a big brother. All these nations are encouraged to adopt a U.S.-style democracy. U.S. policy has been two-pronged. First, all possible Communist-led rebel movements are to be crushed. Second, at the end of every successful military campaign, a democratic form of government is established.

This policy involves the United States in two problems. First, rebel groups are often more motivated by the poverty of the common people than by communism. Second, established governments do not want to change after successfully defeating rebel groups. For the United States to succeed in its Central American policy, the basic character of landowning must be changed. To break up the large landholding in the Central American countries is the equal of a successful revolutionary movement. To distribute free land to the peasants in these countries is the same thing as redividing the wealth in the United States.

The Central American economic–political power structure is not willing to divide up the wealth so that all the members of the lower classes may have equal shares. This type of reform is such pure socialism that it reminds us of the failed economic system of the former Soviet Union. This is the "catch 22" of American policy in Central America.

The United States settles for governments that are friendly. These governments must cooperate with American businesses and Americans resident in their countries. In return, the United States provides economic and military aid. The military aid includes American Military Assistance Groups and Special Forces Units. These military teams are usually located in the Central American country. They are there to support American policy that includes the continued existence of the host country's government.

There is little attention given to the type of government the United States supports. Each Central American nation is encouraged to promote democracy. A record clean of human rights violations is also wanted. Fortunately for the United States, there is always a rebel group in each country that threatens the established government. Communism came in very handy for U.S. foreign policy in this region from 1945 to 1990. Equally fortunate is the arrival of Maoist Communist support from China and North Korea since the collapse of the former Soviet Union. American foreign–economic–military policy has little reason to change.

The basic inequality that is the root cause of the multiple rebel groups throughout Central America remains unchanged. At present, the cries for food, clothing, shelter, and medical care from the millions of suppressed people in the Central American underclasses go largely unheard.

Central America is an area of substantial concern to the United States. All seven nations of this region are suffering severe economic strains. El Salvador and Guatemala are suffering civil wars. Nicaragua is still undergoing revolution and civil war. The Marxist-led junta seems to be out of power. But one set of rebels out in the jungle seems to be a part of Nicaragua's future at least throughout the 1990s. In Honduras, economic stress is constantly aggravated by events in El Salvador and by a large American military presence. Despite the departure of Manuel Noriega, Panama continues to suffer from an economic depression. The current government depends on American support and the presence of a large American troop deployment for its continued existence.

These events see a continuing large volume of U.S. military and economic aid pouring into the region. The appropriate goals and means for U.S. aid to Central America are debated in Congress, in the media, and in the streets every year. Among the disagreements is the need for American military units stationed in Central America. Another hot argument continues on whether military aid is more effective than economic assistance.

So much American time and effort goes into Central America that we will deal with the region one country at a time. Figures are available concerning military aid and economic assistance from 1978. Central America is dominated by American economic interests. It is tied to American foreign policy. In general, Latin American governments exist because of U.S. military aid. Central American people often live because of American economic aid.

Is the United States successful? Are the Central American nations more democratic now than in 1978?

Population and income figures for the region are given in Figure 13.1.

These Central American nations experienced good economic times through the 1945–1973 period. The current economic depression began with the oil shock of 1973. Yet coffee, banana, and other agricultural prices held steady until 1978. Although the annual increase in GNP of the region declined in the early 1970s to less than 3 percent, the various governments were still in the black.

Figure 13.1
Central America, Total Population and per Capita Income (In U.S. Dollars)

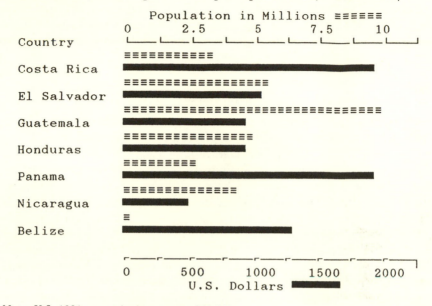

Note: U.S. 1991 per capita income was $21,800.

Real trouble began in 1978 when sharp price declines in sugar, coffee, cocoa, and bananas were accompanied by huge price hikes in imported oil products. The world credit markets also started raising prices. Central American governments found themselves caught between shrinking foreign revenues and increasing foreign debts. By the early 1980s, unemployment was often 20 percent or more throughout the region. Such economic hard times are the breeding ground for social revolutionaries.

The United States responded by increasing military and economic aid. Historically, this is the American way in Central America, where American intervention is a way of life. All of the Central American lands expect the United States to bail them out of economic hard times. Failure to do so gives the rebels their chance to overthrow pro-American governments. Many rebels groups were pro-Soviet simply because the government was pro-American. This pattern is repeating itself as the rebels now turn to the Marxist-Maoist doctrines of China and North Korea. The American dilemma continues into the 1990s.

If the United States has learned anything in this region since 1945, it is that the need for food, clothing, shelter, and medical care for every individual is the root cause of social unrest. These are essential for human beings. Only when these needs are satisfied can the Central American nations build a democracy. We cannot continue to give in to those who argue that American economic interest in Central America is the paramount issue. Experience in this region has taught us that economic progress, democratic institutions, social justice, and human rights can exist only when there is peace and tranquility. A half-starving, sick people have no time for high-flown promises for the future. The revolutionary call for immediate improvement in their day-to-day living conditions is far more appealing.

COSTA RICA

Costa Rica, about the size of West Virginia, borders Nicaragua and Panama and stretches from the Pacific Ocean to the Caribbean Sea. The 3 million people have a per capita average annual income of $1,810. Costa Rica gained independence from Spain in 1821. The government is a democratic republic; and the economy is based on the export of coffee, bananas, sugar, and cocoa. The United States buys 40 to 50 percent of all Costa Rican exports.

Costa Rica's first democratic elections came in 1889. Frederick Tinoco ruled as dictator from 1917 to 1948. In 1948, Jose Figueres led a revolution. More than 3,000 died. Figueres gave Costa Rica a democratic constitution that abolished the army. Elections are free and open. The democratic process is well established. Rarely does a political party win two successive elections.

Costa Rica suffered during the worldwide recession of the late 1970s. Her foreign debt became unmanageable. GNP fell 9 percent just in 1982. Costa Rica needs to reschedule the payment of her large foreign debt.

The United States maintains excellent relations with Costa Rica. From 1950 to 1991 the United States sold Costa Rica $30.7 million in military equipment and construction.[1] From 1978 to 1993 the United States gave economic and military aid to Costa Rica as shown in Table 13.1.

Costa Rica boasts that she has no army. There are 8,000 men in the security forces, the key to political power. Some 4,500 are in the coast guard, and 3,500 more in the rural guard. There are no combat aircraft. The United States has a military advisory group in Costa Rica.

Costa Rica spends less than 1 percent of GNP on her military. GNP rose by 49 percent between 1979 and 1991. She is economically dominated by the United States. She is well within the U.S. forward defense perimeter.

EL SALVADOR

El Salvador, about the size of Massachusetts, borders with Guatemala and Honduras and lies on the Pacific Ocean. The 5 million people have a per capita average annual income of $1,040. El Salvador secured independence from Spain in 1821. Government is a constitutional republic. There are at present six major political parties. All citizens over 18 can vote.

Table 13.1
U.S. Aid to Costa Rica (In U.S. Dollars)

	1978	1979	1980	1981	1982
Military Financing					2,000,000
International Military Education				35,000	58,000
Economic Support Fund					20,000,000
Development Assistance	6,148,000	15,686,000	13,561,000	11,475,000	11,540,000
Food for Peace					19,092,000
Peace Corps	1,317,000	1,464,000	1,461,000	1,746,000	1,007,000
Totals	7,465,000	17,150,000	15,022,000	13,256,000	53,697,000

Table 13.1 (continued)

	1983	1984	1986	1987	1988
Military Financing	2,500,000	2,000,000	3,000,000	3,100,000	2,000,000
International Military Education	125,000	150,000	600,000	250,000	450,000
Economic Support Fund	157,000,000	70,000,000	1,900,000	42,466,000	90,000,000
Development Assistance	27,146,000	15,000,000	6,900,000	16,000,000	12,900,000
Food for Peace	28,000,000	20,000,000	12,400,000	18,000,000	15,140,000
Peace Corps	1,256,000	1,200,000		3,158,000	2,894,000
Totals	216,027,000	108,350,000	24,800,000	82,974,000	123,484,000

Table 13.1 (continued)

	1989	1990	1991	1992	1993
Military Financing	1,500,000				
International Military Education	230,000	336,000	230,000	230,000	230,000
Economic Support Fund	70,000,000	63,544,000	9,705,000	8,000,000	8,000,000
Development Assistance	12,000,000		40,000,000	20,000,000	10,000,000
Food for Peace	15,000,000		15,000,000	10,000,000	10,000,000
Peace Corps	3,411,000		3,040,000	2,187,000	1,193,000
Totals	102,141,000	63,880,000	67,975,000	42,777,000	30,423,000

Source: Figures for 1978–1984, *U.S. Foreign Assistance to Central America*, Library of Congress: Congressional Research Office, March 2, 1984; figures for 1986–1988, Jonathan E. Sanford, *U.S. Aid to Central America*, Library of Congress: Congressional Research Service, June 3, 1987; figures for 1988–1993, United States of America, *Congressional Presentation for Security Assistance Programs, 1988–1993*, Washington, D.C.: GPO, 1988–1993.

149

The economy is based on coffee, sugar, and cotton. The worldwide drop in the prices of these goods during the 1980s brought severe economic depression to El Salvador. About 50 percent of all exports go to the United States.

El Salvador was joined to Mexico in 1822. Guatemala tried to enforce this union with Mexico in 1823. El Salvador asked to become a part of the United States. After a long civil war, El Salvador finally became an independent republic in 1838.

The period from 1839 to 1900 was marked by frequent revolutions and military takeovers; but from 1900 to 1930 there was political stability under the control of the fourteen largest landholding families.

The military seized power in 1931. General Maximiliano Hernandez Martinez became the dictator. Until 1980, the army ruled. Every head of state was an army officer.

In 1969, El Salvador and Honduras fought the Soccer War. This began over a disputed border area. Some 450,000 Salvadorians were working in Honduras. The Organization of American States intervened. A cease-fire remained in place until 1989. The International Court of Justice solved the problem.

Dissident elements took to the jungles in the early 1970s. The United States continued to support the military government. The rebels accepted military aid and training from the Soviets and the Cubans. By 1979, the rebels controlled much of the countryside. Terrorist attacks were common in the cities. Death squads on both sides killed many.

In 1980, a group of young army officers combined to take over the government. Jose Napoleon Duarte led the provisional government until the elections of 1982. Duarte began land reforms. He held honest elections in 1982.

The rebels continue in the field. Government troops, benefiting from increased American military aid, beat back the rebel forces. They have not crushed them. The United States maintains a large military assistance advisors group in El Salvador. Alfredo Cristiani became president in 1989. He called for a direct dialogue between all warring factions.

In 1990 the military situation remained unchanged. The civil war is 20 years old. The government charged nine army officers with killing six Jesuit priests. Two were convicted.

Throughout 1991, human rights abuses occurred on a wide scale. Both sides participated in widespread killing. Public order has been constantly disrupted by military operations, rebel raids, fear, and continued low world prices for coffee, sugar, and cotton.

In 1992 the accords of Chapultepee were signed in Mexico City. A cease-fire went into effect. Both sides began to disarm. Land redistribution began. A U.N. mission now monitors the situation. A new civilian police force began operations.

There were reports in 1993 that the government cut the standing military force by 50 percent. The internal situation is not yet one of peace.

The United States maintains very close relations with El Salvador's government. Support for the Salvadoran ruling junta is firm. From 1950 to 1991 the United States sold El Salvador $875.2 million in military equipment and construction.[2] American economic and military aid is massive, as shown in Table 13.2 (pp. 152–154).

El Salvador maintains armed forces of 45,000 men. The navy is a small coast guard, and there are fewer than 50 war planes. The 40,000-man internal security police is still the key to political power. Equipment is made in the United States. The rebel Marti national liberation front has some 8,000 men. The United Nations has a small observer group in El Salvador.

El Salvador supports her military forces as shown in Figure 13.2 (p. 155).

During the 1979–1991 period, GNP increased by 29 percent. The government of El Salvador cannot survive without continued massive economic and military aid from the United States.

GUATEMALA

Guatemala is about the size of Tennessee. It lies on the Pacific Ocean and its neighbors are Mexico, Belize, Honduras, and El Salvador. The population of 9.5 million has a per capita average annual income of $920. Government is a constitutional republic. There are nine prominent political parties.

The Guatemalan economy is dependent on the world prices of coffee, cotton, and sugar. The decline of these prices during the 1980s led to serious economic depression. The United States buys about 40 percent of Guatemalan exports.

Guatemala declared independence from Spain in 1821. A part of Mexico for a few years, it achieved true independence in 1840. The military controlled the government for the next century. Dissident army officers overthrew General Jorge Ubico in 1944. President Juan Jose Arevalo began liberal reforms in 1945. Colonel Jacobo Arbenz continued this trend.

In 1954, a group of army rebels led by Colonel Carlos Castillo invaded from Honduras. The army stood aside. In 1957, Castillo was assassinated. General Miguel Ydigoras became president in 1958.

A military takeover failed in 1960. The survivors fled to the jungles. Cuba gave them military aid. In 1963, Colonel Enrique Peralta Axurdia gained power. After democratic elections in 1965, Julio Cesar Mendez Montenegro became president. The army opened a major thrust against the rebels. The rebels replied with a terrorist campaign. Many died on both sides.

General Carlos Arana declared a state of emergency in 1970. General Kjell Laugerud Garcia won the disputed elections in 1974. In 1978, General Romeo Lucas Garcia became president. The civil war reached new heights. Torture and murder became normal on both sides.

Despite open rebel-led violence, General Anibal Guevara won the 1982 elections. Dissident military units staged a takeover in 1982. They failed and many died.

Table 13.2
U.S. Aid to El Salvador (In U.S. Dollars)

	1978	1979	1980	1981	1982
Military Financing	25,000	5,000	8,000	25,003,000	33,500,000
International Military Education			247,000	492,000	2,002,000
Economic Support Fund			9,100,000	44,900,000	115,000,000
Development Assistance	7,525,000	6,045,000	43,155,000	32,792,000	36,199,000
Food for Peace	1,584,000	2,593,000	6,269,000	26,277,000	34,887,000
Peace Corps	1,389,000	1,561,000			
Housing Investment			9,500,000	5,500,000	5,000,000
Totals	10,525,000	10,204,000	68,279,000	134,964,000	226,588,000

Table 13.2 (continued)

	1983	1984	1986	1987	1988
Military Financing	33,500,000	45,000,000	121,000,000	133,500,000	119,000,000
International Military Education	1,300,000	1,300,000	800,000	500,000	900,000
Economic Support Fund	140,000,000	120,000,000	177,000,000	236,000,000	200,000,000
Development Assistance	58,540,000	41,300,000	83,900,000	75,500,000	75,600,000
Food for Peace	40,611,000	34,461,000	54,400,000	47,500,000	43,700,000
Peace Corps					
Housing Investment	5,000,000				
Totals	278,951,000	242,061,000	437,100,000	493,000,000	439,200,000

Table 13.2 (continued)

	1989	1990	1991	1992	1993
Military Financing	95,000,000	84,635,000	90,000,000	90,000,000	40,000,000
International Military Education	1,500,000	1,394,000	1,400,000	1,400,000	1,400,000
Economic Support Fund	67,700,000		64,118,000	55,000,000	55,000,000
Development Assistance	185,000,000	130,615,000	180,000,000	120,000,000	160,000,000
Food for Peace	39,771,000		39,886,000	35,812,000	30,000,000
Peace Corps					
Houseing Investment					
Totals	388,971,000	216,644,000	375,404,000	302,212,000	286,400,000

Source: Figures for 1978–1984, *U.S. Foreign Assistance to Central America,* Library of Congress: Congressional Research Office, March 2, 1984; figures for 1986–1988, Jonathan E. Sanford, *U.S. Aid to Central America,* Library of Congress: Congressional Research Service, June 3, 1987; figures for 1988–1993, United States of America, *Congressional Presentation for Security Assistance Programs, 1988–1993,* Washington, D.C.: GPO, 1988–1993.

Figure 13.2
El Salvador's Military Defense Expenditures (In Millions of U.S. Dollars as a
Percentage of GNP)

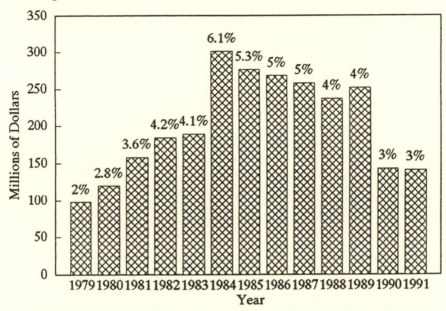

Source: U.S. Arms Control and Disarmament Agency, *World Military Expenditures and Arms Transfers,* Washington, D.C.: GPO, November 1991, p. 61. The figures for 1990 and 1991 are based on Heisbourg et al. *The Military Balance 1991–1992,* London: International Institute for Strategic Studies, 1991, p. 197, and Huldt et al. *The Military Balance 1992–1993,* London: International Institute for Strategic Studies, 1992, p. 178.

General Rios Montt headed a military council. They suspended the constitution. They declared a state of siege. Special death courts operated in secret. All civil liberties remained suspended. Elections were scheduled for 1984.

The army overthrew Rios Montt in 1983. General Humberto Mejia Victores became president. Elections were planned for 1984. A new constitution was in place by 1985. Vinicio Cerezo became president in 1985. The new constitution opened for business in 1986. Jorge Serrano became president in 1991.

Guatemala continues with the problems of a long-lasting civil war and economic depression. Little progress on the twin issues of human rights and land reform is made. There is a minor border dispute with Belize.

The United States guarantees the existence of the current Guatemalan government. From 1950 to 1991 the United States sold Guatemala $66.7 million in military equipment and construction.[3] The massive United States economic and military aid to Guatemala is shown in Table 13.3 (pp. 156–158).

Table 13.3
U.S. Aid to Guatemala (In U.S. Dollars)

	1978	1979	1980	1981	1982
Military Financing	4,000	6,000			
International Military Education					
Economic Support Fund					
Development Assistance	4,215,000	16,500,000	7,764,000	1,207,000	1,688,000
Food for Peace	3,464,000	5,415,000	3,676,000	7,754,000	5,617,000
Peace Corps	1,525,000	1,103,000	1,851,000	2,046,000	1,653,000
Housing Investment					10,000,000
Narcotics Control					
Totals	9,208,000	23,024,000	13,291,000	11,007,000	18,958,000

156

Table 13.3 (continued)

	1983	1984	1986	1987	1988
Military Financing					500,000
International Military Education			600,000	600,000	600,000
Economic Support Fund	10,000,000		1,900,000	2,300,000	2,000,000
Development Assistance	12,500,000	1,600,000	6,900,000	7,300,000	7,300,000
Food for Peace	4,360,000	10,590,000			
Peace Corps	1,905,000	2,100,000			
Housing Investment					
Narcotics Control					
Totals	28,765,000	14,290,000	9,400,000	10,200,000	10,400,000

Table 13.3 (continued)

	1989	1990	1991	1992	1993
Military Financing	5,000,000		5,000,000	2,000,000	
International Military Education	400,000	398,000	400,000	400,000	400,000
Economic Support Fund	80,000,000	56,483,000	60,000,000	30,000,000	10,000,000
Development Assistance	34,000,000		34,295,000	28,225,000	21,000,000
Food for Peace	23,075,000		25,542,000	23,909,000	24,839,000
Peace Corps	3,865,000		4,257,000	2,560,000	2,748,000
Housing Investment					
Narcotics Control					3,000,000
Totals	146,340,000	56,821,000	129,494,000	87,094,000	61,987,000

Source: Figures for 1978–1984, *U.S. Foreign Assistance to Central America,* Library of Congress: Congressional Research Office, March 2, 1984; figures for 1986–1988, Jonathan E. Sanford, *U.S. Aid to Central America,* Library of Congress: Congressional Research Service, June 3, 1987; figures for 1988–1993, United States of America, *Congressional Presentation for Security Assistance Programs, 1988–1993,* Washington, D.C.: GPO, 1988–1993.

Guatemala maintains 40,000 troops. The navy is a coast guard, and the air force has fewer than 20 combat planes. Some 11,000 men are in the security forces, the key to political power. All equipment is American made. The rebel United National Revolutionary Movement of Guatemala might field 1,500 men.

Guatemala spends between 1 and 1.5 percent of GNP on her military forces. Between 1979 and 1991, the GNP grew by 42 percent.

HONDURAS

Honduras, about the size of Tennessee, borders Guatemala, Nicaragua, and El Salvador and stretches from the Caribbean Sea to the Pacific Ocean. The 5 million people have a per capita average annual income of $960. The economy depends on the global price of bananas, coffee, and lead. The United States buys 50 to 60 percent of Honduran exports. The government is a constitutional republic. There are four major political parties.

Honduras declared independence from Spain in 1821. She was the leader of the unsuccessful Central American Federation that failed in 1838. It was not until 1922 that Honduras abandoned efforts to restore this federation. The Honduran military staged over 325 changes of government before 1929.

From 1930 to 1948 General Tiburcio Carias Andino maintained a military government. In 1954, serious trouble began. Radical dissidents caused riots and labor strikes. In 1955, army units installed a new military government. In 1957, free elections led to the appointment of Dr. Ramoa Villeda Morales as president.

Liberal reforms flourished. A military academy was established. In 1963, the army took over after heavy fighting. Many died. Liberal party members were arrested. Many fled the country.

General Lopez Arrellance took power. His National party controlled the country until 1982. Popular discontent was high after the 1969 border war with El Salvador. In 1972, Lopez overthrew his friends. He began land redistribution to the peasants. His government fell in 1975. Charges were brought that he misused international emergency aid after Hurricane Fifi in 1974. He was accused of accepting bribes from the United Fruit Company.

General Melgar Castro was head of state from 1975 to 1978. General Paz García ran the government from 1978 to 1982. They built the military into the largest, best-equipped armed force in Central America. They built bridges, roads, schools, and airfields. Honduras prospered.

In 1980, free elections were held. A new constitution became law in 1982. The Liberal party leader Roberto Suazo Cordoba became president. Nicaragua was a Marxist-Leninist neighbor at this time. El Salvador's civil war offered another danger. Cordoba decided on very close relations with the United States.

In 1986, Jose Azcona Hoyo became president. Rafael Leonardo Callejas became president in 1990. The global economic recession of the late 1980s gave Honduras a large foreign debt. Callejas plans on cutting the traditional economic ties with the United States. He is trying to develop economic ties with Japan and Europe.

Honduras is a client state of the United States. Between 1950 and 1991, the United States sold Honduras $410.9 million in military equipment and construction.[4] The United States has provided economic and military aid to Honduras. American military advisory and training groups are also large. This is in recognition of the threats to Honduras from the Marxist-Leninist leaders in El Salvador.

U.S. aid to Honduras is steady and large, as shown in Table 13.4.

American military and economic aid may decline if Honduras continues her movement toward Japanese and European ties.

The Honduran armed forces contain 18,000 men. Over 13,000 are draftees. The government is reducing the size of the armed forces. There are some 75,000 reservists. The navy is a small coast guard. The air force has about 50 combat planes. There are about 6,000 men in the internal security forces. All equipment is American. The United Nations maintains a small observer team along the El Salvador border. The United States has at least 1,200 military advisors and training personnel in Honduras.

Between 1979 and 1991 Honduras spent between 2.2 and 3.2 percent of GNP on the armed forces. During this same period, the GNP increased by 51 percent. Honduras remains an economic and military client of the United States.

PANAMA

Panama is about the size of South Carolina. Immediate neighbors are Costa Rica and Colombia, and the country stretches from the Caribbean Sea across the narrow isthmus to the Pacific Ocean. The 2.5 million people have a per capita average annual income of $1,980. Her government is a constitutional republic. Her economy is based on bananas, shrimp, coffee, sugar, and Panama Canal fees. The official currency is the U.S. dollar.

Panama gained independence from Spain in 1821 and joined the Republic of Greater Colombia. Between 1826 and 1860, Panama tried to gain independence four times.

After the 1849 discovery of gold in California, Panama became a crossing from the Caribbean Sea to the Pacific Ocean for the gold seekers. In 1855, the transisthmus railway was constructed. From 1880 to 1890, a French company tried to build a canal across the country.

In 1903 Colombia refused the United States permission to build a canal. Coached by the United States, Panama declared her independence from Colombia. American fleet units prevented Colombian troops from landing

Table 13.4
U.S. Aid to Honduras (In U.S. Dollars)

	1978	1979	1980	1981	1982
Military Financing		7,000	11,000		11,000,000
International Military Education	692,000	250,000	441,000	535,000	1,275,000
Economic Support Fund					36,800,000
Development Assistance	12,395,000	20,697,000	45,824,000	25,660,000	36,167,000
Food for Peace	2,038,000	4,625,000	4,829,000	10,088,000	13,961,000
Peace Corps	1,681,000	2,103,000	1,974,000	2,444,000	1,788,000
Housing Investment	10,500,000		10,000,000	15,000,000	
Totals	27,306,000	27,682,000	63,079,000	53,727,000	100,991,000

Table 13.4 (continued)

	1983	1984	1986	1987	1988
Military Financing	27,000,000	40,000,000	69,700,000	76,900,000	80,000,000
International Military Education	800,000	1,000,000	1,000,000	1,300,000	1,500,000
Economic Support Fund	56,000,000	40,000,000	61,200,000	136,400,000	100,000,000
Development Assistance	31,180,000	32,000,000	44,300,000	40,900,000	40,400,000
Food for Peace	13,961,000	11,100,000	18,500,000	17,000,000	16,400,000
Peace Corps	2,788,000	2,983,000			
Housing Investment					
Totals	131,729,000	127,038,000	194,700,000	272,500,000	238,300,000

162

Table 13.4 (continued)

	1989	1991	1992	1993
Military Financing	60,000,000	40,000,000	19,100,000	8,000,000
International Military Education	1,200,000	1,100,000	1,100,000	1,100,000
Economic Support Fund	87,000,000	36,933,000	50,000,000	30,000,000
Development Assistance	40,000,000	80,000,000	41,000,000	31,600,000
Food for Peace	15,122,000	15,601,000	17,432,000	20,051,000
Peace Corps	5,694,000	5,827,000	3,645,000	3,214,000
Housing Investment				
Totals	209,016,000	179,461,000	132,277,000	93,965,000

Source: Figures for 1978–1984, *U.S. Foreign Assistance to Central America*, Library of Congress: Congressional Research Office, March 2, 1984; figures for 1986–1988, Jonathan E. Sanford, *U.S. Aid to Central America*, Library of Congress: Congressional Research Service, June 3, 1987; figures for 1988–1993, United States of America, *Congressional Presentation for Security Assistance Programs, 1988–1993*, Washington, D.C.: GPO, 1988–1993.

163

to suppress the revolution. Panama has been a tributary state of the United States since 1903.

The United States established a constitutional system of government in Panama that lasted until 1968. There was never any doubt that U.S. troops stationed in the Canal Zone ran the country.

In 1968, the United States–trained Panamanian defense force overthrew the government. Brigadier General Omar Torrijos Herrera took power. Elections came in 1972. The military continued to control the government. Formal constitutional government was restored in 1984.

In 1986, the Panamanian defense force again overthrew the government. General Manuel Antonio Noriega came to power. Noriega was indicted as a drug smuggler by U.S. courts in 1988. Noriega claimed victory in the 1989 elections despite widespread fraud.

U.S. troops invaded Panama in 1989. The Panamanian defense force was destroyed. Noriega was captured and taken to stand trial in the United States. He was found guilty. The final sentence and place of imprisonment remain undetermined. Guillermo Endara became the new president. In 1991, President Endara refused to form a new army. A new police force is being constructed. The United States considers Panama to be one of its client states. Between 1950 and 1991, the United States sold Panama $35.8 million in military equipment and construction.[5] The United States has been generous with its economic and military aid before and after Noriega, as shown in Table 13.5.

Panama has a national police force of about 12,000 men. Panama remains a nation occupied by U.S. forces. Panama suffers along with the rest of Central America from the current worldwide recession.

BELIZE

Belize is about the size of Massachusetts. She lies on the Caribbean Sea, and her neighbors are Mexico and Guatemala. Her 190,000 people have a per capita average annual income of $1,250. The economy depends on the world market prices of sugar, citrus fruits, and bananas. The worldwide recession of the late 1980s brought severe economic distress. The United States buys over 50 percent of Belize's exports.

Britain granted independence in 1981. The government is a British-style parliamentary democracy. There are several political parties. Immigration is heavy. There is a longstanding border dispute with Guatemala. It is not considered serious in the military sense.

The United States maintains very friendly relations with Belize. From 1950 to 1991 the United States sold Belize $2.7 million in military equipment and construction.[6]

Belize has received economic and military aid from the United States as shown in Table 13.6 (p. 166).

Table 13.5
U.S. Aid to Panama (In U.S. Dollars)

	1986	1987	1988	1989	1991	1992	1993
Military Assistance	7,500,000	9,800,000	3,000,000				
International Military Education	700,000	750,000	600,000	445,000	75,000		
Economic Support Fund	5,700,000	28,000,000	10,000,000			10,000,000	10,000,000
Development Assistance	18,000,000	18,100,000	19,343,000			17,000,000	8,400,000
Food for Peace	100,000		47,000,000				
Peace Corps						838,000	1,133,000
Totals	32,000,000	56,650,000	32,990,000	445,000	75,000	27,838,000	19,533,000

Source: Figures for 1986, Jonathan E. Sanford, *U.S. Aid to Central America*, Library of Congress: Congressional Research Service, June 3, 1987; figures for 1989–1993, United States of America, *Congressional Presentation for Security Assistance Programs, 1989–1993*, Washington, D.C.: GPO, 1988–1993.

Table 13.6
U.S. Aid to Belize (In U.S. Dollars)

	1982	1983	1984	1986	1987
Military Assistance			500,000	500,000	500,000
International Military Education	26,000	75,000	100,000	100,000	100,000
Economic Support Fund		10,000,000		1,900,000	2,300,000
Development Assistance		6,690,000	4,000,000	6,900,000	7,300,000
Peace Corps	624,000	871,000	909,000		
Housing Development		2,000,000	3,000,000		
Totals	650,000	19,636,000	8,509,000	9,400,000	10,200,000

Source: Figures for 1982–1984, *U.S. Foreign Aid to Central America*, Library of Congress: Congressional Research Office, March 2, 1984; figures for 1986–1988, Jonathan E. Sanford, *U.S. Foreign Aid to Central America*, Library of Congress: Congressional Research Service, June 3, 1987; figures for 1989–1993, United States of America, *Congressional Presentation for Security Assistance Programs, 1988–1993*, Washington, D.C.: GPO, 1988–1993.

Belize maintains a military force of 700 men. Britain keeps some 2,000 troops in Belize. Britain guarantees the existence of the government. The equipment is British. Belize spends approximately 2 percent of her annual GNP on defense activities. Her GNP increases by about 8 percent per year.

NICARAGUA

Nicaragua, about the size of Iowa, borders Honduras and Costa Rica and stretches from the Caribbean Sea to the Pacific Ocean. The 4 million people have a per capita average annual income of $610. Government is a constitutional republic. The economy is dependent on the world market prices of coffee, cotton, sugar, beef, and bananas.

Nicaragua declared independence from Spain in 1821 and became part of Guatemala. Nicaragua became an independent republic in 1838. Political rivalry between liberal and conservative politicians dominated the 1820s.

In 1856, William Walker and 100 American mercenaries seized the government. A civil war drove Walker out in 1857. For 40 years, the conservatives ruled the country.

President Jose Santos Zelaya refused to let the United States build a canal across the country. In 1909, the United States intervened. American troops remained until 1933.

In 1936, the United States–trained Nicaraguan national guard seized the government. Anastasio Somoza García took power. The Somoza family ruled Nicaragua until 1979. They established a military dictatorship.

In 1962, several dissident groups combined to form the Marxist Sandinista National Liberation front (FSLN). FSLN's growing success led to increased government oppression. Gradually the business community came over to the FSLN. The murder of newspaper editor Pedro Joaquin Chamorro in 1978 brought a massive uprising.

Fighting was heavy. The Organization of American States, led by the United States, withdrew support from the government. The last Somoza fled.

The Sandinistas came to power. The economy was a shambles. The cost of the 19-year civil war was 50,000 lives and $500 million in destroyed property. Living standards dropped by 25 percent.

The Sandinista government made improvements in health, nutrition, and the infrastructure. They were not successful in land reform. They adopted the Marxist commune instead of dividing the large landholdings among the peasant farmers. They drew close to the Cuban and Soviet governments.

Opposition groups quickly formed along the mountainous jungle border with Honduras. These groups came to be called the Contras. In 1979, the United States declared an economic embargo on Nicaragua. The impact was devastating. The prices of simple foodstuffs like rice and beans doubled. The price of gasoline tripled. Relations with the United States snapped because of Nicaragua's aid to leftist rebels in El Salvador.

The United States began aiding the Contra rebel groups. These Contras fought the Sandinistas from safe bases within Honduras. American troops began military exercises in Honduras near the Nicaraguan border.

In 1983, the Contras went on the offensive. The Sandinistas declared martial law. Both sides fully mobilized. The Soviet Union supported the government. The United States supported the Contras.

In 1985, the U.S. Congress rejected President Reagan's request for further military aid for the Contras. The aid continued. Private citizens in the United States furnished the money for illegal arms transfers to the Contras. Funds were diverted from secret arms sales to Iran to aid the Contras. These actions in the United States were masterminded by members of the National Security Council. These acts are forbidden by U.S. law.

A peace initiative by several Latin American nations met with success. Gradually deprived of Cuban and Soviet support, the Sandinistas permitted liberalization of Nicaraguan life. Opposition newspapers resumed publication. The Catholic church began radio broadcasting. Antigovernment street demonstrations were permitted.

The Sandinista leader, Daniel Ortega, called for free elections in 1990. He lost. Violeta Barrios de Chamorro won.

A cease-fire began in 1990. It is often violated. The Sandinistas control the armed forces. Many Contra rebel bands retain their arms.

Political stability is precarious, dependent on worldwide economic recovery. Nicaragua suffers from the worldwide recession as does the rest of Central America.

The United States did not support the Sandinista regime. Aid to the government has been limited to humanitarian and economic. In 1987 and 1988, the U.S. government furnished a total of $145 million in military aid to the Contra rebel forces. How much military aid has been channeled to the Contras through illegal means by American citizens in and out of the government is unknown.

All forms of economic aid to Nicaragua in 1992 were $204.7 million. The United States projects $190.7 million in economic aid for fiscal year 1993.[7]

Nicaragua has 31,000 troops. It is said that this army is being reorganized to include both Sandinista and Contra elements. The navy is a small coast guard, and the air force has fewer than 20 combat planes. Equipment is mainly Soviet. Some of the new equipment is North Korean. Air force equipment is Soviet and American. There is a U.N. truce observer team in Nicaragua. Contra rebel strength is estimated at several thousand. The military situation is at best confused.

The support levels for the armed forces is unknown. The United States has not given military aid to the Nicaraguan government since 1979. It is suspected that the Contra rebel bands still receive military aid from private citizen groups within the United States.

NOTES

1. FMS Control and Reports Division, Comptroller, DSAA, *Foreign Military Sales, Foreign Military Construction Sales and Military Assistance Facts, as of September 30, 1991,* Washington, Data Management Division, Comptroller DSSA, 1992.

2. Ibid.

3. Ibid.

4. Ibid.

5. Ibid.

6. Ibid.

7. United States of America, *Congressional Presentation for Security Assistance Programs, Fiscal Year 1993,* Washington, GPO, Jointly Prepared by the Department of State and the Defense Security Agency, 1992.

14

South America

Basically, there are three types of South American countries. The first tier includes Argentina and Brazil which have achieved a level of development that raises them above the conditions of poverty in which the rural and working masses of other South American countries live.

A second tier consists of Chile, Colombia, Peru, and Uruguay where, in spite of the existence of internal contradictions, an encouraging, peaceful revolution has begun, and there is the hope for better levels of living. It is of interest that these are also the countries where the greatest drug traffic occurs. Because of the tremendous amounts of money pumped into the economies of Chile, Colombia, and Peru by various drug cartels, a hothouse situation is developing. Will these countries be able to develop better living conditions for their peoples in the middle of the forthcoming drug wars?

The third tier consists of Bolivia, Ecuador, Guyana, Paraguay, and Suriname where the living conditions of the masses are particularly distressing. These countries do not have the means to escape an underdeveloped state in a reasonable period of time without direct economic intervention by a foreign power, namely the United States.

In this situation, rebel insurgents can act with great flexibility. They adjust their strategies from country to country. Their revolutionary tactics become part of the particular conditions of each country. Redistribution of the land is often the issue. Urban unemployment can also be an issue, as can poor health care and lack of educational opportunity. All these are grist for the rebels' mills.

In Argentina, Brazil, and Venezuela, the left maintains an open struggle, championing the unemployed masses. All these countries have active Communist or leftist political parties that organize and wait their time. Mostly, they try to stay on the right side of the law. In these three countries, there is more trouble from the far right, which has extensive influence over the military. Here the far right includes not just the bureaucrats and large landowners but also the merchant-industrial business class.

In Chile, Colombia, and Peru, Marxist-Maoist groups oppose the governments. These leftist parties try to block government attempts to achieve any form of socioeconomic reforms. The internal politics of these countries are further complicated by the existence of far right landowners and of commercial-industrial ownership classes who also oppose all government-sponsored programs of social betterment. Both extremes try to control the state for their own ends. Generally, the right controls the state while the left forms the armed rebel opposition groups.

In Bolivia, Ecuador, Guyana, Paraguay, and Suriname, rebels take advantage of existing miserable social conditions. Reform propaganda finds favorable ground to dramatize the internal conditions and the unjust division of the nation's wealth. In these countries, armed insurrections based on the masses of the poor are most likely to topple governments.

Given these conditions, the role of the United States in South America will continue to be fourfold. Military aid will be given to all countries where the government is threatened by the left or the right. Rebels will represent the enemy; governments will represent allies. The United States will continue to press all South American governments to operate democratically with regard for human rights. The United States will also press for some redistribution of wealth by giving land to peasant sharecroppers or by increasing the wage levels of the urban working force. The South American countries will also be expected to join the United States in the war on drugs if they expect to receive full economic assistance and military aid. When a South American country adopts all four of the above stances, it will be a friend of the United States and receive a high level of American aid, along with personnel of the Drug Enforcement Agency, the Central Intelligence Agency, and the military advisor and assistance group. Their presence announces that the United States is a guarantor to the continued existence of the government of that South American country.

A short list of these South American countries includes Colombia, Bolivia, Peru, Ecuador, and Venezuela; the most favored five.

South America is an entire continent. It stretches from Colombia in the north to Argentina in the south. The two main languages are Spanish and Portuguese (spoken in Brazil). This continent is a good part of the American economic empire that includes all of North America, Central America, and the Caribbean as well. Population and income figures are given in Figure 14.1.

As a region, South America is one of the wealthier parts of the Third World. It should be a fitting place for American capital and know-how to develop a world superpower in the next twenty years. The developed nations, Canada and the United States, should be able to provide the needed economic stimulus to all the Caribbean and Central and South America to produce one of the great trading blocks in what President Bush of the United

Figure 14.1
South America, Total Population and per Capita Income (In U.S. Dollars)

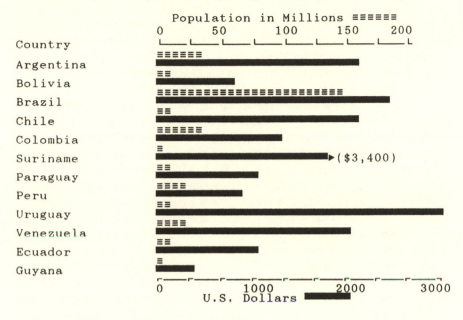

Note: U.S. 1991 per capita income was $21,800.

States called the "New World Order." The opportunity for North and South America to participate as an economic bloc in the new global economy is without parallel in the history of the Western Hemisphere.

To understand the possible problems of the next twenty years, we need to examine the problems of each of the South American countries as they exist today.

ARGENTINA

Argentina is about the size of the United States east of the Mississippi. Neighbors are Chile, Bolivia, Paraguay, Brazil, and Uruguay; and the country lies along the Atlantic Ocean. The 33 million people have a per capita average annual income of $2,134. Spain granted independence in 1816. Government is a constitutional republic. There are several political parties. Universal adult voting is practiced.

The economy depends on the export of foodstuffs. There is an iron and steel industry large enough for domestic needs. The United States buys 20 to 25 percent of Argentina's exports. Argentina suffers from an inflation rate of more than 100 percent a year. The worldwide recession of the 1980s hurt the economy.

The British invested heavily in Argentina in the 1800s. Most of modern Argentine agriculture and industry is built on the British model. The Conservative party ruled until 1916. The Radical party won the election in 1916.

The worldwide depression in 1929 changed the political climate. The Fascist movement found many followers in the 1930s. In 1943, the Fascists overthrew the constitutional government. Colonel Juan Domingo Peron became president. His power base was the General Confederation of Labor.

Peron was reelected president in 1952. Overthrown by the military in 1955, he fled to Spain. Massive social unrest and political street fighting caused by Peron's followers marked Argentine politics from 1955 to 1972.

Peron won the free elections in 1973. His wife, Isabel de Peron, became vice president. Terrorism grew during this period. Peron frequently ruled by martial law. Thousands went to jail without trial. Many died. Some disappeared.

Peron died in 1974. His wife became president. Economic decline led to the military takeover of 1976. The armed forces governed the country until 1983.

The military government lost political credibility as a result of the Falklands' War with the British in 1982. Argentine military forces performed badly. Opposition grew. Riots multiplied. The military promised free elections.

Raul Alfonsin of the Radical Civic Union party won the presidential election in 1983. In 1987 the Peronists ended the Radical Civic Unions parliamentary majority. In 1989 Carlos Menem won the presidential elections. He had the full backing of the military.

The United States usually has good relations with Argentina. During the 1970s, the United States objected to serious human rights violations by the Argentine military government. The United States supported Britain in the Falklands' War.

From 1950 to 1991 the United States sold $229.8 million in military equipment and construction to Argentina.[1] The United States ended economic assistance to Argentina in 1971. Military aid, resumed in 1989, is shown in Table 14.1.

Argentina has 85,000 in her armed forces. Some 20,000 are draftees. There are another 400,000 in various reserve formations. The navy consists of one carrier task force and several submarines. The air force has about 180 combat planes. There are some 6,000 marines. There are some 30,000 internal security police. Equipment is a mixture of British, French, American, and Argentine manufacture.

Argentina has observer units with U.N. peace-keeping forces in Angola, Central America, Lebanon, and Kuwait.

Argentina supports her armed forces as shown in Figure 14.2 (p. 176). Preliminary figures for most recent years show a further decline in defense level toward the 2 percent of GNP. During the same period, the GNP increased by 26 percent. The loss of the Falklands' War in 1982 did not lead to a large increase in military funding. The present Argentine government is dependent on military support.

Table 14.1
U.S. Aid to Argentina (In U.S. Dollars)

	1989	1991	1992	1993
Military Assistance		1,000,000	1,000,000	1,000,000
International Military Education	125,000	150,000	200,000	200,000
Food for Peace				913,000
Totals	125,000	1,150,000	1,200,000	2,113,000

Source: United States of America, *Congressional Presentation for Security Assistance Programs, Fiscal Years 1989–1993,* Washington, D.C.: GPO, 1989–1993.

Table 14.2
U.S. Aid to Bolivia (In U.S. Dollars)

	1989	1990	1991	1992	1993
Military Financing	5,000,000	39,200,000	35,000,000	40,000,000	40,000,000
International Military Education	400,000	500,000	900,000	900,000	900,000
Internal Narcotics Control		7,800,000			
Economic Support Fund	11,800,000	33,400,000	76,800,000	25,000,000	
Development Assistance	24,600,000	24,200,000	23,800,000	22,500,000	25,600,000
Food for Peace	33,300,000	33,800,000	36,700,000	33,300,000	31,930,000
Peace Corps			1,238,000	1,262,000	1,697,000
International Narcotics Control	10,000,000	15,700,000	15,700,000	15,700,000	17,000,000
Totals	85,100,000	154,600,000	190,138,000	138,672,000	117,126,000

Source: Figures for 1989–1992, U.S. Department of State, *Fact Sheet: U.S. Economic, Military and Counter-Narcotics Program Assistance*, U.S. Department of State Dispatch, March 2, 1992, p. 167; figures for 1993, United States of America, *Congressional Presentation for Security Assistance Programs*, 1993, Washington, D.C.: GPO, 1993.

government is a constitutional federal republic. Portugal granted independence in 1822. There are many political parties, including two different Communist parties.

Brazil's economy is based on the export of manufactured goods. Brazil has a large and rapidly expanding arms industry. The United States buys 25 to 30 percent of Brazil's exports. Brazil maintains a strong independent foreign policy.

On independence, Brazil became an empire. Dom Pedro I was the first emperor until his death in 1831. His son, Dom Pedro II, ruled until his death in 1889. Brazil then became a republic.

Until 1930, Brazilian politics were democratic in nature. The military overthrew the constitutional government in 1930. Getulio Vargas became the military dictator. He lasted until 1945. After initial hesitation, Vargas joined the American side in World War II.

From 1945 to 1961, a civilian government functioned normally. Radical political groups grew in power. After serious rioting, the army moved in 1964. Marshal Humberto Castello Branco became president. Other generals succeeded him.

The army permitted some liberalization in politics during the 1960s and 1970s. Brazil became the leading industrial nation in Latin America. Democratic elections were held in 1985. Normal constitutional government began again.

There is a large and growing poverty-stricken class in Brazil. Inflation and poverty led to severe economic problems in the late 1980s. Brazil's foreign debt is one of the largest in the world. There is no serious rebel insurrectionist threat in Brazil at present.

Brazil and the United States have correct diplomatic relations. Although the United States is Brazil's most important trading partner, Brazil is not a U.S. client state. Between 1950 and 1991 the United States sold Brazil $606.6 million in military equipment and construction.[3] Other than a few officers trained in some years, Brazil jealously guards her military independence from U.S. influence.

Brazil maintains some 300,000 in her armed forces. Nearly 130,000 are draftees. Nearly 2 million reservists are said to exist. The navy has a carrier task force and many other warships. The air force has about 325 combat planes. Military equipment is a mixture of French, American, and Brazilian. There are nearly 250,000 men in her public security forces, which have important political influence.

Brazil spends on her armed forces an average of 7.5 percent of GNP. The GNP grew by 55 percent between 1979 and 1991.

CHILE

Chile, about twice the size of California, borders Argentina, Bolivia, and Peru and lies on the Pacific Ocean. The 13 million people have a per capita average annual income of $2,130. Chile has a republican form of government. There are ten registered political parties. All forms of Marxism are prohibited.

Chile's economy is based on copper, iron ore, and nitrate exports. The United States buys 20 to 25 percent of Chile's exports. The recession of the late 1980s brought economic chaos to Chile.

Bernardo O'Higgins led Chile to independence from Spain in 1818. Society did not change much in the 1880s. The large landowners, supported by the Roman Catholic church, dominated the country. Opposition gradually increased. The civil war of 1891 saw the power of the landowners somewhat curbed.

Chile expanded her territory by a series of wars that brought the military to the prominent position it still enjoys. The Mapuche Indians in the south were crushed by 1881. The 1879–1883 War of the Pacific gave Chile control of the rich nitrate areas in the north which had been in Bolivia.

The early 1900s saw a further rise in the importance of the military. Marxism-Leninism began to make headway in the 1920s. A military takeover resulted. General Carlos Ibanez ruled by military decree from 1924 to 1932.

The Great Depression saw a rapid fall in the price of nitrates. Economic chaos resulted. Troops were often used in the streets. Many died. This distress saw the rise of the Radical party. From 1932 to 1964 Chile was ruled by a series of coalitions between the Conservatives and the Radicals. Marxist-Leninist groups were suppressed by the army.

In 1964, Eduardo Frei of the Christian Democrat party became president. By 1967 Frei was encouraging Marxist-Leninist groups. Little land reform was started.

In 1970, the Marxist-Leninist Salvador Allende won the presidential elections. The government began taking over industries, banks, and mining operations. Peasants were forced onto collective farms. By 1973, Chile was in an economic depression. The economy was in a state of collapse.

The military seized power in 1973. Allende died, supposedly a suicide. The military government began to exterminate Marxist-Leninists. Repressive measures continued throughout the 1980s. The military promised elections as soon as the Marxist-Leninist threat was crushed.

In 1980, General Augusto Pinochet lost the elections. The military permitted a peaceful change to an elected constitutional government. In 1989, Patricio Aylwin Azocar won the presidential elections. The military remains a political force to be reckoned with. The least sign of the government turning left will bring a military takeover.

The United States has a problem with Chile. The Chilean government has yet to restore full human rights to all segments of the population. Chile does not fully help the United States in the war on drugs. The United States watches the Chilean military who, in turn, watch the Chilean government.

From 1950 to 1991 the United States sold Chile $180 million in military equipment and construction.[4] Chile is still allowed to buy arms and munitions in the United States. In recent years American military aid to Chile has consisted in training a few army officers. No further military aid is contemplated for 1993.

Chile maintains nearly 100,000 men in her armed forces. Almost 35,000 are draftees. The navy consists of old American and British surplus warships, and the air force has about 100 combat planes. Military equipment is a mixture of British, French, and American. Chile has 30,000 security police charged with keeping law and order and running down dissidents.

Chile participates in U.N. peace-keeping efforts along the India-Pakistan border, in Lebanon, and in Kuwait. There are two very small Marxist rebel groups. No serious rebel opposition exists at the present time. Support for the military is 3 to 4 percent of GNP. From 1979 to 1991 GNP increased by 74 percent.

COLOMBIA

Colombia is about the same size as Texas, Oklahoma, and Arkansas. With Panama, Venezuela, Brazil, Peru, and Ecuador for neighbors, Colombia lies along the Caribbean and Pacific coasts. The 34 million people have a per capita average annual income of $1,300. The government is a constitutional republic. There are three major political parties. All adults can vote.

Colombia's economy is based on coffee and illegal drugs. The United States buys over 50 percent of Columbia's legal exports. Most of the cocaine produced in Colombia also finds its way into the United States.

Colombia won independence from Spain in 1813. Simon Bolivar was the first president. At that time, Colombia led the Republic of Greater Colombia which also included Panama, Venezuela, and Ecuador. Venezuela and Ecuador gained independence in 1830. Panama, with U.S. assistance, revolted in 1903.

There have been only two political groupings in Colombian history, the Conservatives and the Liberals. They alternate power every few years. The military is less powerful in Colombia than in many other South American nations. The military have taken power only three times, in 1830, 1854, and 1953.

Despite this, there were two very bloody civil wars. From 1899 to 1902, the War of the Thousand Days saw more than 100,000 die. In the 1940s and 1950s, during the first stage of the Violence, some 300,000 to 400,000 died.

General Gustavo Rojas Pinilla took power in 1953. He ended the Violence for a time. He was overthrown in 1957 by both the Liberal and Conservatives groups. Laureano Gomez became president. A national front government began. Leftist political groups have few followers.

The Violence returned in the 1970s with the growing influence of the

Medellin-based drug smuggling cartel. Attempts at land reform did not succeed. The vast amounts of money available to the drug lords made corruption and bribery commonplace in the government and the military. Those who do not accept bribes are silenced by fear or with a gun.

Sparked by massive American military aid, the government began a crackdown on the Medellin drug cartel in 1989. This led to a series of assassinations of judges, local officials, military officers, and private citizens. Even a minister of justice resigned out of fear for the safety of her children.

In 1990, two presidential candidates were slain. Cesar Gaviria Trujillo was elected president. The war on drugs goes on. Recently, police headquarters in Medellin was blown up by the drug lords. The very existence of the civil authority is in question in Colombia.

U.S. drug enforcement agents, operatives of the Central Intelligence Agency, and military advisory and assistance groups are all operating with the Colombian authorities against the drug lords. So far these efforts are not successful.

The United States sold Colombia $245.9 million in military equipment and sales from 1950 to 1991.[5] Colombia cooperates with the United States in the war on drugs. The U.S. aid to Colombia is shown in Table 14.3.

Colombia has 140,000 men under arms. Some 45,000 are draftees. In addition, 120,000 trained reserves are claimed. The navy is in the small warship class. Most of the ships were purchased from the U.S. mothball fleet. The air force has some 70 combat aircraft. Colombia has 85,000 men in her internal police force, a powerful political factor. Colombia participates in the U.N. peace-keeping operations in Egypt and in Nicaragua.

There are several Maoist-Marxist rebel groups. They may number 7,000 men. The serious challenge to the government is the illegal cocaine drug cartel based in the city of Medellin.

The Medellin cartel is the new economic force in Colombia. Since 1981, it has virtually controlled the economy. All the U.S. money and all Colombia's soldiers are unable to defeat the drug cartel.

Colombia spends only about 2 percent of GNP on her military forces. From 1979 to 1991, GNP rose by 55 percent. Without continued massive U.S. military aid, the Medellin cartel could easily seize control of the Colombian government.

SURINAME

Suriname, about the size of Georgia, has Brazil, French Guiana, and Guyana for neighbors and lies on the Atlantic Ocean. The 400,000 people have a per capita average annual income of $3,400. The government is evolving—midway between a military dictatorship and a constitutional republic. The Dutch granted independence in 1975.

Table 14.3
U.S. Aid to Colombia (In U.S. Dollars)

	1989	1990	1991	1992	1993
Military Financing	7,100,000	71,700,000	27,100,000	58,000,000	58,000,000
International Military Education	1,000,000	1,500,000	2,500,000	2,300,000	2,200,000
Internal Narcotics Control	65,000,000	20,000,000			22,000,000
Excess Defense Spending			2,400,000		
Economic Support Fund	2,900,000	2,100,000	50,000,000	50,000,000	
Development Assistance		7,500,000	4,100,000	3,800,000	
Food for Peace		200,000			
International Narcotics Interdiction	9,400,000	18,900,000	18,500,000	18,300,000	82,200,000
Drug Prevention and Education		200,000	300,000	300,000	
International Narcotics Program Development	600,000	900,000	1,200,000	1,400,000	
Totals	86,000,000	123,000,000	106,100,000	134,100,000	144,600,000

Source: Figures for 1989–1992, U.S. Department of State, Fact Sheet: U.S. Economic, Military and Counter-Narcotics Program Assistance, U.S. Department of State Dispatch, March 2, 1992, p. 167; figures for 1993, United States of America, Congressional Presentation for Security Assistance Programs, 1993, Washington, D.C.: GPO, 1993.

The economy is based on bauxite, rice, and sugar exports. The economy was hurt by the worldwide economic recession of the late 1980s. The United States buys 30 to 40 percent of Suriname's exports. The Dutch account for most of the rest.

The military overthrew the constitutional government in 1980. Sergeant Desire Bouterse assumed power by 1982. A number of opposition leaders were killed.

In 1988, military rule ended. Ramsewak Shankar became president. In 1990, Bouterse led another military takeover. Military rule ended because of the Maroon insurgency.

The Maroons are a people, descended from runaway slaves, who live deep in the interior. Ronnie Brunswijk brought the Maroons together with other dissident elements in 1987. Although the army practiced genocidal warfare on the Maroons, they were unable to suppress the rebellion.

Political pressure from the Dutch and Americans was brought to bear on the military government. A peace agreement between the military government and the Maroons began in 1991. At present there is a transitional government in power. The future role of the military is being severely limited. Universal suffrage is the law. In 1992, a treaty of cooperation was signed with the Dutch.

The United States maintains correct but frosty diplomatic relations with Suriname. Continuing human rights abuses make good relations something for the future. No economic or military aid arrives from the United States.

Suriname has 2,500 men in the armed forces. The navy is a small coast guard and river patrol service, and the air force has fewer than five combat planes. Brazil provides some military assistance. Most equipment is made in Brazil. Brazil provides military aid and maintains a training unit in Suriname.

Information concerning military expenditures in unavailable.

PARAGUAY

Paraguay, a landlocked country about the size of California, has boundaries with Argentina, Brazil, and Bolivia. The 5 million people have a per capita average annual income of $1,110. The government is a constitutional republic with a very strong head of state. All adults can vote. There are four major political parties. Spain granted independence in 1821.

The economy is based on the export of food products. The United States buys less than 5 percent of Paraguay's exports. The major trading partners are Brazil, Argentina, and the European Economic Community.

The Lopez family dominated Paraguay from 1814 to 1862. The War of the Triple Alliance, 1864–1870, saw Paraguay lose half her population to Argentina, Uruguay, and Brazil. Brazilian troops occupied Paraguay until 1874.

From 1880 to 1904, the Colorado Political party governed the country.

The Liberal party stayed in power from 1904 to 1940. Politics was corrupt. Paraguay built a government based on military rule and isolation from all foreign influences.

General Alfred Stroessner held power from 1954 to 1989. He was elected president seven consecutive times. Gradually the country changed. Opposition political parties came into being. Corruption in the government declined. Free municipal elections were held. A new constitution arrived in 1967.

General Andre Rodriguez overthrew Stroessner in 1989. He was elected president in 1989. Paraguay has no important rebel movement.

The United States maintains correct relations with Paraguay. America sold Paraguay only $1 million in military equipment and construction between 1950 and 1991.[6] In 1989, the United States began training a few Paraguay Army officers each year. The Peace Corps is active in Paraguay.

Paraguay maintains 18,000 men in the armed forces. Some 11,000 are draftees. Paraguay claims 50,000 trained reserves. The navy is a river patrol, and the air force has perhaps ten combat planes. There are 8,000 men in the special police force, an important power in national politics. Most military equipment is made in Brazil.

Paraguay spends about 1.5 percent of GNP on her military. From 1979 to 1991, GNP increased by 59 percent.

PERU

Peru, three times the size of California, borders Chile, Bolivia, Brazil, Colombia, and Ecuador and lies on the Pacific Ocean. The 22 million people have a per capita average annual income of $898. Her government is a constitutional republic. There are three major political parties. All adults can vote.

Peru's economy is based on fruits and illegal drug exports. The United States buys 35 to 40 percent of Peru's legal exports. Undoubtedly a majority of Peru's cocaine exports also wind up in the United States. Peru is a member of the United States–led South American coalition war on drugs.

Jose de San Martin proclaimed independence from Spain in 1821. Peru has clashed with her neighbors several times since independence. The War of the Pacific, 1879–1883, saw Chile defeat Peru and Bolivia. Important nitrate deposits passed to Chile. In 1941, the border dispute with Bolivia saw the United States intervene to reestablish peace. As late as 1981, there was shooting along this border.

The military rule in Peru. Civil government is often overthrown by the military. No civil government can last without the military's support. From 1968 to 1980, a series of generals ran the country. In 1985 Peru held free elections for the first time in 40 years. The military continue to watch the government closely.

Peru has a long history of dissident rebel groups. Now there is the war on drugs. The drug lords form a large and powerful rebel group. There is also a Marxist-Maoist rebel group known as the Shining Path. Despite the recent capture of the Shining Path's leader, Abimael Guzman, this rebel movement continues to terrorize the capital, Lima. Many of the remote Andean provinces are under the control of the drug lords, the Shining Path, or a combination of the two. In some areas, there is a three-way civil war as the government forces fight both the drug lords and the Shining Path. The two rebel groups also often fight each other. Peru is often on the brink of complete chaos. Guzman's capture by police only increased the level of country-wide acts of violence by the Shining Path. Bombings in Lima are commonplace.

Peru suffers from the worldwide recession that began in the late 1980s. In 1989, the annual inflation rate was 2,775 percent. In more recent years, the economy verges on chaos.

U.S. relations with Peru have been strained over the last 25 years. Peru emphasizes its national sovereignty and protection of its national resources in its foreign policy. American concerns over the war on drugs have brought renewed interest in Peru. Tension is on the rise between the two countries.

The United States has three major concerns about Peru: (1) curbing drug production and smuggling, (2) combatting the Marxist-Maoist Shining Path rebels, and (3) promoting human rights. Most human rights violations stem from the Shining Path's terrorist tactics and the government's repressive counterinsurgency methods. The United States plans to increase its role in combating the Shining Path. Although American plans include some human-rights instruction, the main American effort will be against narcotics trafficking.

At present, Drug Enforcement Agency personnel, Central Intelligence Agency operatives, and military advisory and assistance groups all operate in Peru. There are also private-enterprise military units contracted by the U.S. Department of Defense to fight in the war on drugs. With little additional effort, Peru can become a client state of the United States much like several other Central American republics.

The current Peruvian president, Alberto Fujimori, has supervised free elections. Fujimori calls the war on drugs futile. The military support Fujimori for the present.

Between 1950 and 1991, the United States sold Peru $197.3 million in military equipment and construction.[7] As a partner of the United States in the war on drugs, Peru has been favored with American aid as shown in Table 14.4.

Peru maintains 110,000 men in her military forces. Some 75,000 are draftees. The navy is in the medium warship class. There are two cruiser battle groups, and the ships are all second-hand purchases from various nations. The air force has about 120 combat planes. There are some 75,000 men in her internal security forces, a potent political force.

Table 14.4
U.S. Aid to Peru (In U.S. Dollars)

	1989	1990	1991	1992	1993
Military Financing	2,500,000	1,000,000	24,000,000	39,000,000	34,000,000
International Military Education	500,000	500,000	500,000	900,000	740,000
Economic Support Fund	2,000,000	3,300,000	59,100,000	100,000,000	
Development Assistance	17,700,000	16,000,000	9,700,000	15,700,000	26,500,000
Food for Peace	30,000,000	50,800,000	88,400,000	72,000,000	72,777,000
International Narcotics Control					19,000,000
International Narcotics Interdiction	7,700,000	6,900,000	13,600,000	13,600,000	
Crop Production Control	2,000,000	2,200,000	4,200,000	4,300,000	
Drug Prevention and Education	100,000	100,000	200,000	100,000	
International Narcotics Program Development	800,000	800,000	1,000,000	1,000,000	
Totals	63,300,000	81,600,000	200,700,000	246,600,000	163,017,000

Source: Figures for 1989–1992, U.S. Department of State, *Fact Sheet: U.S. Economic, Military and Counter-Narcotics Program Assistance, U.S. Department of State Dispatch*, March 2, 1992, p. 167; figures for 1993, United States of America, *Congressional Presentation for Security Assistance Programs, 1993*, Washington, D.C.: GPO, 1993.

The Shining Path may have 5,000 armed rebels. Current support levels for the military are not available. In past years, Peru has spent about 4 percent of GNP on her defense forces. The civil-military balance in Peru is always precarious. The need for fighting both the war on drugs and the Shining Path Marxist-Maoist revolutionaries at the same time is placing a severe strain on the entire country. Nothing is operating on a peacetime standing.

URUGUAY

Uruguay, about the size of Oklahoma, borders Brazil and Argentina and lies on the Atlantic Ocean. The population of 3 million has a per capita average annual income of $2,970. There is a republican form of government. All adults can vote. There are three major political parties.

Uruguay's economy is based on the export of food products. The United States buys 15 to 20 percent of Uruguay's exports. Argentina and Brazil buy 30 to 40 percent.

Jose Gervasio Artigas led the war of independence against Spain in 1811. Uruguay was part of Brazil from 1821 to 1825. Argentine troops helped to defeat the Brazilians in the 1825–1826 revolt. Uruguay became independent in 1828. A constitution emerged in 1830.

Civil war between the Colorado and the Blanco political parties marked most of the period from 1830 to 1865. The Colorado party controlled the government from 1865 to 1958.

Battle y Ordonez was president from 1903 to 1907 and from 1911 to 1915. He began widespread social reforms that continue today.

In 1959, the Blanco party returned to power. This began another political battle much like the one of the early 1800s. In 1973, the military established its own government. In 1977, the armed forces announced a timetable for a return to the republican government. The military maintained tight control through 1983.

Jose Maria Sanguinetti won the presidential elections of 1984. By 1989, Uruguay had a civilian government. The Blanco party won the 1989 elections. Luis Alberto Lacalle became president.

Uruguay's economy suffers from the worldwide recession of the late 1980s. Her foreign debt was recently refinanced. There are no noteworthy rebel movements in Uruguay.

The United States maintains friendly relations with Uruguay. The United States supplied most of Uruguay's military equipment until the military takeover in 1973. The 1990 inauguration of President Lacalle began a gradual return of American military aid, as shown in Table 14.5.

Uruguay maintains 25,000 men in her armed forces. The navy is in the small warship class, and the ships are second-hand purchases from the United States. The air force has fewer than 40 combat planes. Military equipment is mostly American made. There are 2,500 men in various inter-

Table 14.5
U.S. Aid to Uruguay (In U.S. Dollars)

	1992	1993
Military Financing	1,000,000	500,000
International Military Education	325,000	330,000
Peace Corps	647,000	1,012,000
Totals	1,972,000	1,842,000

Source: United States of America, Congressional Presentation for Security Assistance Programs, Fiscal Years 1992 and 1993, Washington, D.C.: GPO, 1992–1993.

nal police units. Uruguay participates in U.N. peace-keeping ventures in Egypt, along the India-Pakistan border, and in Kuwait.

Uruguay usually spends 2 to 3 percent of GNP on her military forces. Between 1979 and 1991, Uruguay's GNP increased by 38 percent.

VENEZUELA

Venezuela is about twice the size of California. Neighbors are Brazil, Guyana, and Colombia, and the coast stretches along the Atlantic Ocean and the Caribbean Sea. The government is a federal republic. The 20 million people have a per capita average annual income of $2,150. All adults can vote. There are nine political parties.

Venezuela's economy rests on oil and coffee exports. There is a growing drug-smuggling problem. Much cocaine leaves Venezuela for markets in the United States. The United States is Venezuela's most important trading partner. Venezuela is a member of the American-led South American nations coalition fighting the war on drugs.

Simon Bolivar led Venezuela to independence from Spain in 1821. Venezuela was a part of Gran Colombia until 1830. The 1800s and the 1900s in Venezuelan history are marked with frequent periods of political instability, military rule, and rebel movements.

Romulo Betancourt was the first democratically elected president to complete his term of office from 1959 to 1964. Betancourt survived several attempted military takeovers, Marxist-Leninist dissidents supported by Cuba, and civilian political opponents. He modernized the state and began needed land reforms.

Raul Leoni, president from 1964 to 1969, continued Betancourt's efforts. Things were peaceful and progressive enough until the glut in the world oil market brought economic distress in the 1980s. President Jaime Lusinchi took office in 1984. He was faced with declining oil revenues and a rising national debt. He launched several austerity measures. Charges of corruption in the government were everywhere.

Carlos Andres Perez won the presidential elections in 1988. His austerity actions in early 1989 included raising the price of gasoline and transportation to breakeven levels.

The urban population rose in revolt. The military crushed the revolt in the streets after heavy and often hand-to-hand fighting. At least 500 died in Caracas alone. A stunned population awaited another chance.

In February 1992, rebel military paratroopers attacked the presidential place in Caracas. Loyal forces crushed the rebels. Hundreds died. In November 1992, rebel military forces tried again to overthrow Perez. The presidential palace was bombed. Radio stations were seized. Again loyal troops crushed the rebels. Hundreds died.

The political situation in Venezuela is mixed. The economic crisis continues. Although discontent with the Perez government is widespread, a well-organized Marxist-Maoist revolutionary movement does not exist.

The United States maintains friendly relations with Venezuela. From 1950 to 1991, the United States sold Venezuela $935.9 million in military equipment and construction.[8] Venezuela receives aid as a member of the American-led South American nations in the war on drugs, as shown in Table 14.6.

Continued destabilization of Venezuela's government will see further decline in American aid. Currently the Central Intelligence Agency, the Drug Enforcement Agency, the military advisory and assistance group, and several Department of Defense civilian contractors all operate in Venezuela in the war on drugs.

Venezuela maintains 80,000 men under arms. Some 20,000 are draftees. Another 25,000 are in the national guard. The regular army has only about 14,000 troops. The navy is in the small warship class, and the air force has about 110 combat planes. Venezuela participates in U.N. peace-keeping forces in Nicaragua and Kuwait.

From 1979 to 1992, Venezuela used an average of 1 percent of GNP in support of her military. Preliminary estimates show a rapid rise in 1993 to between 2 and 3 percent of GNP. The GNP rose by 35 percent during this period.

ECUADOR

Ecuador, about the size of Colorado, lies on the Pacific Ocean with Peru and Colombia for neighbors. The 10.75 million people have a per capita average annual income of $1,040. There is a republican form of government. All adults between 18 and 65 can vote. There are at least fifteen large political parties.

Table 14.6
U.S. Aid to Venezuela (In U.S. Dollars)

	1989	1990	1991	1992	1993
International Military Education	100,000	100,000	400,000	200,000	175,000
International Narcotics Interdiction	600,000	800,000	800,000	1,700,000	1,500,000
Drug Prevention and Education				100,000	
International Narcotics Program Development	100,000	200,000	200,000	300,000	
Totals	800,000	1,100,000	1,400,000	2,300,000	1,675,000

Source: Figures for 1989–1992, U.S. Department of State, *Fact Sheet: U.S. Economic, Military and Counter-Narcotics Program Assistance,* U.S. Department of State Dispatch, March 2, 1992, p. 167; figures for 1993, United States of America, *Congressional Presentation for Security Assistance Programs,* 1993, Washington, D.C.: GPO, 1993.

Ecuador's economy is based on oil and shrimp exports. The country suffers from the long recession of the late 1980s. Ecuador is a member of the American-led South American countries war on drugs.

Simon Bolivar led Ecuador to independence from Spain in 1821. From 1822 to 1830, Ecuador was a part of Gran Colombia. From 1830 to 1948, Ecuador endured 62 successive military-backed governments.

The election of Galo Palza Lasso as president in 1948 brought Ecuador's first political stability since independence. This civil government lasted until 1968. Dr. Velasco Ibarra won the elections in 1968. In 1970 he suspended the constitution. In 1972 the military overthrew Ibarra. General Rodriguez Lara became head of state. In 1976 Admiral Alfredo Poveda replaced Lara.

In 1979, free elections saw Jaimer Roldas become president. He died in a plane crash in 1981. Despite the increase in drug smuggling operations and the earthquake of 1987, the civil government is still in power.

Rodrigo Borja became president in 1988. He began a program of land reform and respect for human rights. There is a longstanding border dispute with Peru that last saw shooting in 1981. Trouble between the United States and Ecuador last surfaced in 1981 over the seizure of U.S. tuna boats said to be fishing in Ecuadoran waters.

The United States maintains friendly relations with Ecuador. From 1950 to 1991, the United States sold Ecuador $157.8 million in military equipment and construction.[9] As a member of the American-led coalition in the war on drugs, Ecuador receives massive U.S. aid, as shown in Table 14.7.

Ecuador has 60,000 men in her armed forces and claims a trained reserve of 100,000. The navy is in the small warship class, and the air force has about 80 combat planes. Equipment is a mixture of French and American. Ecuador supports U.N. peace-keeping efforts in Central America.

Ecuador spent 4 percent of GNP on her military in 1979. She spent 2 percent in 1989. Most recent estimates indicate little change. Her GNP increased by 53 percent during this period.

GUYANA

Guyana, about the size of Idaho, lies on the Atlantic Ocean, with Suriname, Venezuela, and Brazil as neighbors. The 750,000 people have a per capita average annual income of $380. Guyana is the poorest country in South America.

Guyana's economy is based on sugar and rice exports. The worldwide economic recession of the late 1980s caused economic difficulties. The United States buys 25 to 30 percent of Guyana's exports. Britain accounts for another 50 percent.

Guyana is a republic within the British Commonwealth of Nations. Britain granted independence in 1970. There are five major political parties.

Table 14.7
U.S. Aid to Ecuador (In U.S. Dollars)

	1989	1990	1991	1992	1993
Military Financing	4,000,000	500,000	2,000,000	5,000,000	5,000,000
International Military Education	700,000	700,000	800,000	800,000	800,000
Internal Narcotics Control	3,000,000				
Economic Support Fund	9,000,000				
Development Assistance	17,200,000	16,300,000	15,600,000	15,000,000	14,280,000
Food for Peace	700,000	3,200,000	10,500,000		
Peace Corps					2,706,000
International Narcotics Interdiction	800,000	1,200,000	1,300,000	2,600,000	2,000,000
Crop Production Control				100,000	
International Narcotics Program Development	200,000	200,000	200,000	300,000	
Totals	35,600,000	22,100,000	30,400,000	23,800,000	24,786,000

Source: Figures for 1989–1992, U.S. Department of State, *Fact Sheet: U.S. Economic, Military and Counter-Narcotics Program Assistance,* U.S. Department of State Dispatch, March 2, 1992, p. 167; figures for 1993, United States of America, *Congressional Presentation for Security Assistance Programs,* 1993, Washington, D.C.: GPO, 1993.

Forbes Burnham ruled Guyana until his death in 1985. Desmond Hoyte followed him. State socialism was the driving political force until 1990. The economy is a shambles. Hoyte began to encourage private business. He wanted to sell the state-owned telephone, electricity, and airlines, among others. He tried to end Guyana's longstanding election frauds. His successor (1992), Dr. Cheddi Jagan, continues these policies.

The United States maintains correct diplomatic relations with Guyana. The long history of election fraud and one-party rule is not in keeping with American democratic practices. Guyana has received only enough U.S. military aid to train a few army officers in most years. She has benefited from the Food for Peace and Economic Development Assistance programs from time to time.

There are border disputes with both Venezuela and Suriname. At present, neither is a serious threat.

The Guyana defense force has 2,000 men. There is a people's militia of another 2,000. The navy has two patrol boats, and the air force has no combat planes. There are no serious rebel organizations.

Guyana spends from 2 to 3 percent of GNP on the military. From 1979 to 1991, GNP fell by 53 percent.

NOTES

1. FMS Control and Reports Division, Comptroller, DSAA, *Foreign Military Sales, Foreign Military Construction Sales and Military Assistance Facts, as of September 30, 1991,* Washington, Data Management Division, Comptroller DSSA, 1992.
2. Ibid.
3. Ibid.
4. Ibid.
5. Ibid.
6. Ibid.
7. Ibid.
8. Ibid.
9. Ibid.

15

The Pacific Area

Third World nations in the Pacific area are all tiny specks on the map. None appear to be of any great significance to the rest of the world. These are nations that before 1945 were all islands belonging to various imperialist powers such as Britain, the United States, Australia, New Zealand, and Japan. Some of these new nations do not have military forces. Names like Fiji, Papua, Tonga, and Samoa evoke visions of tropical paradises. Travel agencies would have us flock to these islands for sun-kissed, unspoiled beaches. Names like New Guinea, Nauru, the Solomon Islands, Kiribati, Tuvalu, and Vanuatu evoke World War II memories to the older generations.

Yet these island nations have been of importance twice in the present century. They were essential supply bases and fortresses as long as ships needed to stop for supplies on their crossings of the Pacific Ocean. In World War II, these islands were either supply bases or killing grounds. Most atomic experiments are carried out on one island or another in the Pacific. Atomic tests are the greatest single worry among the Pacific area independent Third World nations.

After World War II, these islands gradually acquired their independence. One by one, most have become members of the United Nations.

This is the area of the Third World to which the United States gives the least attention. Support for these new members comes from other countries. Population and income figures are given in Figure 15.1 (p. 196).

FIJI

Fiji is a series of islands in the South Pacific located 1,700 miles northeast of Sydney, Australia; 1,100 miles north of Auckland, New Zealand; and 2,800 miles southeast of Hawaii. The nearest neighbors are Tonga to the east, Vanuatu to the west, and French-held Wallis and Funtuna islands to

Figure 15.1
Pacific Area, Total Population and per Capita Income (In U.S. Dollars)

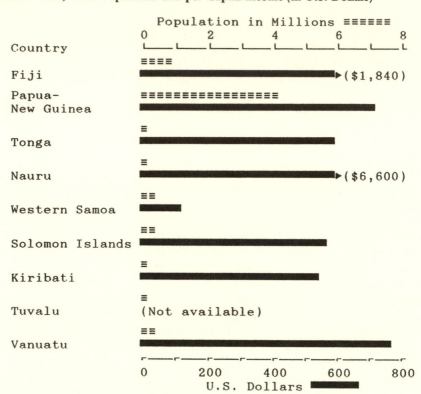

Note: U.S. 1990 per capita income was $21,800.

the north. The total land area is smaller than Vermont, and the 775,000 people have a per capita average annual income of $1,840.

Fiji is an independent republic within the British Commonwealth of Nations. Her government is a parliamentary democracy. Britain granted independence in 1970. Fijian political history is marred with racial hatred.

Fiji's economy is based on sugar exports and tourism. Members of the European Economic Community buy over 90 percent of Fiji's exports.

Fiji became a part of the British Empire in 1874. British rule was marked by the spread of plantation agriculture and the introduction of Indian indentured laborers. This marked the beginning of the current racial trouble. Tension remains high between native Fijians and Indians. During British rule, the Indian minority came to dominate the sugar industry.

The British gave Fiji a constitutional government in 1966. At independence, Ratu Kamisire Mara, an Indian, became prime minister. Constant racial tension led to a 1987 electorial victory for Timoci Bavadra. He was the first native Fijian to hold high office. He appointed a majority of Indian ministers.

The military overthrew Bavarda one month later. Bavadra and Mara agreed to form a coalition government. The military rebelled again. General Stivena Rabuka took power. He resigned in late 1987. He appointed Penala Ganilau, the former British governor general, as president. Rabuka still controls the police, the army, and the government.

Fiji maintains close ties with Britain, Australia, and New Zealand. Relations with the United States are normal since 1988. In 1993, the United States furnished only enough military aid to train six army officers. Fiji receives some economic aid from the United States. The Peace Corps operates in the Fiji islands.

Fiji maintains possibly 5,000 men in the armed forces. There is a small patrol-boat navy. The vast majority of the soldiers are native Fijians. Fiji maintains 1,200 men in various U.N. peace-keeping units along the Afghanistan-Pakistan border, in Egypt, in Lebanon, and in Kuwait.

In 1979 Fiji spent less than 1 percent of GNP on her military forces. She spent 2.2 percent in 1989. The expenditures have hovered between 2 to 2.5 percent of GNP since 1989. Her GNP increased by 43 percent during this same period.

PAPUA–NEW GUINEA

Papua–New Guinea, about the size of Oregon and Idaho, consists of the eastern half of New Guinea, the Bismarck Archipelago, and Bouganville. The 4 million people have a per capita average annual income of $725. The government is a parliamentary democracy. There are ten major political parties. All adults can vote. Britain granted independence in 1975. Papua–New Guinea remains a member of the British Commonwealth of Nations.

The economy depends on coffee and copper exports. Germany, Japan, and Australia are the major trading partners. The United States buys less than 5 percent of Papua–New Guinea's exports. The economy is healthy and growing.

Papua–New Guinea has an interesting multicolonial history. In 1884 Germany took possession of part of New Guinea. In 1914, Australian troops defeated the small German garrison. The British took control in 1921 on a mandate from the League of Nations. The Japanese invaded in 1941. In 1946, Britain combined Papua and New Guinea into a single administrative unit.

In 1972, the name was changed to Papua–New Guinea. Elections gave Michael Somare power. Elections in 1977 confirmed Michael Somare's coalition government in power.

In 1980, Sir Julius Chan became prime minister. Paias Wingti replaced him in 1985. Rabbie Namaliu replaced Wingti in 1988. Papua–New Guinea is a genuine democracy.

The United States maintains excellent diplomatic relations with Papua–New Guinea. Papua–New Guinea is the South Pacific island region's largest and most populous nation. The United States enjoys a wide range of cooperative programs with this island nation. In 1990 a memorandum of understanding concerning possible future combined military actions came into being. Papua–New Guinea offers the United States a military base. At present, U.S. military aid is limited to training a few army officers each year.

Papua–New Guinea maintains about 4,000 men in its armed forces. The navy is a coast guard. The air force has no combat planes. Most equipment is Australian. Australia maintains about 125 troops in Papua–New Guinea.

There is a separatist movement on the island of Bouganville. This could become serious because of the economic importance of the copper deposits on this island. The Bouganville Revolutionary Army claims about 2,000 men. This rebel group shows little activity at present.

Papua–New Guinea spends about 1 percent of GNP on her military forces. Between 1979 and 1991, the GNP increased by 49 percent.

TONGA

Tonga is located on 36 inhabited islands in the South Pacific Ocean; 400 miles southeast of Fiji, about 150 miles to the south of Western Samoa, and 1,100 miles northeast of Auckland, New Zealand. Her 110,000 people have a per capita average annual income of $725. The government is a constitutional monarchy. Britain granted independence in 1970. There are no political parties. All adults can vote.

Tonga's economy depends on the export of copra and bananas. Her trading partners are Australia and New Zealand.

In 1845, after his conversion to Christianity, King George Tupou I established a constitution and parliamentary government. In 1862, he abolished serfdom. He redistributed the land.

Tonga became a British protectorate in 1900. Britain handled foreign affairs and protected the islands. During World War II, 2,000 Tongans fought with New Zealand troops in the Solomon Islands. United States and New Zealand troops were stationed in the islands during World War II.

King Tupou IV now rules Tonga. The king is interested in developing tourism.

The United States does not have an embassy in Tonga. Diplomatic affairs are handled by the embassy on Fiji. The United States does not give military aid to Tonga, except for training several army officers each year.

The small 400-man Tongan defense force is commanded by a New Zealand Army officer. The navy consists of a small coast guard.

Tonga spends less than 3 percent of GNP on her defense force. There are no rebel opposition groups.

NAURU

Nauru, the smallest nation in Asia, is an 8-square-mile island in the South Pacific lying 2,200 miles northeast of Sydney, 2,450 miles southeast of Honolulu, and 150 miles southeast of the Island of Tarawa of World War II fame. Her 9,000 people enjoy a per capita average annual income of $6,600. The government is a republic. The Democratic party is the only political party. All adults can and must vote.

Nauru does not publish import or export figures, nor does she reveal her GNP. Her major trading partners are Australia, New Zealand, and Japan. Nauru uses Australian money. The economy is based on phosphate mining.

In 1881, Germany occupied the island. In 1914, Australia took over. The Japanese landed in 1942. They deported some 1,200 Nauruans as forced laborers; fewer than 800 returned.

In 1947, Nauru became a United Nations trust territory administered by Australia. Nauru became independent in 1968. Nauru is a functioning parliamentary democracy.

The U.S. ambassador to Australia handles affairs with Nauru. The United States does not furnish military aid to Nauru. Australia assures the defense of the country. Nauru maintains a police force of some 75 men.

WESTERN SAMOA

Western Samoa, about the size of Rhode Island, is made up of several islands in the Southeast Pacific. Auckland, New Zealand, is some 1,600 miles distant. The nearest neighbors are American Samoa, Tonga, Fiji, and French Wallis Island. The 75,000 people have a per capital average annual income of $115. Her government is a parliamentary democracy. There are two political parties. Voting is by traditional family groups. New Zealand granted independence in 1962.

Western Samoa's economy is based on the export of copra and hardwoods. Her major trading partners are Australia and New Zealand.

The 1889 Final Act of the Berlin Conference on Samoan Affairs gave Samoa independence and neutrality. In 1900, Germany took Western Samoa. The United States took Eastern Samoa.

In 1914, New Zealand troops took Western Samoa. In 1919, the League of Nations made Western Samoa a New Zealand Trust. There was some civil disturbance to New Zealand's rule in the 1930s.

In 1946, the Samoans asked for independence. They went through the process of developing a democratic government. There is no organized political opposition to the government of Malietoa Tanumafili II.

The United States maintains a consulate in Western Samoa. The United States does not furnish military aid to Western Samoa.

Western Samoa does not support a military force. There are no military agreements with other countries. New Zealand accepts responsibility for the country's defense.

SOLOMON ISLANDS

The Solomon Islands are in the southeast Pacific Ocean. They are about the same size as Maryland. The largest island is Guadalcanal of World War II fame. The nearest neighbors are Papua–New Guinea and the New Hebrides Islands. The 350,000 people have a per capita average annual income of $570. The Solomon Islands are in the British Commonwealth of Nations. The government is a parliamentary democracy. Britain granted independence in 1978. There are several political parties. All adults can vote.

The economy is based on the export of fish and bananas. Major trading partners are Australia, Japan, Singapore, and Britain.

In 1885, Germany took over the northern Solomon Islands. The British took the southern Solomon Islands in 1893. Germany ceded her islands to Britain by 1900.

World War II brought widespread destruction to the Solomons. A strong antiforeigner sentiment arose. There is no rebel opposition group operating at the present time.

The United States and the Solomon Islands maintain good relations. American military aid trains a few students each year.

The Solomon Islands does not maintain a military force. There is a police force of about 550 men. Britain assures the defense of the country.

KIRIBATI

Kiribati is made up of three island groups in the Gilbert Islands. These islands are scattered over 1 million miles of the mid-Pacific Ocean. The total land area is less than 700 square miles. Only Tarawa, of World War II fame, has a large population. The 70,000 people have a per capita average annual income of $514. The government is a constitutional republic. There is one political party. All adults can vote. Britain granted independence in 1979.

The economy was based on phosphate mining until 1979. Since then, the major exports have been copra and bananas. Major trading partners are Britain, the United States, and Japan.

In 1892, the Gilbert and Ellice islands became a British protectorate. In 1978, the Ellice Islands became the independent nation of Tuvalu.

In 1979 Ieremia T. Tabai became president. Reelected in 1983 and 1987, he stepped down in 1988. Tennaki Teatoa is the current president.

Kiribati signed a treaty of friendship with the United States in 1979. The United States does not give military aid to this country.

Kiribati maintains only a small interisland police force.

VANUATU

Vanuatu is made up of over 80 islands, formally known as the New Herbrides, in the southwest Pacific Ocean. They stretch from the Solomon Islands to New Caldonia. Their land area is about the size of Connecticut. The government is a parliamentary democracy. There are three political parties. All adults can vote. The British and the French granted independence in 1980.

The economy is based on the export of copra and fish. Tourism is growing. Major trading partners are Holland, Japan, France, and Belgium.

In 1906, Britain and France agreed to jointly administer the New Hebrides Islands. An antiforeign cult grew up during and after World War II.

The United States maintains normal diplomatic relations with Vanuatu. American military aid trains a few people each year.

Vanuatu remains strongly tied to Australia, New Zealand, Britain, and France. Australia provides most of Vanuatu's military aid. Vanautu maintains only a small 300-man interisland police force. There are no rebel groups at the present time.

TUVALU

Tuvalu consists of nine islands, formally known as the Ellice group, scattered over the western Pacific Ocean. The total land area is about 10 square miles. There are about 9,500 Tuvaluans. The average annual income is unknown, as is the GNP. Tuvalu is a member of the British Commonwealth of Nations. The government is a parliamentary democracy. All adults can vote.

The economy is based on the export of copra. Tourism began in the 1980s but has recently slumped.

Britain assumed control of these islands in 1875. In 1916, Britain set up one administration for both the Gilbert and Ellice islands. In 1978 the Ellice Islands were granted independence by Britain. Their name was changed to Tuvalu.

Relations between the United States and Tuvalu are normal. The United States does not give military aid to Tuvalu.

There is a very small police force. Britain guarantees Tuvalu's defense.

MARSHALL ISLANDS

The Marshall Islands are located in the central Pacific Ocean. The 42,000 inhabitants enjoy a per person average annual income of $1,600. There is a republican form of government. Until World War I, the Marshalls were a German protectorate. Japan ruled these islands until the end of World War II. In 1947, the United States agreed to act as the U.N. trustee. The Marshall Islands received independence in 1990. They became a member of the United Nations in 1991.

The Marshall Islands have no military establishment. Independence is guaranteed by the United States. There is a large U.S. missile test range on Kwajalien Atoll. The entire economy is based on U.S. grants-in-aid and rent on this missile base.

Appendix: Important Events for the Third World since 1945

1945

World War II ends. European colonial powers begin leaving Third World countries. United Nations begins. Argentina, Bolivia, Brazil, Chile, China, Colombia, Costa Rica, El Salvador, Egypt, Ethiopia, Guatemala, Haiti, Honduras, India, Iran, Iraq, Lebanon, Liberia, Mexico, Nicaragua, Panama, Paraguay, Peru, Philippines, Saudi Arabia, South Africa, Syria, Uruguay, and Venezuela are members of the United Nations.

1945–1950

Cold War begins between the United States and the Soviet Union. Retreat of European colonial powers from the Third World continues. Communists win the civil war in China. Soviet Union develops the nuclear bomb. Afghanistan, Pakistan, Israel, Indonesia, Myanmar, Thailand, and Yemen join the United Nations.

1950–1960

Korean War between the United States–led U.N. forces and the North Koreans aided by the Soviet Union and mainland China. Japan begins economic revival. French ousted from Vietnam by Communists. United States becomes involved in Vietnam. Iran is first Middle East country to nationalize oil fields. Fidel Castro establishes Communist government in Cuba. U.S. economic and military aid program to non-Communist governments in full swing. Egypt seizes control of the Suez Canal. Israeli, French, and British troops invade Egypt but forced to withdraw by the United States. Cambodia, Ghana, Guinea, Jordan, Libya, Laos, Malaysia, Morocco, Nepal, Sri Lanka, Sudan, and Tunisia join the United Nations.

1960–1970

United States becomes deeply involved in Vietnam. Soviet economic and political penetration of the Third World continues—for example, Cuba, Algeria, and Guinea. The United States backs military takeovers in Ghana, Indonesia, and Zaire, among others. Israel becomes a major Middle East power. The United States intervenes in Yemen civil war by sending support through Saudi Arabia. The Soviet Union does the same through Egypt. The United States fails to oust Castro from Cuba in the Bay of Pigs invasion. Cuban missile crisis erupts between the United States and Soviet Union. A defeated United States leaves Vietnam. U.S. Marines intervene in the Dominican Republic. Israel occupies the Golan Heights and the Gaza Strip. Mainland China becomes a nuclear power. North Korea seizes the U.S.S. *Pueblo*. Civil war begins in Nigeria. Ideological differences between mainland China and the Soviet Union split the Communist world. Botswana, Algeria, Burkina Faso, Burundi, Cameroon, Benin, Central African Republic, Chad, Congo, Equatorial Guinea, Gambia, Guyana, Ivory Coast, Gabon, Kenya, Kuwait, Lesotho, Madagascar, Malawi, Maldives, Mali, Mauritania, Mauritius, Niger, Nigeria, Rwanda, Senegal, Sierra Leone, Singapore, Somalia, Swaziland, Tanzania, Trinidad and Tobago, Togo, Uganda, Zaire, and Zambia join the United Nations.

1970–1980

Vietnam unified by the Communists. "Boat people" began to flee southeast Asia. The United States backs non-Communist military takeovers in Chile, Argentina, Bolivia, and Peru, among others. Russian military involvement obvious in Afghanistan, Angola, and Ethiopia, among others. Similar French involvements exist in Chad, Morocco, and Zaire, among others. Cuba sends thousands of troops to Angola and Mozambique, plus military advisors to Grenada and El Salvador, among others. Tribal warfare reaches new heights in many African states such as Nigeria. The United Nations and the United States pressure South Africa to drop the "blacks are second class citizens" policy. The United Nations expels the Taiwan government and seats Red China in its place. The U.S. offer of friendship is accepted by Red China. Moslem terrorist activities against Israel and her friends begin. The United States ceases all war activities in Vietnam, Cambodia, and Loas. U.S. military and economic aid to non-Communist countries increases around the world. Arabs and Israelis fight again. Israeli commandos free hostages in raid on Uganda's Entebbe Airport. U.S. Marines are blown up in Lebanon. Khmer Rouge kill millions of Cambodians. Iranian religious fanatics seize the U.S. embassy and hostages in Iran. Angola, Bahrain, Bangladesh, Bhutan, Cape Verde, Comoros, Djibouti, Dominica, Fiji, Grenada, Guinea-Bissau, Mozambique, Oman, Qatar, St. Lucia, Sao Tome and Principe, Seychelles, Solomon Islands, Vanuatu, United Arab Emirates, Vietnam, and Western Samoa join the United Nations.

1980–1990

American hostages are released by Iran. Collapse of the Soviet Union. Cold War ends. The United States continues its system of military and economic aid to governments who practice democracy and assure human rights. Iraq-Iran war kills millions. The United States aids Britain in her Falklands' war against Argentina. The United States bombs Libya to end support for terrorists. The United States invades Granada to end a Communist takeover. Israel bombs Iraq nuclear factory, invades Lebanon, and fights an internal Palestinian uprising. Lebanon dissolves in a permanent civil war. The United States backs Contras (anticommunists) in El Salvador's civil war. Great famines in Africa. Forces seeking to end South Africa's antiblack laws won much ground. Chinese military forces shot students in Tiananmen Square demonstrations. There was notable rise in assignations among heads of state—Egypt, India, Lebanon, Pakistan, and Argentina, among others. Japan became an economic superpower. United States invaded Panama and seized Noriega. Belize, Brunei Darussalam, and Zimbabwe joined the United Nations.

1990–

South Africa released Nelson Mandela. A United States–led U.N. force fights the Desert War with Iraq. Continued famine in Somalia, coupled with a total breakdown of the government, led to a United States–led U.N. military intervention. Marshall Islands, Namibia, North Korea, South Korea, and St. Kitts and Nevis joined the United Nations.

Selected Bibliography

GOVERNMENT DOCUMENTS

Air University Library. *Index to Military Periodicals,* Maxwell Air Force Base, Ala.: Air University Library. Quarterly. The most complete reference work of its kind. Free to all libraries.

Area Handbook Series: Country Studies. Washington, D.C.: Federal Research Division, Library of Congress. Each country study is updated every few years.

Budget of the United States Government. Washington, D.C.: Office of the President of the United States. Annual. Good for the overall impact of foreign military assistance.

CSIS Africa Notes. Washington, D.C.: Center for Strategic and International Studies. Monthly plus occasional papers. Country studies are valuable.

Congressional Research Service. Washington, D.C.: Library of Congress. Various papers on foreign countries, foreign aid, and military assistance.

Early Bird. Washington, D.C.: American Armed Forces Information Service (AFIS/OASD-PA). Weekly. A summary of the American press on military topics and events. Invaluable. Many libraries carry this publication under the title, *Current News.*

FMS Control and Reports Division, Comptroller, DSAA. *Foreign Military Sales, Foreign Military Construction Sales and Military Assistance Facts as of September 30, 1991.* Washington, D.C.: Data Management Division, Comptroller, 1992. Useful in establishing the rhythm of U.S. assistance.

Foreign Economic Trends and Their Implications for the United States. Washington, D.C.: GPO, U.S. Department of Commerce. Country-by-country approach. Usually updated every two years.

Report of the Secretary of Defense to the President of the United States. Washington, D.C.: GPO. Annual.

Supporting U.S. Strategy for Third World Conflict. Report by the Regional Conflict Working Group submitted to the Commission on Integrated Long-Term Strategy. Washington, D.C.: The Pentagon, 1988. Gives the rationale for this strategy.

Thesis, 1988.

Neuman, Stephane. *Military Assistance in Recent Wars: The Dominance of the Superpowers.* New York: Praeger, 1986.

Pach, Chester J., Jr. *Arming the Free World: The Origins of the United States Military Assistance Program, 1945–1950.* Chapel Hill, N.C.: University of North Carolina Press, 1991.

Wah, Chin Kin. *Defense Spending in Southeast Asia.* Singapore: Institute of Southeast Asian Studies, 1987.

Wesson, Robert, ed. *The Latin American Military Institution.* New York: Praeger, 1986.

OTHER RESOURCES

Cultural and Military Attaches of Each Foreign Country. A letter to each embassy service will bring economic and military information as well as the history of the foreign country as seen by the present government. A valuable source for updating country files. To be used with discretion and after files are already established.

Index

ABOUT THE AUTHOR

CLAUDE C. STURGILL, Professor of History, University of Florida, is well known for his studies of the French military system and contemporary topics in world military history. His most recent books include *Low-Intensity Conflicts in American History* (Praeger, 1994), *Reflections sur l'Administration Fiscale de l'Armée des Bourbons: Le Budget du Secretaire d'Etat à la Guerre de 1720 à 1792* (1994), and *Dictonnaire d'Art et d'Histoire Militaires* (1988).